CW00766659

WHERE BORDERS BLEED

WHERE BORDERS BLEED

An Insider's Account of INDO-PAK Relations

RAJIV DOGRA

RUPA

First published by
Rupa Publications India Pvt. Ltd 2015
7/16, Ansari Road, Daryaganj
New Delhi 110002

Sales Centres:
Allahabad Bengaluru Chennai
Hyderabad Jaipur Kathmandu
Kolkata Mumbai

Copyright © Rajiv Dogra 2015

The views and opinions expressed in this book are the author's own and the facts are as reported by him/her which have been verified to the extent possible, and the publishers are not in any way liable for the same.

All rights reserved.
No part of this publication may be reproduced, transmitted, or stored in a retrieval system, in any form or by any means, electronic, mechanical, photocopying, recording or otherwise, without the prior permission of the publisher.

ISBN: 978-81-291-3573-5

Fourth impression 2021

10 9 8 7 6 5 4

The moral right of the author has been asserted.

This edition is for sale in the Indian subcontinent only

Typeset by SÜRYA, New Delhi

Printed at Saurabh Printers Pvt. Ltd, Noida

This book is sold subject to the condition that it shall not, by way of trade or otherwise, be lent, resold, hired out, or otherwise circulated, without the publisher's prior consent, in any form of binding or cover other than that in which it is published.

To my daughter Radhika, who gave me the idea for this book, and who persisted for five long years until I agreed to write it

Contents

1
Prelude to Pakistan

The root of all complexities is loneliness and that solitude feeds the imagination. It makes the mind wander and think the unthinkable. Would the following have been written in normal circumstances, amid the biases and passions of a work day?

> By the time I was twenty-three, I had read *Glimpses of World History* four times. Nehru was one of the most polished writers of English prose of our times. There was inspiration and music in his words.
>
> From Jakarta, I warned you in that letter written fourteen years ago, that I was not emulating him... He was a freedom fighter, the great leader of Indian masses, the Cambridge-educated aristocrat with a trail of glory. He was not a petty murderer, an embezzler of the state, a nobody from a village of Larkana languishing in a death cell...
>
> Nehru was kept in jail by our alien rulers in some place with honour and respect... His daughter was a thirteen year old little girl who had made her contribution to the politics of that time by organising what she called 'monkey brigades'...
>
> But you are caught in the middle of a fire and it is the fire of a ruthless junta... There is therefore a world of difference... The similarity, if any, lies in the fact that you, like Indira Gandhi, are making history. I can claim to know Indira Gandhi quite well... I respect her qualities very much but I have not been one of her greatest admirers... True, she became the Prime Minister of India and remained in that high office for eleven years... She was called a goddess when she seized East Pakistan.
>
> Knowing all these things, I have no hesitation in saying that my daughter is more than a match for the daughter of Jawahar Lal Nehru, the goddess of India...
>
> One thing you have in common; both of you are equally brave. Both of you are made of pure damescene steel...[1]

---

[1]Zulfikar Ali Bhutto, *My Dearest Daughter: A Letter from the Death Cell.*

Interesting, isn't it? These are the opening paragraphs of a long letter dated 21 June 1978 by Zulfikar Ali Bhutto to his daughter Benazir. He wrote it in District Jail, Rawalpindi. The surprise, however, is not in guessing the identity of the writer, but the fact that he should have written in admiration of Nehru and his daughter.

Bhutto, after all, was a virulent India baiter for most of his active political life. When he was in power, he had talked of waging a thousand-year war against India. It was he who said that Pakistanis would eat grass if that was the sacrifice needed to make a nuclear bomb. Had he got one, while he was the prime minister, the history of the subcontinent may have been different. With his whimsical turns and Machiavellian love for intrigue, anything was possible.

Bhutto was impetuous and unpredictable. He pushed two military dictators into wars with India—Ayub Khan in 1965 and Yahya Khan in 1971. Then, in defeat, he spared no effort in running them down to his political advantage. All along, he excelled in badmouthing India internationally and in clawing back diplomatically some of what had been lost on the battlefield.

After a lifetime of tricking and trapping India, why did he change track at the fag end of his life? What was it that brought about this softening in Bhutto? Or was it just a temporary phase, a momentary rush of blood, because later in this long letter to Benazir he resumes his strident rhetoric. Still, this temporary and rare departure from the usual is worth noting.

Was it motivated by a desire to be objective while writing to an impressionable young girl? Or, as he claims further on in this letter, was it on account of the fact that, 'With the exception of your father, the Qaid-e-Azam and perhaps Suhrawardy, either charlatans or captains have run this country.' With such a paucity of local heroes, he may have wanted his daughter to follow those from the other side (India) as her inspirational figures.

Once again, and even here, his ego prevailed. In Bhutto's universe how could anyone else be better than his daughter? It wasn't, therefore, a flippant flourish of his pen that led him to write, 'Knowing all these things, I have no hesitation in saying that my daughter is more than a match for the daughter of Jawahar Lal Nehru, the goddess of India.'

Still, let's give him the benefit of the doubt. Let us assume that in prison Bhutto had undergone a change of heart. If instead of being hanged to death by General Zia ul-Haq, he had somehow survived and become the prime minister of Pakistan again, would he have changed that admiration for Indian leaders into something more substantial? Would he have toned down the confrontational posture against India? It is difficult to predict what a hugely ambitious man like Bhutto may have done—and he was both mercurial and imperious.

An impetuous man is capable of taking bizarre turns. Bhutto was such a man; he could change the course of his nation's history to suit his whim. Therefore, it is quite possible that Bhutto, who was largely responsible for the bitterness that led to the creation of Bangladesh, could also achieve quite the opposite result if fancy struck him and his instincts told him that he could profit politically from a particular move.

It is often said that the partition of India may not have taken place had Muhammad Ali Jinnah been offered the prime ministership of undivided India. Is it beyond the realm of possibility that Bhutto, too, may have been tempted by such a prospect? If he is faulted for the intrigues that directly or indirectly led to the break-up of a nation, wasn't he capable of reverse engineering too? If there was one leader who could sway Pakistani people to his logic, perverse or otherwise, it was Zulfikar Ali Bhutto.

A hugely ambitious leader like Bhutto would have relished the prospect of ruling 1.5 billion people. As prime minister of a united India he would have been the master of the biggest nation in the world; a state larger in population than China, the country that he adored and cultivated.

Let us for a moment consider it done, with or without Bhutto. Let us also assume that at a not too distant date in the future, India and Pakistan (Bangladesh as well) somehow succeed in forgetting the bickering of their past and decide that the time has come to start a new chapter, that like united Germany they, too, should give union a chance. Such a thought, dear reader, isn't unique to you and me. Others in the past have considered it too.

Writing to London about his reservations regarding the partition of India, Lord Louis Mountbatten asserted:

> The most we can hope to do, as I have said before, is to put the responsibility for any of these mad decisions fairly and squarely on the Indian (pre-partition India) shoulders in the eyes of the world, for one day they will bitterly regret the decision they are about to make.[2]

---

[2]Nicholas Mansergh and Penderel Moon, *Constitutional Relations between Britain and India: The Transfer of Power, 1942–47: The Mountbatten Viceroyalty Formulation of a Plan, 22 March–30 May 1947.*

Within a year of the partition Pandit Nehru was in a revisionary mode. He said:

> Perhaps we acted wrongly... The consequences of that partition have been so terrible that one is inclined to think that anything else would have been preferable... Ultimately, I have no doubt that India and Pakistan will come close together...some kind of federal link... There is no other way to peace. The alternative is...war.[3]

Nor was Nehru alone in thinking that the partition was a horrible mistake. Jinnah, the cause of it all, despaired quickly of what he had brought about. According to his doctor, when the dying Jinnah saw Pakistan's prime minister, Liaquat Ali Khan, he told him: 'Pakistan was the biggest blunder of my life.'[4] Jinnah also added in a slurred whisper, 'If now I get an opportunity I will go to Delhi and tell Jawaharlal (Nehru) to forget about the follies of the past and become friends again.'

It wasn't just Nehru and Jinnah who wanted to rewrite history. In fact, the history of the subcontinent would have been written vastly differently had Mountbatten shown some bureaucratic sloth; instead of advancing the date of partition if he had delayed the announcement, the division may never have taken place. Jinnah, after all, died thirteen months after the partition. And his right-hand man and successor, Liaquat Ali Khan, wasn't convinced that partition was such a good idea.

What Mahatma Gandhi had in mind was an undivided India; one that included in its embrace the areas that became Pakistan. Let us for a moment assume that the Mahatma's wish had been granted, and that the country had not been divided.

It's easy to list the benefits. One that comes immediately to mind is the saving of human lives; at least one million people were killed in the orgy of violence before, during and after the partition. It wasn't a sporadic act but systematic, organized and premeditated violence on a massive scale. These were slaughters of the kind that should have invited mass trials by an international commission and the harshest of punishment to the perpetrators.

It wasn't just the Hindus and Sikhs who were slaughtered, Muslims too, were massacred. Men, women and children from both sides died

---

[3]For Nehru, the consequences of the partition, see Stanley Wolpert, *India and Pakistan—Continued Conflict or Cooperation*.

[4]Alex von Tunzelmann, *Indian Summer—The Secret History of the End of an Empire*.

in the anger of retribution. Many of them were killed or driven out of their homes in East and West Punjab, besides Karachi, in a calculated move at ethnic cleansing. Others were put to sword due to an element of greed. The properties that got vacated could then be taken over by the evil forces which had set their eyes on them.

If ever 'might' had a field day, this was it. There was no appeal and no redress—the strongest took it all. Yet by the twisted logic of communal hatred it was a mere redistribution of wealth—to each according to his strength. All of this happened in the anarchy of division in a lawlessness sanctioned by the law of revenge.

Such a celebration of violence and loot would not have happened in a united India. In that India cruelty would not have been a virtue, nor mercy considered a flaw. Communal tensions may have simmered and even boiled over occasionally, as they had done in the past, but there wouldn't have been slaughter and massacres of the type that the partition brought about.

Let us put our more practical thinking cap on and consider the issue from an economist's viewpoint. The industrial base in pre-partition India was built on the basis of geographic advantage and economies of scale. After partition, the economies of the two countries had to be recast and started all over again. New industries had to be built and makeshift towns established to accommodate the migrants and their fledgling new enterprises.

It can be argued that this was a great new opportunity for entrepreneurs of both sides. It could have led to the setting up of brand-new industries fitted with the latest technology, and that race to install the best should have fostered a fine sense of competition between the two countries. This ought to have been the case in an ideal situation, but it rarely is. And it certainly wasn't the case with India and Pakistan.

People investing in industry were refugees who had fled with very little beyond what they could hold in their hands. They, therefore, set up new industries on lean, shoestring budgets. Instead of getting the best equipment that money could buy, they had to cut corners and manage with whatever was available at the cheapest price. This resulted in ill-planned townships and makeshift industries. Had India not been partitioned, there wouldn't have been any need to make such compromises.

Obviously then, the partition generated the economics of compromise—of making do with whatever little was available. It also caused great agony. Besides the one million who were killed, there were another seventeen million or so who were displaced. They had to start life all over again; their struggle for a new beginning led to some success stories but there were many more who couldn't make it. Theirs are the forgotten stories; their struggles the private grief to be agonized over in the privacy of whatever spot they called their home.

One could say cynically, so what? There are no guarantees in life; they could have lost it all in any number of ways. There could have been a natural disaster and they would have had to start life all over again. After all, many millions died during the Bengal famine. Well, that is true but the partition was no natural disaster—it was man-made, pre-planned and the result of an arbitrary decision by a handful for which millions had to suffer.

Some persist in maintaining to this day that Pakistan was insufficiently imagined and that its raison d'être was suspect from the beginning. They point also to the needless suffering the partition caused to millions of people, and the lingering bitterness between the two states. Was all that really necessary? Wouldn't it have been better to emerge in independence as a single entity?

The globe would have been India's stage then. A united India will have become the largest nation of the world. It, rather than China, would have been offered one of the Permanent Seats in the UN Security Council. As an equal participant at the global high table, the worries of the world would have engaged it and its counsel sought on all the major international issues. This elevation may not by itself have had any significant effect on India's economy or its domestic politics, but the sense of pride and responsibility that comes from being in the big league would have permeated the country too.

As second to India in terms of population, and in international standing, China may not have made its aggressive moves against India. It may even have hesitated and perhaps decided against moving into Tibet. It is also possible that the humiliation of 1962 suffered by India may not have happened at all. Still, if a war had broken out, the scores may not have been so one-sided.

Moreover, a united India would have seen a fine balance of aggression and softness in its foreign relations; the unbridled aggression of the present-day policymakers in Pakistan blended with the soft approach of Indian leaders would have made it an excellent mix.

If this united India was to adopt secularism as its guiding principle and tolerance as the medium of social dialogue, as has largely been the case with modern India, then terrorism and jihad in their present-day form may not have flourished. Like the Maoists in India, they might have caused localized eruptions, but they would have spent themselves in the enormous cushion that democracy provides. Agitations and rebellions in India take place in localized silos and run out of steam there because of the vast heterogeneity of races and creeds.

The Taliban and Al Qaeda would not have prospered in a united India, in the way they have done in Pakistan.

Democracy, even in a frustratingly slow format, provides enough safety valves for people to shout and for their anger to be vented safely. Moreover terrorists, and their organizations, have flourished because of the sanctuaries provided to them in the Afghanistan–Pakistan region. That facility, and the freedom of movement, would not have been available to them in an environment that discourages violence and radicalism. Equally importantly, the need to invent a terror-positive Inter-Services Intelligence (ISI) would not have arisen. In the absence of a state organization like the ISI and its protective patronage, the Taliban and Al Qaeda may never have come into being. If by some chance they had managed to sprout somehow, their nuisance value would at best have been marginal and its effect temporary.

Such a pacific Indian nation could not be a 'state sponsor' of terror and that would have been good news for the world. There wouldn't have been a 9/11 in the United States or a 26/11 in India, and the world would have been a far more tranquil and safe place.

Afghanistan, too, may have been spared the devastation that it has suffered for over thirty years. In the absence of war, and without the destructive influence of the Taliban, its people may have lived life differently, more benignly. The Soviet Union's misadventure in Afghanistan may not have taken place at all, and it may not have broken up to splinter into multiple pieces as it did eventually. If you extend this logic further, isn't it possible that a benign India may not have sheltered Osama bin Laden?

The influence of a democratic and industrially advanced India may have led Afghanistan to be a democracy and an important tourist destination for the world. All this may sound far-fetched but is it really beyond the realm of the possible? Is the possibility, and its benefits, not tempting enough to give it a fair try even now?

The biggest benefit would have been on the issue of peace and stability in the region. Thus far periodic armed conflicts, and tensions have led to the expenditure of billions of dollars in procuring arms and maintaining large armies. It is true that China, too, has been a factor in the continually increasing defence expenditure by India, but not on the same scale as that due to Pakistan, and not till recently. For a united India the only borders requiring vigil and defence would have been those that adjoin China.

This united country's defence expenditure would have been 60 or a maximum of 70 per cent of what India, Pakistan and Bangladesh are spending on their soldiers and armaments today. Moreover, the Indian army would have remained subordinate to the political authority as is the case in today's India and Bangladesh, rather than the other way round as has been happening in Pakistan.

There would have been no need then for the two million men-plus army that the three countries maintain. The money thus saved could have been used for education and better health care for people; the budgetary deficits would have been smaller thereby making more money available for infrastructural development and the like.

Consider yet another aspect of it. A terror-free world would have been prosperous and less prone to setting up multiple agencies to tackle terror. The money thus saved could be put to productive use. India has suffered enormously from terrorism. Besides the huge loss of lives, it has also imposed major financial costs on the country. To give just one example, the Indian government, industry and businesses have been forced to employ nearly 9 million security personnel as a check against terrorism. The expenditure on this alone must amount to a couple of billion dollars annually; this is a large sum of money for a poor part of the world to afford. These billions could have been employed productively and elsewhere. To this one must add the expenditure on paramilitary outfits and other bodies like anti-terror agencies.

That is the expenditure on preventive measures. But there is also the loss suffered in human and material terms every time a successful terror strike takes place. There is no known computation of it yet, but if one were to be made then the loss, since the early 1980s, would be a huge financial sum. Add to it the cost of opportunities lost because of the closure of businesses and industry every time a terror strike takes place and a frightening picture emerges. It is doubtful if, and to what extent, Pakistan has gained by this negative drag on India, but it is certain that the subcontinent has lost tremendously.

Had it been otherwise, wouldn't a democratic, secular and united India be more than a match to the economic giant that China is today?

Consider the possibility, the very serious instance, where the West had a choice of investing either in an opaque and communist China or a chaotic and anarchic but vibrantly democratic united India.

The foreign investor would surely have chosen to invest in a terror-free and united India, rather than in inscrutable China. It is true that corruption in such an India would have been all-pervasive; perhaps much more so than it is in the three separate units. It is also possible that the bureaucracy may have been far more frustrating and obdurate. Still, the thought of investing in a democracy, and the idea of it being the largest market in the world, would have been major pluses for a foreign investor. A united India may also have traded with Afghanistan, Iran, and Central and Southeast Asia in a hugely significant manner.

Foreign financial investors would have placed their bets on such an India. If that was so, isn't it possible that given a choice again, the people who divided India might choose differently the second time?

Like Nehru, but for an altogether different reason, Jinnah came to regret the horrors of partition. It is said that during a flight to survey the extent of the refugee crisis in the Punjab, he held his head in his hands and remarked, 'Oh my God, what have I done?'[5] Would he, with the benefit of hindsight, have chosen a different course? Perhaps he might have.

One day, within months of the partition, Jinnah asked the first Indian high commissioner to Pakistan, Sri Prakasa, to convey a personal message from him to Pandit Nehru. 'Tell Jawaharlal not to break my heart.' Jinnah said almost pleadingly, writes Sri Prakasa in an account of that meeting, 'You do not know how much I love Bombay. I still look forward to going back there.'[6]

High Commissioner Sri Prakasa was taken aback. Had he heard Jinnah correctly? Was he actually planning to return to Bombay to live there? After the mayhem and bloodshed of the last few months, and violence the like of which had rarely been seen in the history of the world, Jinnah—the cause of it all—seemed to have changed his mind. The man who wanted a separate 'homeland' for himself and others of his faith now wanted to abandon that 'homeland' for the city he loved and for the house he had built there.

His house in Bombay was now an evacuee property. By law, the title of such a property ceased to be with the previous owner if he had

---

[5]Mahir Ali, 'A case of mistaken identity', *The Hindu*.

[6]For Jinnah wanting to go back to Bombay, see Sri Prakasa, *Pakistan: Birth and Last Days*.

migrated to Pakistan. The same rule applied in Pakistan to all the properties left behind by those who had migrated to India. Therefore, what Jinnah was seeking was against the law that the two countries had adopted. As a lawyer, and one of repute, Jinnah should have known that what he was seeking was not legal and that if an exception was to be made in his case, millions of others could also step forward to reclaim businesses and properties they had left behind. It would have set in motion more slaughters and countless claims and counterclaims. The violence and confusion of the partition would have revived all over again to carry on indefinitely. Jinnah must have known the implications of his request. Yet he did not hesitate in making the demand and telling the Indian high commissioner that he wished to go back to Bombay!

'Really, Mr Jinnah!' said Sri Prakasa. 'You desire to go back to Bombay. I know how much Bombay owes to you and your great services to the city. May I tell the prime minister that you want to go back there?'

'Yes, you may,' Jinnah replied.

A few weeks later, Sri Prakasa saw Jinnah again. Pandit Nehru had responded positively, but it was with the expectation that Jinnah would make up his mind within six months. It is difficult to guess what might have happened if he had returned to India. Would he and the other leaders have rewritten the chapter of partition, countering all the arguments they had advanced earlier in its support, erasing the fault lines of division? Jinnah himself never made his ultimate choice known. He died before the six-month period was over.

Was Jinnah's death before his final response to Sri Prakasa an ominous sign? Was it nature's way of conveying that nothing in the world is utterly perfect, that a united India was an impossible dream? Perhaps it was so, because the subsequent history can hardly be called promising. It does not encourage the hope that there would be amity between India and Pakistan, that first essential step towards greater goals.

It might also mean that we are better off as separate entities because Pakistan's chosen path is vastly different from India's. However, if by some magic wand a united India were to come about, the world is likely to be deeply suspicious of a country that remains continually on edge; where communal fault lines are prominent and simmer all the time. Moreover, even if the benefits of a union outnumber the negatives of it, the nays will have their way because their voice is shriller and their message fiercely potent.

Let's for a moment also consider the social dimension of it; the intercommunity relations would have been complicated and short of goodwill. Mutual accommodation may have required a constant effort just to keep the national fabric in one piece. Yet there is no harm in dreaming of a united India, because without dreams reality would lack hope.

*

According to a *Times of India* report of 19 July 1947, for the first six months at least from 15 August 1947, the inhabitants of India and Pakistan were not going to be reminded that they were foreigners in each other's country. 'They will be able to travel freely from Lahore to Delhi and from Calcutta to Chittagong without having to produce passports and visas,' the report said. 'They will have the same common currency and there will be a free flow of trade between the two countries. The railways will run from India to Pakistan as now, without interruption.'

If everything was to be as before what then was the point of the partition? Well, nothing was the same as before. This special dispensation was a temporary measure to give people some more time. Those who could not cross over in time got a few extra months and that was it. Then the gates clanged shut. Thereafter, people could contemplate borders, not cross them. But even then, even as the spilt blood reminded them constantly that India's partition was violent and destructive, people thought that it was not definitive. They hoped that once passions had cooled they could go back to the homes they had left in a hurry.

Ironically though, that was not the view of the principal actors. If Nehru and Jinnah considered the erasable quality of the partition one moment, they changed their mind the next. If the human dimensions of the tragedy troubled them in the morning, their ego clashes willed them in the opposite direction by the evening.

Perhaps it was a personality issue. Nehru's visceral hatred of Jinnah was recorded in his diaries. A man who was otherwise extremely careful with his choice of words was in this particular case uninhibited and bluntly scathing. Consider, for example, this:

> Jinnah...offers an obvious example of an utter lack of the civilized mind... With all his cleverness and ability, he produces an impression on me of utter ignorance and lack of understanding... Instinctively I think it is better to (have) Pakistan or almost anything, if only to

> keep Jinnah far away and not allow his muddled and arrogant head from interfering continually in India's progress.[7]

What did Jinnah think of his counterparts? Jinnah labelled Nehru '...an arrogant Brahmin who covers his Hindu trickiness under a veneer of Western education'.[8] And he called Mahatma Gandhi '...a cunning fox, a Hindu revivalist'.[9]

There were other instances where personality and the subjective judgement of leaders played a huge part, affecting millions. Thus, within three months of taking over as the viceroy of India, Mountbatten decided to advance the date of British departure from India to 15 August 1947. Since this announcement was made on 3 June 1947, it meant that the British were committed to quit India in the next ten weeks.

Government officials require more time than that to wind up their affairs in a routine transfer from one city to another. Here, lives of millions were going to be affected and in this case there was no pressing need to hurry things. Prime Minister Clement Attlee of the UK had earlier declared that Britain would leave India by June 1948. So where was the need to rush matters? June 1948 would have given Mountbatten a full year, and his officials would have had enough time to plan for it all. Yet he advanced by ten months the date of division, reducing by that much the chance for people to prepare themselves for the cataclysm.

One explanation could be that his intentions were to safeguard British and his interests. During a press conference on 4 June 1947, he said, 'Waiting would only mean that I should be responsible for law and order.' At a later date when Mountbatten was asked why he chose the earlier date, he boasted, 'The date I chose came out of the blue. I chose it in reply to a question. I was determined to show that I was the master of the whole event.'

But Mountbatten was mistaken in assuming that he alone was the master. Nehru may have been an atheist; he may have personally stayed away from practising religion or subscribing to ritual, but in matters of national destiny, he was willing to make a compromise. For him, at least in this one instance, God rather than Mountbatten was the master in the matter.

---

[7]For Nehru's hatred of Jinnah, see Richard Bourke and Raymond Geuss (eds.), *Political Judgement: Essays for John Dunn*.

[8]Sankar Ghose, *Jawaharlal Nehru*.

[9]William Shirer, *Gandhi: A Memoir*.

Legend has it that he consulted Goswami Ganesh Dutt, the president of the Sanatan Dharam (traditionally the largest non-political Hindu organization), and a leading Hindu seer. After looking at the astrological charts, he shook his head sadly and said that both the dates suggested by Nehru, 14 and 15 August, were inauspicious. Both indicated a life of strife and uncertainty if India came into independent existence on either of these dates. Pandit Nehru had no choice beyond these two dates and told him so. Nehru asked him to consult the charts again and suggest the more favourable time, or the least troublesome time, within that two-day period.

It was then that Goswami Ganesh Dutt came up with the suggestion of ringing in independence at the midnight hour. According to his calculations a birth at that time was the most propitious in an otherwise bad period. But he also warned Nehru, 'This doesn't mean that India will be free of troubles. It only means that it will face less of them in comparison to Pakistan, but it too will face problems because that is destined in the charts.'

Mountbatten was not troubled by the worries of inauspicious signs and their bleak connotations. Nor was he bothered by the fact that there was hardly any time for the two nations to organize themselves administratively or for their leaders to prepare for the task of governance. His priority was to get the 'mission partition' accomplished quickly.

When he was asked on the eve of the partition if he had not shown undue haste, Mountbatten remarked flippantly, 'The best way to teach a youngster to cycle was to take him to the top of a hill, put him on the seat and push him down the hill—by the time he reached the bottom of the hill, he'd have learnt to cycle.'[10]

Why did Mountbatten advance the date of independence? It is clear that he was not under any pressure from London to do so, nor were the Indian leaders pressing for it. Why then did he do it? A clue to this lies in his background and in his anxiety to please the royal family. Louis Mountbatten's family wasn't particularly wealthy; it was Edwina who had inherited immense wealth. As a royal he was related to almost every royal family in Europe, yet as forty-eighth in the line of succession he was only a second-class royal in Britain. Add to it the fact that his father, Prince Louis of Battenberg, was removed from his position as the First Sea Lord because he was one German too many in the British hierarchy when the First World War started.

---

[10]Louis Mountbatten, *Time Only to Look Forward*.

That humiliation came as a shock to young Louis Mountbatten. Thereafter, the driving ambition of his life became the ability to make a mark in life.

He cultivated his personality around that central theme; a great gift for storytelling at the cost of economizing sometimes on truth, stage-managing publicity coups and inveigling himself into the good books of the king and the princes became the principal instruments of that ambition. But ability was not one of his principal virtues; *HMS Kelly*, the first ship he commanded, was sunk by the Germans.

Another of his traits was the desire for grand gestures with little regard for human lives; the bizarre plan to attack the Germans head-on to conquer the Dieppe port was one such disaster which resulted in large losses for the Allies. When he learnt of the disaster at Dieppe, Lord Beaverbrook, minister of aircraft production in Winston Churchill's government, went so far as to call Mountbatten a murderer.[11] Despite that, his royal connections ensured that he was beyond reproach. Soon, he was made the supreme allied commander in Southeast Asia. On hearing the news, Field Marshal Bernard Law Montgomery remarked dismissively that he was unfit to be a supreme commander. Admiral Andrew Browne Cunningham put it even more bluntly, 'I think most people in the service have just laughed.' As it happened, he was not trusted with any real military matters because he was considered a hopeless strategist. Historian Andrew Roberts depicted 'Dickie' Mountbatten as a psychopathically ambitious, vain, disingenuous, manipulative, adrenaline junkie and a man who was utterly careless of other peoples' lives.[12] This same Louis Mountbatten, known in the navy as the 'Master of Disaster', was made the viceroy of India.

Like Mountbatten, Jinnah too, was in a rush but for an altogether different set of reasons. He was suffering from tuberculosis and cancer of the lungs, and his health was failing rapidly. But history maintains that only the closest of his confidants were privy to this secret. Jinnah was worried that if the news of his illness leaked out, the Congress leadership would delay giving consent to the partition plan. Moreover, having single-handedly carved out a nation for himself in less than a decade, he did not want to push his luck. Delay could have led to change. He wanted his creation to take shape during his

---

[11]Robert Langton, 'The war time raid that shamed Mountbatten', *Daily Express*.

[12]Ibid.

lifetime. In any case, Jinnah wasn't interested in consulting astrologers or in seeking more time to prepare for a smooth transition. He was a man in a hurry.

Yet, Mahatma Gandhi didn't give up. Even though Mountbatten showed little interest in exploring the alternatives, Gandhi suggested at one of their meetings that the existing interim government led by Nehru be dismissed and Jinnah invited to form a new one.

'What would Jinnah say to such a proposal?' Mountbatten wondered.

'If you tell him I am the author, he'd reply, "Wily Gandhi!"'

That was the end of the matter. Even for Gandhi it must have meant the end of the road for reconciliation. Had Mountbatten given the proposal a sincere try, perhaps it may have changed the course of history.

While all this was going on, people were kept scrupulously out of the loop. None of these leaders of men, some of whom had great faith in democratic traditions, thought it necessary to consult people on the partition of their land, nor did they consider it prudent to give them notice. Had the masses been told in advance that they had to decide between one or the other country by mid-August 1947, it is possible that some of the mayhem may have been avoided.

If there was adequate notice, had the administrative machinery enough time to chalk out a plan to shift populations, the magnitude of the tragedy may have been lessened. But people were caught unawares. They were ignorant about the gathering storm. In fact most were busy making holiday plans for the summer vacations. June to July was the time of the year for children to pay an annual visit to at least one set of grandparents. It was time too to go for a swim with a large party of cousins. A nearby river or a pond was enough to cool off and enjoy water-cooled mangoes thereafter. So, as they did every year, schoolchildren went to their separate holiday destinations bidding each other fond goodbyes; the Muslim children to their relatives and the Hindu and Sikh children to their extended families. However, the summer wind of 1947 was unusually warm; and it began to carry the first intimations of the approaching cataclysm. Yet no one, not even the most experienced or the worldly-wise, had anticipated that those initial sparks would soon become an all-consuming fire.

Post-partition, Jinnah may have wondered if his moth-eaten Pakistan was worth the slaughter and the suffering of people. But that doesn't take away from the fact that there is hardly any other example in history where a handful of people arbitrarily decided to amputate a country, resulting among other depredations in a million deaths. It is this arbitrariness that the people's anguish was about.

The British rulers were skilled at manipulating ethnic divisions in South Asia, but in 1947 they chose artificiality based on religion rather than ethnicity, thereby spawning in Pakistan an implausible gaggle of Bengalis, Sindhis, Punjabis, Baluchis and Pashtuns lumped together. Had the British used the same culture/language/ethnicity criteria as happened in Europe, would Pakistan exist? Instead, there might have been 'Pushtunistan', 'Baluchistan', and even a 'Sindh'.

The British did find the time to hold a referendum in the North-West Frontier Province (NWFP) to find out if the people wished to join the new nation called Pakistan. It is alleged that the referendum was flawed, that the hugely popular Khan Abdul Ghaffar Khan boycotted the referendum and along with all his followers stayed away from voting. If such a large number of people stayed away from polling, the result was obvious. Then there is the doubtful principle of the exercise. The British decreed that a simple majority was enough to consider it a verdict of the people. Was that fair?

In a matter as significant as the destiny of a province, is a simple majority of one vote enough? Shouldn't the will of at least two-thirds of the people have been made the minimum criterion? And was there enough time to persuade Khan Abdul Ghaffar Khan and his followers that the boycott of the referendum was a suicidal step—one that would hand over victory on a platter to the partitionists?

It is also alleged that Jinnah's agents engineered massive rigging and the stuffing of ballot boxes. Wali Khan details the instances and the extent of it in his book *Facts are Facts: The Untold Story of India's Partition*. To illustrate the size of rigging, he mentions that in one case a woman had cast one hundred ballots in favour of the NWFP joining the new state of Pakistan!

It is this kind of suspect behaviour that is hard to live with; angst bubbles over loudly and tearfully every time. This is exactly what happened. Resentment and anger kept multiplying. When the swords came out, every neck from the other religion was a target. Guns were quicker still and they could kill many more. Women suffered the most; the young among them were not killed, they were taken away to live the life of the living dead in what was soon to become another country.

Amrita Pritam, a leading Punjabi poet of the time, conveys it heart-rendingly in her lament to Waris Shah, an eighteenth-century Sufi poet,

Today, I call Waris Shah, 'Speak from your grave,'
And turn to the next page in your book of love,
Once, a daughter of Punjab cried and you wrote an entire saga,
Today, a million daughters cry out to you, Waris Shah,
Rise! O narrator of the grieving! Look at your Punjab,
Today, fields are lined with corpses, and blood fills the Chenab...

But partings need not be brutal and India's was not the only partition the world has seen. In many cases there was an understanding that if there has to be a parting of ways, it should be done without fuss. The break-up would definitely cause a wrench but that's about it.

The Soviet Union broke up into fifteen parts without major eruptions. There were no massacres, nor any great bitterness. And it happened suddenly—the decree was signed one late night by a very drunk Boris Yeltsin and the next morning they were on their own. There was hardly any notice, nor a great period of transition to prepare the leaders for their new role. There was bewilderment definitely, but hardly any rancour. There was migration too, but it was like the flow of water that finds its own level. The splintering of the Soviet Union was a loss of a large empire for the Russians, and it still causes a huge wrench when you ask them about it. But that's it; they just shrug and carry on as do people in the other fourteen states. No one there talks of a thousand-year war.

Almost similar was the case with Czechoslovakia when it split into two parts, the Czech Republic and Slovakia. They called it a velvet divorce, a most civil parting of ways where one evening people raised their glasses of wine together and went their separate ways the next morning.

Even the bitterly divided Greek and Turkish Cypriots have adjusted to their cheek-by-jowl but separate existence. They might occasionally scowl at each other, but there is hardly ever a stage where there is a call to arms.

Then why was the Indo-Pak parting so bitter?

You could fatalistically say that it was willed in our stars; that it was destined to be this way. Perhaps that was so. It is possible that we may have had malignant stars. There must be a grain of truth in that, otherwise why should friends of yesterday be suddenly at each other's throats?

It could also be asked why this happened in 1947 when for centuries under the alien Mughal rule people could find a modus vivendi of coexistence. It is true that there were riots and violence even in those times and during the invasions before the Mughals conquered India.

Entire cities were put to torch and religious shrines desecrated every time a foreign army marched down the Afghan mountains in search of loot. But the riots and pillage then couldn't be resisted. Once the local army had been defeated, it was a surrender of the meek to the invaders; the citizens had no choice. But the partition was different; this time it was a surgical incision across the Indian heart. And this wasn't an invading army that did it, it was self-willed and self-wrought.

It would also be fair to say that the British drove us to such a pass; their policy of divide and rule could only have led to an abyss. The British needed a suitable instrument to carry out their design; someone who had immense ambition and the ability to mesmerize people with the power of his argument. Jinnah was just the man they were looking for. Together, with him, they could stir the cauldron.

Another, and perhaps frank, explanation for the violence during the partition might be the unleashing of the feral force during that period. The smell of blood is difficult to resist. Once it starts to flow, it becomes an unstoppable stream. It pollutes sophisticated debate, consumes argument. This in the end seems to have happened in 1947. In any case where was the scope for debate when throats were being cut en masse?

The scale of that violence and its sheer brutality is the stuff that family lores are made of—stories that are told between sobs of shame and pain. Generally speaking, Indians are a forgiving lot. Unlike some other races, Indians do not carry rancour and their grudges perpetually. They tend to forget the unpleasant. The partition, however, was different; the bitterness was so intense that the hurt continues to linger. So does the feeling of revenge. It is as if the Indo-Pak ground is not yet satiated with all the blood that has already seeped into it.

I recall spending a pleasant evening in a vast Karachi home. As with all such prosperous evenings the place was buzzing with gossip and good humour. At some point a young man was introduced to me. I asked him about his profession in the inquisitive manner that is peculiar to us in the subcontinent. He said he had graduated earlier that day from the prestigious Naval Academy of Karachi and that now he was a commissioned officer of the Pakistani navy. I congratulated him and wished him well in his career. We chatted a little more. When he found out that I was from India, he enquired if there would ever be good relations between our two countries. I replied encouragingly and said that given the goodwill on both sides there would surely come a time when we would begin to live in peace as two such closely connected neighbours should.

At this he stiffened. There was puzzlement in his eyes and with the innocence of youth he asked, 'Then what will happen to the oath that I took earlier this evening?'

Having said it he checked himself. He realized that it was a red line he shouldn't have crossed, not even in a friendly environment. He bid a quick goodbye and drifted away to join a group of young Pakistanis. Later I found out that a part of the oath for all newly commissioned defence officers of Pakistan calls upon them to engage in a jihad against India.

Since then I have often wondered at the wisdom of administering such an oath to impressionable young men. Even if these officers are trained to fight and kill, must their minds be prejudiced and poisoned at such a young age? Moreover, what will happen if in pursuit of that oath their objectives clash with those of a political leader who wants to live in peace with India? The oath that this young man took, and its part about jihad, continued to trouble me for a long time. Where would such indoctrination lead to? Does it not circumscribe the role of diplomats? Will such a constriction ever offer hope for normalization of relations between the two countries?

Given this background, the chances are that we will constantly be at each other's throats. To me that call for jihad was a real mind bender. The bigger and more dangerous question that I kept asking myself was this—what if they were to act in accordance with that oath?

Would that successful jihad end up breaking India? I was bewildered by the medieval mentality of that oath and I asked myself repeatedly if what I had heard from that young man was actually of this time and age? Sadly, it was.

Many years later I posed a similar query, but in a different context, to two young Indian girls. My enquiry was not Pakistani jihad related, it was more general in tone.

'Do you think India will ever break up again?' I asked.

'Oh no. Definitely never,' they protested.

I had not finished yet. So my next question followed quickly, 'Do you think Pakistan will break up again?' I asked this time.

They didn't reply, but both giggled spontaneously.

2

Breaking Up

Is the break-up of the other side an unfulfilled wish in people's minds? Is that the reason why we rush to draw arms so readily? Sometimes it would seem so. Alas, what should have been only sometimes has been happening rather often. A misstatement, a terror strike, a skirmish across the borders is enough to fuel passions. Even a rumour suffices.

In 1527, a Mughal ruler had built the Babri Masjid in Ayodhya after demolishing a temple that had stood there from ancient times for the holiest of Hindu gods, Ram. The destroyed temple commemorated the exact spot where Lord Ram was born. Its replacement, the Babri structure, remained largely unused and continually excited religious passions among Hindus. Following the demolition of the Babri mosque in India on 6 December 1992, Pakistan reacted quickly. It need not have but the timing was convenient for domestic political reasons. Nawaz Sharif was the prime minister then, and he had already been put on notice by the army establishment for maladministration and corruption. Moreover, Benazir Bhutto as the principal opposition leader was gaining political ground.

Benazir had recovered from the shock of her ouster from the government and had set in motion a credible campaign to get her back into power. Unlike in the past, this time she was not averse to keeping a line open with the army as also with the ISI. Her public rallies were attracting crowds and the media was beginning to take her seriously again; it had forgotten the misdeeds for which it had pilloried her and the frequent accounts of corruption by her husband Asif Ali Zardari and the rest of her Cabinet. The political wind was beginning to turn in her favour one more time.

But first she had to trip Nawaz as often as possible and get him eased out of power. Nawaz, on the other hand, needed to divert people's attention from his administrative inadequacies and get the national focus away from the style of his governance, in which cronyism was the norm and economy was on a wild ride. Both Benazir and the army were sniping at him. Since he was under attack from all sides, the Babri incident was just the type of diversion he needed. The fact that it would be transient, a passing phase of a few days before the national focus shifted back to the inadequacies of his government hardly mattered. The possibility that it might derail Indo-Pak relations yet again was of no consequence either. The important thing was not to miss this opportunity.

Nawaz Sharif addressed the nation on 7 December 1992 and in the course of that emotionally charged television address against India, he asked Benazir Bhutto, 'Will you remain silent at the martyrdom of Babri?'

His intent was obvious—to challenge Benazir to shed her allegedly doveish approach towards India and to join in the chorus of India-bashing. For good measure he also declared 8 December 1992 a day of mourning and a national holiday. The mobs came out in all their fury that day and over 200 Hindu and Sikh temples were torched or destroyed across Pakistan.

But such destruction of temples is routine in Pakistan; during Zia ul-Haq's time eighty-four temples were razed to the ground because they happened to be in the proposed alignment for a new highway between Karachi and Islamabad.

Zia was a rigid Islamist, but he could also be practical when it suited him. It is said that a mosque stood on the grounds where a new hotel, Pear Continental, was to be built in Karachi. When the owner of the hotel approached Zia with this dilemma, he advised the hotel owner to get that mosque brought down under the cover of a dark night and to have it rebuilt at a more convenient location nearby.

Such generosity of spirit is not extended to India. Any act or misact on India's part is good enough to rouse passions in Pakistan. Sometimes it seems that rumours feed and incite the highest too, affecting their judgement.

A few weeks after the Babri incident, I happened to be at a dinner with Benazir. Suddenly, out of the blue she asked me, 'Is India at the point of breaking up?'

'Why do you presume that?' I enquired.

'I am not saying that. It is your prime minister [Narasimha Rao] who said so,' Benazir replied.

It is true that after the Babri Masjid was brought down, Narasimha

Rao had said that the fabric of India was woven together by the thread of secularism, and that if secularism was dented the national fabric, too, would get damaged. It wasn't as if he had any doubt about India's unity or its stability. He was emphasizing the importance and the place of secularism in the Indian ethos. I explained the context accordingly to Benazir and our conversation moved on to other issues.

Later, I wondered about Benazir's query. She had a sharp mind and a well-honed politician's instinct to focus on the big picture. Yet she had asked that question with obvious conviction. Did she really believe in it? Or was it an illustration of the fact that an information gap can develop quickly even between two people who were one till 1947?

She had clearly misunderstood Narasimha Rao's lament. Or was it that in the absence of secularism in Pakistan, the otherwise liberal-minded Benazir found it hard to empathize with a neighbour's concern for a secular polity? It could have been one or a combination of these reasons because our misunderstandings have taken multiple forms over the years.

It wasn't always like that.

*

Following the mutiny against the British in 1857, there was a conscious effort by many Muslim leaders to identify with and promote Hindu–Muslim unity. Sir Syed Ahmed Khan, the founder of Aligarh Muslim University, had this to say in his address to the Indian Association in Lahore in 1884:

> I heartily wish to serve my country and my nation faithfully. In the word Nation I include both Hindus and Mohammadans, because that is the only meaning I can attach to it... There are different grounds upon which I call both these races which inhabit India by one word i.e. Hindu, meaning to say that they are inhabitants of Hindustan.[1]

It was the right antidote against British efforts to divide the two communities. But it also pointed to the uncertainties of the period; what was said one day could be reversed the next day. Because of the confusion prevailing then, it was the age of flip-flops. Some people changed positions and their views in line with the prevailing wind;

---

[1]M.G. Chitkara, *Rashtriya Swayam Sevak Sangh: National Upsurge.*

Sir Syed was no exception. He, rather than Muhammad Iqbal, is acknowledged by many as the father of the two-nation theory.[2]

Sometimes momentary passions, often perceived slights, and more devastatingly, the incitement by the British were instrumental in these turns. It was all so bewildering to those who decided to make these about-turns and even more so for those who thought that the people who had made the initial about-turn were really on their side. Many among them weren't even sure why they were abandoning the secular tradition of centuries. In the Hindi/Urdu heartland of India, in provinces like Uttar Pradesh and Bihar, people prided themselves on their Ganga–Yamuna tradition, these words being an allusion to the centuries of togetherness between Hindus and Muslims. It is true that there were occasional riots, and there were taboo areas between the communities. But they were aberrations rather than the norm. If sentiments bonded them together, emotions tore them apart sometimes.

The traditionalist and the more rigid among Hindus hesitated to share a meal or water with a Muslim. Yet, it was also quite normal to see Hindu and Muslim friends share food from the same plate. Everyday life may have had its red lines, but they were gently drawn. An unintended transgression was not reason enough for a call to communal arms.

The differences needed a more potent spark to erupt—an interfaith marriage, or a fight for turf between mafia dons belonging to different religions. The riots that followed killed some and injured many others. But the law and order machinery stepped in quickly and the community elders were cajoled to get into the act and stop the riots from spreading. With that ointment, the temporary surge of blood was reversed so it could flow at its normal, placid pace.

Still, some hurt feelings lingered. Consequently, there were reservations, taboo areas and discreetly drawn red lines. Some resentments persisted, leading to the fear of the other. All this was fed into the institutional memory, but none of it was so serious that it couldn't be healed by a vow of forgive and forget. As time went by, people accommodated the past and its trespasses, as they had done for centuries. That healing touch was the essence of the Ganga–Yamuna tradition—the acceptance of and respect for the other.

Jinnah understood it all; that's why Sarojini Naidu had once called him the ambassador of Hindu–Muslim unity. But his ambition got in

---

[2]Hari Dev Sharma (ed.), *100 Significant Pre-Independence Speeches—1858–1947.*

the way; he was a man in a great hurry and a politician with very high aims. Though intellectually he continued to be swayed by the Ganga–Yamuna culture, as a man with a mission he had neither the patience for its elaborate niceties, nor the inclination for compromise.

Accommodation carried with it the risk of giving up his ambition and he did not want to be number two to Gandhi and certainly not to Jawaharlal Nehru. He had at least given Gandhi the courtesy of adding 'Mr' whenever he addressed him in the initial years. But later, even that was missing. And in so far as Nehru was concerned, that was never in consideration in the initial years because Motilal Nehru was his contemporary and a friend and Jawahar just a friend's son. But in later years, when they became political rivals, Jinnah's hatred of his friend's son was visceral. In one phase they had not spoken to each other for five years and in another phase they did not speak with each other for seven years.

Was Jinnah then the villain that he was made out to be by a vast majority of Indians post-partition?

It is easy to castigate popular opinion; after all, it is not based on clinically tested facts. Still, much like common sense, general perception takes its strength from numbers. Indian people were convinced that had it not been for Jinnah the partition of their country would not have taken place.

Was it really so, or were Gandhi and Nehru also responsible for pushing Jinnah into an intransigent position? Or was the truth a halfway house, somewhere between the two sides? Let's also not forget the third party in this divorce. Would the British have left India united? Though a small island, battered to bare bones by the Second World War, Britain still had the pretensions of a world power, a status that it aimed to preserve for a long time to come.

Was it a part of this grand strategy that a portion had to be hived off from India to keep it in check? Moreover, that portion could become Britain's calling card to the Islamic world. Was Jinnah essential to the success of this British scheme? Or to put it in another way, had there been no Jinnah, would the British have invented one? Let's complicate the picture further and ask whether the British were given this suggestion about Pakistan being vital to their future strategic interests by Jinnah. Was it he who fed them the idea that Pakistan would be an ideal interlocutor for the British with the Islamic world?

Now that we have shaken the kaleidoscope, let's try and get the bigger picture.

3

Beginning the Divide

The crunch came in 1920. It was about a matter that did not concern India directly. Britain had invaded Turkey and in protest, the Ali brothers—Maulana Mohammad Ali and Maulana Shaukat Ali—had launched the Khilafat Movement in defiance against the British. On 1 August 1920, Gandhi decided to join in and began 'non-cooperation' against the British and in support of the Khilafat Movement. At first Mahatma Gandhi did not get ready support from his party for this move; there were even appeals by some Congressmen that he should withdraw the Non-Cooperation Movement. Those ranged against him made a formidable line-up. Besides the old guard of the party like Annie Besant, C.R. Das, Bipin Pal and Lala Lajpat Rai, there were also the relatively new Congressmen such as Motilal Nehru and Jinnah who opposed Gandhi on the issue.

Gandhi disagreed. He said, 'For me to suspend non-cooperation would be to prove untrue to the Musalman brethren.'[1]

When the matter was put to vote at a special session of the Congress party in September 1920 in Calcutta, Gandhi managed to win approval by only a narrow margin.

However, the doubts of the Congress leadership were not shared by the masses. The pro-Gandhi mood among them became a virtual storm when the Congress met in December 1920 for its regular annual session in Nagpur. Anti-Gandhi leaders were shouted off the stage. Jinnah, in particular, was booed with the cries of 'shame, shame'. Gandhi, on the other hand, could barely be heard because of the loud cheers in his favour. This Congress session attracted the largest number of Muslim delegates ever.

The year 1920 was to prove a year of some seminal changes in

---

[1]D.G. Tendulkar, *Mahatma: Life of Mohandas Karamchand Gandhi*.

Indian politics. Gandhi became the Mahatma, the undisputed leader of the Indian masses and the guiding light of the Congress party. The old guard had been vanquished and a disgusted Jinnah walked out of the Nagpur session.

The Khilafat Movement also unnerved the British rulers. Their first counter to it came through a 'firman' by the Nizam of Hyderabad. He declared the Khilafat Movement anti-Muslim and hence illegal. When Gandhi and the Ali brothers went to Aligarh Muslim University to get support for the Khilafat Movement, the British instigated the Muslim population of the city to riot against the Hindus.

The British also found ready support where they needed it. Mohammad Shafi, a member of the Viceroy's Executive Council, presented the viceroy with a two-pronged scheme:

i) To weaken the movement for a united India, it was essential to lure away the Muslims; this could only be done if the British signed the peace treaty with Turkey.
ii) An Anglo-Mohammadan unity programme in the interest of the British Empire should be organized.

This was just the kind of input that would have pleased the British colonialists. On 21 September 1922 the then viceroy of India, Lord Reading, wrote to the secretary of state for India in London:

> I have just sent you a telegram, which will show you how near we have been to a complete break between Muslims and Hindus. I have been giving the greatest attention to this possibility, and I have had the greatest assistance from [Mohammad] Shafi on my Council, who is a highly respectable Mohammadan.[2]

The British plans worked perfectly thereafter; the wedge between the two communities became steadily deeper. It must have delighted the viceroy sufficiently to have taken time out on a New Year's day (1 January 1925) to write to the secretary of state, 'The bridge Gandhi had built to span the gulf between the Hindus and Mohammadans has not only broken down, but I think it has completely disappeared.'[3]

Those in London were fully in tune with this project. On 22 January 1925, the secretary of state for India, Lord Birkenhead, wrote to the viceroy:

---

[2]Wali Khan, *Facts are Facts*.

[3]Ibid.

> The more it is made obvious that these antagonisms are profound, and affect an immense and irreconcilable section of the population, the more conspicuously is the fact illustrated that we and we alone can play the part of the composers.[4]

Still, the major point of worry for the British was the absence of a leader in the Muslim community who was capable of uniting the community. They were looking for someone who was charismatic enough to take on the Congress leaders.

*

By 1929, the British were convinced that they had found a counter to the Congress leaders, and that Muhammad Ali Jinnah was the leader they were looking for. In fact, Jinnah had started talking of parting with the Congress from mid-1928 when he returned from Paris without his wife Ruttie (she did not go back to him ever again). Towards the end of the year he had publicly begun talking of parting of ways and for the first time used the expression 'Muslim India'. With that the self-proclaimed nationalist had become a 'collaborationist'.

The viceroy wrote on 20 May 1929:

> I had a long talk with Jinnah a few days ago, which made it very clear to my mind that he and all the Bombay people, who are not disposed to Congress, are disposed to swing towards our direction if we can give them help later.[5]

A little over a year later Jinnah decided to quit it all. But this wasn't the only flip-flop of his life. He had done it before and he would do it again, including on the substance of that famous speech on 11 August 1947 delivered by him to the Pakistan Constituent Assembly in Karachi and on his shift from Bombay to Pakistan. The only objective that he remained steadfast on was his ambition to carve out a separate land for himself and Muslims.

However, the Muslim League was not attracting the numbers. There were more Muslims with Gandhi than with Jinnah or any of the others. (In 1927, the Muslim League's membership was only 1330. Even in 1933 its annual expenditure did not exceed Rs 3000.) The December 1930 session of the Muslim League presided over by Sir Muhammad Iqbal in Allahabad was a flop because of low attendance. Jinnah attended the session but he was fed up by its inconsequence.

---

[4]Ibid.

[5]Ibid.

Disheartened, he decided to shift to London with his daughter Dina and sister Fatima. His long-term intentions were clear because he took a passport which showed an address in London as his residence. For the next five years he ran a successful legal practice in London. It was lucrative enough for him to live in considerable style. There was still enough money left for him to purchase seven apartments in London in addition to his house in Hampstead. Despite these comforts, and despite his love for theatre in London, he missed the attention and the politics of India. The Muslim League was floundering and its leaders kept trying to convince Jinnah to come back to India. Finally, Jinnah gave in to their entreaties and in April 1936 he decided to return. This time there was no holding back and he went on the offensive from the moment he took over the reins of the party.

'Islam is in danger' and 'Free India would mean Hindu Raj' became his battle cry. On 3 January 1937 he said at a public meeting in Calcutta that he represented the third party in the country, the Muslims, the British and the Congress being the other two!

Nehru had not met Jinnah for over five years, but he was quick to rebut him. On 16 January 1937 he responded:

> All those people who talk in terms of Hindu rights and Muslim interests are job-hunters, pure and simple, and fight for loaves and fishes of office. How long are you going to tolerate this nonsense, this absurdity... There are only two forces in the country, the Congress and the Government. Those who are standing midway will have to choose between the two.[6]

Even a year after his return from London the prospects for the Muslim League and his own political leadership were not promising. In the prestigious province of Punjab, for example, the Unionist Party led by Sir Sikandar Hayat Khan had been in power since 1920. Theirs was a non-communal platform and they didn't want anything to do with the Muslim League provoking Jinnah to vow, 'I shall never come to Punjab again; it is such a hopeless place.' Yet, he returned to Punjab repeatedly, most notably in 1940 to Lahore for the famous League session.

Punjab, however, was not the only problem. Jinnah had other, more serious difficulties on his health front. The tuberculosis which had first affected his lungs was now beginning to spread to the other

---

[6]Jawaharlal Nehru, *Selected Works*, vol. 8.

parts of his body. But Jinnah was consumed by his pursuit of Pakistan and tuberculosis would have to wait till his dream was fulfilled.

The pursuit of this dream made him tear at the long-standing Indian traditions. He decided that one sure way of achieving his objective, and getting attention, was through the Ganga–Yamuna heartland. Muslims were in a majority in Punjab and Bengal, but in both they formed the government, so they could not agitate against themselves. The United Provinces and Bihar were different—there, Muslims were in a minority and had grievances that could be scratched raw. Jinnah set about exploiting those sore spots.

15 October 1937 was an important day for Jinnah. That was also the day when Jinnah exchanged his Saville Row suit for the dress worn by the Muslim elite in the United Provinces, a sherwani on top of a kameez and pyjama. On the way to the League session he noticed the cap that his host, the Nawab of Mehmoodabad, was wearing. He took that and put it on his head. From that day, this black aristocratic cap was his answer to the homespun Gandhi cap. A sartorial distinction had now been added to the League's list of differences with the Congress party.

At last, the political tide too was turning in his favour. Things were beginning to fall in place precisely according to Jinnah's plan. He was already the president for life of the League and after the massive show of numbers at the Lucknow session, the League and his will were synonymous; his word was law. On 10 December 1938 Maulana Mazharuddin Ahmad announced in his Urdu paper *Al-Aman* that Jinnah should henceforth be known as Qaid-e-Azam, the great leader. It fitted his stern image.

The toothless Mahatma Gandhi, with his impish smile, remained a humble Bapu to the Hindu and Muslim masses.

By early 1939 Jinnah had already discussed with some of his closest confidants his plan to seek the partition of India. The approaching world war was to be his great chance. Unlike Gandhi who refused to help the British with their manpower needs for the army, Jinnah readily stepped forward with an offer to get them Muslim youth to fight. But it was to be one part of a bargain; he expected the British to pay a price for it.

An opportunity presented itself when Nehru's friend Chaudhuri Khaliquzzuman, who had now become a Muslim Leaguer and a confidant of Jinnah, went to London. On 20 March 1939, his last day there, he met Lord Zetland, the secretary of state for India. Zetland asked him about the plan he had to prevent the enslavement of Muslims.

Khaliquzzuman had the Jinnah-scripted answer ready. He said, 'You may partition the Muslim areas from the rest of India and proceed with your scheme of federation of the Indian provinces without including the Muslim areas, which should be independent from the rest.'[7]

Lord Zetland sat with his visitor for nearly ninety minutes and listened carefully, for the proposal had possibilities. Obviously, the British couldn't stir the Indian pot when they were about to go into the Second World War. But there was no harm in letting hope germinate in the League's upper circles.

Mahatma Gandhi was already wary and in a note of 30 October 1939 he wrote, 'Janaab Jinnah Saheb looks to the British power to safeguard the Muslim rights. Nothing that the Congress can do or concede will satisfy him.'

A week later the Mahatma was even more direct. Writing in the 7 November 1939 issue of the *Harijan*, he remarked, 'I hope the League does not want to vivisect India.'

The Mahatma may have hoped against hope that the seemingly inevitable was not going to happen. But Harry Coomer (Hari Kumar), the Anglo-Indian protagonist of Paul Scott's *Raj Quartet*, sees it all coming when he writes to an English friend in 1940:

> I think that there's no doubt that in the last twenty years—whether intentionally or not—the English have succeeded in dividing and ruling, and the kind of conversation I hear...makes me realise the extent to which the English now seem to depend upon the divisions in Indian political opinion perpetuating their own rule at least until after the war, if not for some time beyond it. They are saying openly that it is no good leaving the bloody country because there's no Indian party representative to hand it over to. They prefer Muslims to Hindus (because of the closer affinity that exists between God and Allah than exists between God and the Brahma), are constitutionally predisposed to Indian princes, emotionally affected by the thought of untouchables, and mad keen about the peasants who look upon any Raj as God...

India's destiny, sadly, was going to follow the course set in Paul Scott's fictional account, not entirely but largely.

Vivisection was the precise plan of the Muslim League; one that it was going to make public in 1940 in Lahore. Even then the bulk of the Indian population, Hindu, Muslim, Sikh, Christian, and others, were

---

[7]Sankar Ghose, *Jawaharlal Nehru*.

far too occupied with the daily routine of existence to worry much about the complications of politics. For them the present was all that mattered, and the present meant the world war and British colonial rule.

But Jinnah was glad that his scheme was working; his idea of independence for a community as opposed to the country was beginning to get the attention he wanted. While he was happy now to share this secret with the world, he was keeping his fingers crossed that his other, and more personal, secret about tuberculosis should remain one. Occasionally, and surprisingly for Jinnah, he also sent out a prayer that independence for Pakistan should precede his ultimate journey.

Thus far life had granted him his every wish, immense riches, every luxury that an Indian could dream of, a beautiful wife, a caring sister and a delightful daughter. He had also got every high position that one could want. But Pakistan was his ultimate ambition; he could then enter history books not merely as a footnote that he was a brilliant lawyer, but as a leader who had shaped history.

Jinnah's vanity demanded nothing less.

4

'Give Me Pakistan'

Janet Morgan brings out the contrast between Jinnah and Nehru in her book, *Edwina Mountbatten: A Life of Her Own*. She narrates what Dickie (Mountbatten) said after his first interview with the Muslim leader: 'My God, he was cold.'

She goes on to write, 'With Nehru there were no such difficulties. Charming and cultivated, he was never at a loss for the right phrase or gesture. He was fit and trim—he practiced Yoga—and unlike Jinnah, who was gaunt and sickly with bad teeth, Nehru was good looking.'

She could have added that Jinnah was fiercely ambitious to the extent of adopting unconventional means to achieve his objective. Nehru was trusting and sometimes naïve in his judgement. Like his mentor Gandhi, means were as important to him as the end.

Jinnah was a man of few words. There were long spells of silence when he just looked into distant space, which unnerved and baffled others. He was such a private person that neither friend nor foe could claim to understand him. He wrote no book and kept no diary. He wrote no memoir and was not known as a prodigy of learning. He confided in no one except in the Raja of Mehmoodabad, Nawab Mohammad Ismail Khan. Obstinate and uncompromising himself, his favourite book, from which he often quoted in his public speeches, was John Morley's *Compromise*, which emphasizes that compromise is to politics what devotion is to friendship.

Jinnah was stern to the point of being rude even to children. When he visited Karachi he stayed often at the Haroon House, which belongs to the family that owns the *Dawn* newspaper. *Dawn* was also actively involved in promoting the cause of Pakistan from the very beginning. It was, therefore, convenient for Yusuf Haroon and Jinnah to be together. But the Haroon children positively dreaded these visits. The story has it they used to hide behind any big furniture or under a bed just to escape Jinnah's notice. He terrified them.

In contrast, Nehru loved children. They in turn called him Chacha Nehru, Uncle Nehru. He could dance with them with the same ease as he donned a Himachali cap to dance with the hill people. Nehru too had a short fuse. He was quick to lose his temper, and he did so frequently, even with his father. He was also prone to jumping in a crowd to control them, a crowd of party followers or even that of baton-wielding policemen. But his anger was that of milk simmering on low heat; forever threatening to spill over, but never actually doing so. Nehru's was a non-violent temper. Had it been violent, he might have reacted to the League's subterfuges with greater cunning than mere hot words.

Jinnah put his legal training to full use in pursuing his political objective. He was rapier-sharp in argument and intent upon winning his case, the pursuit of Pakistan being the biggest case of his life. And that case was going to be decided in the Imperial Majesty's court. Though ethics would have advised him not to approach the judge to influence him, Jinnah dropped any reservation that he might ordinarily have had. He approached the viceroy and any other imperial authority who he thought could help influence the decision in favour of Pakistan. The British themselves were not averse to his approaches, or to his suggestion for a mutually beneficial arrangement.

Nehru, by family tradition, and through his grounding at Harrow, was committed to a sense of fair play. Things had to be above board. Matters may have taken a different turn had he been a practising lawyer like Jinnah before joining politics. Then, he may have been inclined to take short cuts and a more practical view of matters. He did practise law initially, but it was just a passing phase. It was all too brief to expose him to the tricks of the trade. Nehru insisted on playing politics like he played cricket—as a gentleman.

Jinnah was not averse to applying pressure, even strong-arm tactics if it served his purpose. In July 1945 he began to stress that only he and Pakistan stood between Muslims and slavery under Hindus in an independent India. Any Muslim who differed was branded a traitor. Simultaneously, the League also began to prepare for violence. This private army was called the Muslim National Guards.

By the time the Cabinet Mission came to India in March 1946, the British had decided to concede Pakistan. But had the father of this notion thought the idea through? Sir Akbar Hydari asked Jinnah at a meeting with this Mission, 'Could you define Pakistan?' Jinnah did not have a clear-cut answer to that question.

Viceroy Archibald Wavell favoured Jinnah but even he found him exasperating at these meetings. As Wavell wrote in his diary, 'Jinnah spent an hour on a largely fanciful history of India and on differences between the Hindus and the Muslims.' On the overall presentation by Jinnah and his Muslim League colleagues to the Cabinet Mission, Wavell writes, 'The only thing they were articulate about was their "Hymn of Hate" against the Hindus.'[1]

What Wavell said fitted in precisely with the theory of Sigmund Freud. He wrote in an essay concerning 'the narcissism of the minor differences', that the most vicious and irreconcilable quarrels often arise between peoples who are to most outward appearances nearly identical. Neither Jinnah nor Gandhi/Nehru nor Wavell/Mountbatten could have imagined the extent of viciousness that their decisions would soon unleash between identical people who once swore by the idea of India.

Jinnah was still uncomfortable with the fact that the Pakistan which was likely to come his way would be a moth-eaten one, closer to the one envisaged by Iqbal in 1930, rather than the grander version he wanted. He had wanted a large-sized Pakistan that could compare favourably in size with India. But the one that seemed feasible was more wild than manageable.

Baluchistan was sparsely populated and largely barren, the NWFP wild and historically untamed, while Sindh had some promise it was Punjab that was the jewel of India. But the large numbers of Hindus and Sikhs in Punjab presented a problem for him—what if they were to migrate en masse to India? Would the Muslim minorities from other parts of India then migrate to Pakistan, presenting the new state with a huge problem of resettlement? Would Pakistan be able to accommodate 90 million Muslims who were then spread all over India? It was issues such as these which brought out the contradictions in Jinnah's scheme. He didn't want the 90 million to migrate to Pakistan.

The Muslim homeland that he was going to create should not be cluttered by too many of them. Rather, he wanted them to remain in India as a guarantee of Pakistan's safety. On the other hand, he wanted the minorities in Pakistan to thin out. Yet they were needed there in some numbers, as a security to ensure the safety of Muslims who chose to stay on in India. His idea of partition, ruinous as it was for millions, was remarkably complicated in its objectives.

Nor were the means towards his objective simple. Jinnah set about

[1]Penderel Moon (ed.), *Wavell: The Viceroy's Journal.*

using those means with the same ruthlessness as he employed in suppressing those who differed with him. 'The Muslim League Army' was one of the strategic means that he was to employ with successful effect.

Why was a resort to arms necessary? Was it because of the apprehension that the Congress party might somehow influence the British even at this late stage and get them to agree that the partition would only result in misery for people? Or was it a tactic to put pressure on the British to give a larger share of territory to Pakistan? It could have been one or a combination of these motivations. The Muslim League in any case had decided on action.

At a League session in Delhi in April 1946 Jinnah made every delegate sign a pledge in the name of Allah that he would do anything necessary to achieve Pakistan.

Hussain Shaheed Suhrawardy was then the prime minister of Bengal. The resolution for the pledge was moved by him and while he proposed it, he said, 'I have long pondered whether the Muslims are prepared to fight. Let me honestly declare that every Muslim in Bengal is ready and prepared to lay down his life.'[2]

On 16 July 1946, Jinnah gave the call for Direct Action. When asked about what the League intended by Direct Action, Jinnah replied evasively, 'I am not going to discuss ethics.'[3]

Exactly a month later, Suhrawardy declared a holiday on 16 August in Bengal. Since the 16th coincided with the weekend, all government offices were closed for three days. On that day, the British brigadier in charge of troops in Calcutta ordered them to stay in their barracks for the day. There was not a policeman in sight as a sea of Muslim Leaguers began their march through the city. Then there was mayhem, with looting and killing starting soon after. In his address to the mob later that afternoon the prime minister of Bengal urged the looters to carry on! This behaviour fitted in well with his reputation for violence. Viceroy Wavell had accurately described Suhrawardy in his diary as 'crooked, dishonest, shifty and unprincipled'.

The riots in Calcutta continued for three days, leaving a smell so powerful that the army needed masks to ward off the stench from the corpses. Almost 15,000 people were massacred in Calcutta. In her biography of the photojournalist Margaret Bourke-White, Vicky Goldberg describes the violence thus:

---

[2]Sankar Ghose, *Jawaharlal Nehru.*

[3]Ayesha Jalal, *The Sole Spokesman.*

> At first light, the Moslem mobs swarmed up out of the filthy slums. Screaming, burning, rampaging for five days without stop, they clubbed to death thousands of Hindus, leaving the streets clogged with mutilated bodies and the Hooghly River awash with bloody corpses. News of the massacre spread like fire in high wind… The savagery of religious fanaticism in Calcutta changed history in India, unleashing hatreds and reprisals that in time split the country apart.[4]

Margaret had gone to Calcutta to cover the aftermath of violence for *Life* magazine. What she saw and photographed was nauseating. Days after the massacre, she could see vultures feeding on bodies of dead Hindus on the streets of Calcutta. Their feast was so plentiful that fattened by it some of the vultures were too heavy to fly.

All the officers of military and civil authority blamed Suhrawardy for the riots and recommended that he be replaced. This was easily achievable because his stay in office depended upon the support of the British votes in the Assembly.

But the British vote stayed on his side.

Meanwhile rioting had spread to other parts of India. It was nowhere near as deadly as that in Calcutta. But all over India it was the same story, cities were in flames; the communal violence seemed unstoppable. 5000 people were killed in the Noakhali district on 10 October. Even then, violence could have been controlled and stopped altogether if like the Congress party, the Muslim League had given out a call for restraint.

Instead, on 10 November 1946 Jinnah gave out the statement, 'Give me Pakistan, otherwise the riots will not stop.'

This wasn't just a verbal flourish. Jinnah meant every word of what he had said. He had plans and backup plans, ready just in case the main one misfired. But as it was the dice were falling his way no matter how recklessly he threw them. Even as the country was on fire, Jinnah was working on something even more special for the NWFP. In February 1947, he called Iskander Mirza the man he had chosen for this special task.

As Wali Khan writes about this episode in his book *Facts are Facts: The Untold Story of India's Partition*:

> Jinnah told Iskandar Mirza that he was not going to get Pakistan unless some serious trouble was created and the best place to do this

---

[4]Vicky Goldberg, *Margaret Bourke-White—A Biography*.

> was NWFP and the adjacent tribal areas... Jinnah wanted him to resign from the [Government] service and go into the tribal areas to start a Jehad.

Wali Khan writes further, 'Communal riots had pulverised the nation. But Jinnah wanted to play a most dangerous game and that too in the Frontier Province.'

Then Wali Khan quotes a passage from first president of Pakistan Iskander Mirza's biography:

> This could only take the form of raids on the border villages in the settled area...yet I decided to fall in line with Qaid-e-Azam's plan. I had no desire to be branded as a man who was found wanting when the time for action came. With the liberal expenditure of money I would be able to cause some trouble in Waziristan Tirah and Mohamand country. I gave my estimate of money as one crore.[5]

The first instalment of Rs 20,000 came from the Nawab of Bhopal. With that amount as the seed capital, Mirza collected a team from Dera Ismail Khan and Peshawar. But before they could get into action, word came from Jinnah in May 1947 that since Pakistan was going to be conceded, the scheme should be abandoned. This association gave him the chance to get close to Jinnah. After the partition, Mirza claims to have suggested to Jinnah that 'special consideration should be given to Leaguers as they had brought in Pakistan'. Jinnah was quick to retort, 'Who told you that the Muslim League brought in Pakistan? I brought in Pakistan with my stenographer.'[6]

By mid-April 1947, it was clear to the new Viceroy Louis Mountbatten that Jinnah could not be persuaded to agree to anything less than complete independence for Pakistan. Though Mahatma Gandhi did suggest to Mountbatten on 31 March 1947 that he should try and persuade Jinnah to accept the leadership of the interim government on whatever terms he wished, the idea failed to pass muster during Mountbatten's consultations with his advisers. The basic difficulty was in the approach of the two principals—if Gandhi had a solution for every problem, Jinnah had a problem for every solution. Jinnah used every subterfuge and covered every angle to stay a step ahead of the Congress leaders. And it included the destabilization of Muslim-majority provincial governments.

---

[5]Humayun Mirza, *From Plassey to Pakistan: The Family History of Iskander Mirza.*

[6]K.C. Yadav, *India Divided.*

The prime minister of Punjab, Khizar Hayat Tiwana, was bitterly opposed to the Muslim League. However, all of a sudden he resigned on 2 March 1947, to the chagrin of the Congress and Akali leaders whom he didn't care to consult. It seems that it was the handiwork of Jinnah's emissary Sir Muhammad Zafarullah who persuaded Tiwana not to betray his community. Tiwana's letter of resignation was also drafted by Sir Zafarullah.

Jinnah also masterminded the Civil Disobedience Movement in Punjab and the NWFP. His object was to topple the Tiwana and Khan Sahib[7] ministries and to disturb the communal ratio in Assam so that he could grab for Pakistan the largest possible area. Two members of the Viceroy's Executive Council, Abdul Rab Nishtar and Ghazanfar Ali Khan, were his collaborators in this project. The Civil Disobedience Movement had popular support in which a large number of students of Aligarh Muslim University, burqa-clad women, pirs and *sajjada-nashins* (descendants of pirs or Sufi saints who were hereditary administrators) participated.

It wasn't just in India that Jinnah was exerting himself; he had secretly been in touch with Winston Churchill too. One of their meetings was held on 22 May 1947, about two weeks before the partition plan was to be announced. They stayed in touch through letters too. Since Churchill did not want to be discovered corresponding directly with him, Jinnah's communications were addressed to Churchill's secretary. And these consultations continued till almost a week before independence. Jinnah's dependence on British connivance was so deep that once Churchill had commented, 'By God, Jinnah is the one man who can't do without British help.'[8]

In retrospect, Jinnah seems to have played a clever card. By seeking British help and by ingratiating himself with leaders like Churchill, his need for a separate homeland captured British sympathy and his case their understanding. When Jinnah accepted the partition plan that was announced on 3 June 1947, the die was cast. All that remained was to trace a line over a map. The borders that were soon to emerge were an imperial arbitration that took no account of the historical evolution of states and societies.

As Marya Mannes put it in her poem:

---

[7]Dr Khan Sahib was the chief minister of the NWFP.

[8]Arthur Herman, *Gandhi and Churchill*.

Borders are scratched across the
hearts of men
By strangers with a calm, judicial
pen,
And when the borders bleed we
watch with dread
The lines of ink across the map
turn red.

5

A Divisive Agenda

Sir Cyril Radcliffe was the stranger chosen to wield the red pen. There is no real explanation for why he was chosen for the task, except perhaps some inordinate faith in the possibility that a new broom would sweep clean. But was his arrival in India absolutely necessary? To this day, people wonder whether the train towards partition could have been stopped somehow, whether enough efforts were made by people to give unity one last chance.

That was the fatal flaw. The people of India were never given a real chance; they were informed of the decision made by a few that henceforth they must live their lives differently. The humiliation of living in a colony was soon going to be replaced by the trauma of partition. But all through, Mahatma Gandhi kept trying to preserve a united India. As the Indian poet Ali Sardar Jafri was to write at a later time, and in a different context, Gandhi too believed that there was hope provided:

> *Guftagu band na ho*
> *Baat se baat chale*
> *Subh tak shaam-e-mulaaqat chale*
> (Keep the conversation going,
> One word leading to another,
> The evening rendezvous lasting till dawn)

Sadly, that conversation was the missing link. A divisive agenda instead of common cause, emotions rather than reason prevailed. Naturally, then, the lines drawn on the ground turned indelible. Yet there is no harm in making the enquiry that David Page makes in the introduction to his book, *Prelude to Partition*. He writes:

> Why did relations between Hindus and Muslims deteriorate to the point where partition became a necessity? It was undoubtedly a

> presumptuous and foolhardy quest, as I was told quite firmly by Sir George Abell, private secretary to the last two Viceroys... He said, 'I was in India for twenty years and I didn't manage to get to the bottom of it and you certainly won't in three.' His words were still ringing in my ears five years later and do so even today.

George Abell and David Page are not the only ones bewildered by the puzzle. People in the subcontinent still shake their heads in disbelief that the partition should have happened. Whether the British have any regret for what they did, and the way it happened, remains a mystery. The few accounts about the partition that have been written have concentrated on the consequences rather than the cause of it. In any case, the versions written by the British have tended to be sympathetic to the British masters of the time, while the handful of accounts penned by Indian and Pakistani writers have tended to focus on the human aspect of the tragedy.

There is another vital difference. The British made the mess and left the Indian shores to concentrate on other things. Indian and Pakistani people had no choice; they had to pick up the pieces from a complex disaster zone. That avoidable trauma is the reason why the question resurfaces every so often—why did it have to happen the way it did?

Mushirul Hasan writes in *Partition Narratives*:

> Pacifying enraged mobs was relatively simple; for the Gandhian charisma still worked (March 1947)... But Jinnah...was a hard nut to crack. Allaying his apprehensions proved to be a nightmare for his political adversaries. Meeting his demands was doubly difficult... Gandhi did not expect to convert Jinnah to his creed, but he counted on his party comrades (Nehru and Patel) to pay heed to his warnings. What if they had done so?

For the sake of argument let's assume that they had done so. Would it have made any difference? Could their combined efforts have stopped the partition of the country? It seems highly unlikely because the British had made up their mind to divide the country. Moreover, Jinnah was just not willing to concede to any compromise—he wasn't even interested in the crown of India, an offer that was made to him. He wanted a separate land for himself.

Since we are talking in hypothetical terms about a history that cannot be refashioned, let's at least look at it in yet another way.

Between December 1921 and August 1942, Jawaharlal Nehru went to jail nine times, spending 3262 days there, or about nine years. Then from August 1942 to June 1945 he was jailed for another 1040 days. Therefore, altogether, he spent nearly half of that twenty-four-year period in jail. So did many of the other Congress leaders.

It also means that during this long period, while the Congress leaders were in jail, they were politically inactive. Sealed inside the four walls of a prison they could neither mobilize people nor interact with the British to counter Jinnah, and project the Congress's point of view. In contrast, Jinnah did not spend a single day in jail. These years also happened to be the period when he became most active politically. This suited both the British masters and Jinnah's Muslim League—Jinnah had the entire political field to himself and the undivided attention of the British.

Let's shake that kaleidoscope a bit more and ask—what if Gandhi, Nehru and Patel had not spent years in prison and they too had been free? Would the partition plan have still come to fruition in the manner that it did? Alas, that was not to be; going to jail was an essential part of their plan. You might call it self-willed hara-kiri, but their form of protest involved the awakening of people, and going to jail was an important part of spreading that awareness. In the process they antagonized the British, who in turn, denied them a level playing field.

Would equal opportunity have made any difference at all? Well, we can always speculate. After all, it's easy to embroider history, and easier still to rage against leaders from this distance in time. One can also skilfully play historical echoes against each other to suit whatever shape we want to give to the journey. But all our contortions would not address the fundamental difference between the two approaches—for Congress leaders the journey was as important as the destination, for Jinnah the end point was arrival. Like Groucho Marx he too might have said, 'I have principles. If you don't like them, I have others.'

Sadly, it must be admitted that even if the Congress leadership had shown maximum accommodation, Jinnah had set for himself a political trajectory that ruled out compromise. It wasn't as if no one had made the effort to convince him. The Unionist Party led by Sikandar Hayat Khan and later by Tiwana in Punjab did its best to argue in favour of a united India, but instead of convincing Jinnah, they were converted to his side.

On a few occasions, when the British made the effort they were stonewalled by Jinnah. Mountbatten used every argument that he could possibly think of to dissuade him against a complete break, but in the end he concluded that Jinnah was 'a psychopathic case'. He said:

> In fact until I had met him [Jinnah] I would not have thought it possible that a man with such a complete lack of administrative knowledge or a sense of responsibility could achieve or hold...so powerful a position.[1]

Why did Mountbatten come to this conclusion? As a leader of men in war, he must have constantly judged people in different conditions, and evaluated his officers for their administrative skills. This ability must have been at work as he met political leaders in India. As a new and supposedly impartial observer he may also have been convinced of the impracticality of partition; it was certainly going to leave many questions unanswered.

Did Jinnah care about the larger number of Muslims who were going to be left behind, Muslims who constituted no part of his two-nation theory? Or even for the Muslims who were used for agitations by the Muslim League. The fact is that he had no intention of accommodating them in his Pakistan because it would have made Pakistan unviable with the administrative burden and financial responsibility for a people who were relatively poor. The Pakistan he wanted was not going to be encumbered by these hungry masses.

Jinnah created a country not because history demanded it or a vast majority felt the necessity of it; he created it for himself and his ego. As he told Mountbatten, 'I do not care how little you give me as long as you give it to me completely.'[2]

Political scientist Ishtiaq Ahmed criticizes the Congress for its tactical mistakes:

> The truth is that two Congress decisions proved to be colossal mistakes: resigning the ministries in September 1939 and then the ill-fated Quit India movement of August 1942 whose chief merit was that the Congress was nowhere around to make a difference while the Muslim League filled that space and secured a mandate from the Muslims of India for a separate state. Had the Congress not earned the contempt and wrath of the British who considered the lack of support during the war as a betrayal that was tantamount to treason, the course of history would have been very different.[3]

---

[1]Latif Ahmed Sherwani, *The Partition of India and Mountbatten*.

[2]Tariq Ali, *The Clash of Fundamentalists*.

[3]Dr Ishtiaq Ahmed, 'Splitting India–iii', *The Friday Times*.

Sometimes people still speculate and ask that if Jinnah wasn't there, would Pakistan have come about? Well, speculations are difficult to respond to with any degree of accuracy; unless one says fatalistically that it was destined to happen. But more rationally, it could be said that if Jinnah had not been a leader then, the chances of a Pakistan happening may have reduced considerably. Or to apportion the blame equally, it should also be said that leaders like Nehru need not have shied away from asserting themselves and their position less idealistically and more forcefully. Perhaps they should have also found a way of neutralizing Jinnah's stormtroopers.

Then there is the other imponderable. Jinnah had been suffering from severe ill health for over a decade. It had been kept a secret all this while. Would people have reacted differently had it become public knowledge, say in 1940 before the Lahore resolution was passed, or even in the years after that? Had the British known about his medical condition in the early stages, would they still have chosen Jinnah as their confidant and close collaborator?

While researching for *Freedom at Midnight*, Dominique Lapierre and Larry Collins met the Indian doctor (J.A.L. Patel) who had treated Jinnah. When they showed Mountbatten a copy of the medical report that Dr Patel gave them, he gasped:

> Good God! If I had known all this at the time, the course would have been different. I would have delayed the granting of independence for several months. There would have been no partition. Pakistan would not have existed. India would remain united. Three wars would have been avoided...

These were noble sentiments indeed. But was Lord Mountbatten speaking the absolute truth? Let us consider a few facts.

Jinnah, it may be recalled, had been having health problems for many years before Mountbatten became the viceroy of India. That medical condition was *not* a secret. Considering the political plans the British had for him from the 1920s, is it not possible that they would have been interested in monitoring Jinnah's health?

Later, in the 1930s, for five years, Jinnah was a resident of London. He would have had regular medical check-ups there. It is also possible that the first signs of pleurisy may have been detected during that stay in London. Is it not likely that the British secret services may have monitored his medical reports at least in the London clinics?

Akbar S. Ahmed writes in his book, *Jinnah: Pakistan and Islamic Identity*:

> From 1938 onwards he was to be found complaining of 'the tremendous strain' on his 'nerves and physical endurance' (Jinnah's letter to Hassan Ispahani, 12 April 1938). From then on he regularly fell ill... He remained unwell for much of the first half of 1945. Later in the year he admitted: 'The strain is so great that I can hardly bear it' (to Ispahani, 9 October 1945).

B.R. Nanda writes in his book, *Road to Partition: The Life and Times of Mohammad Ali Jinnah*:

> While travelling by train with his sister Fatima from Bombay to Delhi in the second week of March (1940) Jinnah complained of pain in the middle of his back and spinal cord. He was examined by his doctor and told that he was suffering from pleurisy and required bed rest for at least a fortnight.

Jinnah did not follow the doctor's advice because he had an appointment to keep with the viceroy on 13 March. And a week later he had to be in Lahore for the Muslim League session which was to pass the resolution demanding a separate nation for Muslims. Jinnah was determined not to miss either of these appointments, especially the second one. But it is hard to believe that the news of his illness in the train did not reach the viceroy and the Congress leadership.

Rajmohan Gandhi gives another instance in his book, *Eight Lives: A Study of the Hindu–Muslim Encounter*:

> Gandhi a month under 75, and Jinnah close to 68 (in 1944) were both ill...the frail Jinnah had just learned that there was 'unresolved pneumonia' in the base of his lungs. Calcium injections, tonics and short wave diathermy had helped him; still pneumonia in India of the mid-forties was a disease to dread.

Yet, even this serious episode seems to have escaped the attention of the British administration and the Congress cadres.

Frank Ryan, an American doctor specializing in tuberculosis, writes in his book, *Tuberculosis: The Greatest Story Never Told*, 'Dr. J.A.L Patel first diagnosed Jinnah with "chronic cavitating pulmonary tuberculosis" in June 1946.' Dr Ryan categorized the disease as a sentence of death.

Now, that was a full year before Mountbatten announced his partition plan. That apart, isn't it too much of a coincidence that every time there was a major medical episode, Jinnah launched something radical, as if he was racing against the time allotted to him by destiny? The Pakistan Resolution of 1940 and the Direct Action of 1946 both followed the news of his grave medical condition.

Prior to handing over charge, Lord Wavell had informed London that Jinnah was suffering from tuberculosis. Would he not have briefed his successor Lord Mountbatten that the president of the Muslim League was suffering from a debilitating disease? Let us give him the benefit of doubt and grant that pressures of departure may have made him forget this detail in his briefing of Mountbatten. Even if that was the case, what about the written papers and the message that Wavell had sent to London about Jinnah's medical condition? Surely, Mountbatten had access to that official correspondence. Finally, wouldn't the aides have advised the new viceroy about the medical condition of such an important leader as Jinnah?

The British secret service in India was one of the most famed of its time in the world. How is it that despite the episodes mentioned above, British intelligence chose to ignore them all?

Let's consider another piece of evidence. As *Freedom at Midnight* details further, Jinnah was barely able to walk the few steps up the aircraft ladder as he emplaned for Karachi prior to independence. It is reasonable to assume that his frail health condition had been in evidence for some time. Even a casual glance at the photographs of Jinnah from that period shows that he had been reduced to a skeleton frame from the healthy, handsome man of the 1920s.

The British pride themselves for their ability to read body language. How is it that, over a period of at least ten years, they ignored the signals from Jinnah's body that he was very sick; that his pale skin and gaunt looks conveyed something more than a starvation diet of a pauper? With his sunken cheeks and skeletal frame Jinnah looked, in his last decade, the picture of a man ravaged by some serious disease. Pleurisy, tuberculosis and cancer of the lungs can hardly be kept a state secret for such a long time.

Or is it that Mountbatten wasn't entirely truthful when he told Lapierre and Collins that he had not known of Jinnah's illness. Did he pretend ignorance on purpose? Were the British complicit in keeping Jinnah's health condition a secret?

Isn't it a fact that a swift transfer of power was the clear brief given by Prime Minister Attlee to Mountbatten when he was appointed the viceroy of India? Isn't it also a fact that the partition was a political act on the part of the British and not a bifurcation made necessary by a religious need?

After the Second World War, the British hold over India was weakening. The recruitment to the steel frame, the Indian Civil Service (ICS), had stopped in 1943. The soldiers of England's conscript army in India, exhausted by the world war, were no longer keen to serve in India. Moreover, Mountbatten was haunted by the violence of the Direct Action Day in Calcutta (August 1946) by the Muslim League. Yet, Mountbatten had claimed to Larry Collins and Dominique Lapierre that 'there would have been no Partition'. Was he trying to rewrite history in his favour by making this assertion? Why did he claim that he was ignorant of the crucial fact that Jinnah was very sick and dying? Was he concerned about history assigning him his share of the responsibility for the horrors that followed?

What about the Congress party? There were doctors among its leadership. Would they not have noticed that Jinnah was no longer able to take much physical strain? A person affected by tuberculosis and cancer of the lungs gives out loud and obvious signs of ill health. Did no one in the Congress suspect that something seemed seriously wrong with Jinnah's body? Even otherwise, Bombay society can rarely keep a secret for long. Were they all sworn to silence? Could no one notice in India that this much-photographed man was steadily looking drawn and sickly?

Either it was a slip of a vast magnitude, or a huge conspiracy of silence on the part of the British, the Congress leadership and Bombay society. Otherwise, how could so obvious a medical condition be ignored? How could they not note that there was something very wrong with a man who found it difficult to take a few steps without gasping for breath?

These mysteries of history are difficult to rewind with great accuracy. What is certain, however, is the fact that despite Mahatma Gandhi's frequent lament, especially during the weeks before August 1947, that no one listened to him any more, the fact is that his was still the commanding voice. The Indian masses simply worshipped the ground he walked on. His effect on people, the media and everyone else he came in contact with was magical. American photographer Margaret Bourke-White was fascinated by Mahatma Gandhi, and in one photograph at least she claimed to have captured an 'apostle-like aura' around his head, or so she thought.

But even Gandhi could not have stopped Radcliffe from coming to India. He had a mission to accomplish and he was given a limited time frame for it. Radcliffe was appointed the chairman of the Boundary Commission to delimit the India–Pakistan boundary. He was Lord Chancellor William Jowett's nominee. Jinnah too had suggested his name but Nehru had wanted Maurice Gwyer to be the chairman.

Radcliffe had never visited India before. He knew no Indian language, nor did he possess Reginald Coupland's grasp of the Indian constitutional problem although he was a brilliant Oxford product, and a reputed lawyer. Known for his long stretches of silence, in India he did not meet any political leader. He did not attend any hearing of the claimants to the disputed areas. Motilal Setalwad told him the entire procedure adopted by him in respect of the Boundary Commission proceedings was strange and farcical.

Still, Radcliffe completed his work in thirty-six days and left India after he destroyed his papers. Later, when asked whether he would return to India, he said, 'God forbid, not even if they ask me. I expect they would shoot me out of hand, both sides.'[4] The possibility that someone might have taken the cue and actually shot him was not put to test because Radcliffe never returned to India. But the shot that he had fired to divide India was to set the subcontinent ablaze. W.H. Auden has described it thus in his poem on the partition.

Unbiased at least he was when he arrived on his mission,
Having never set eyes on this land he was called to partition
Between two peoples fanatically at odds,
With their different diets and incompatible gods.

[...] He got down to work, to the task of settling the fate
Of millions. The maps at his disposal were out of date
[...] But in seven weeks it was done, the frontiers decided,
A continent for better or worse divided.

The next day he sailed for England, where he quickly forgot
The case, as a good lawyer must. Return he would not,
Afraid, as he told his Club, that he might get shot.[5]

---

[4]A.N. Wilson, *After the Victorians.*

[5]See 'W.H. Auden's Unsparing Poem on the Partition of India', *Scroll*, in <http://scroll.in/article/674238/WH-Auden's-unsparing-poem-on-the-partition-of-India>; also 'Partition', *Outlook*, in <http://www.outlookindia.com/article/Partition/212914>.

6

Leading Up to 15 August

The last judgement on the departing British was best given by Nirad Chaudhuri in his autobiography *Thy Hand, Great Anarch!*

> By what the British administration did and also what they did not, they stultified two hundred years of British rule in India by disregarding two of its highest moral justifications: first, the establishment and maintenance of the unity of India; secondly, the enforcement of Pax Britannica to save the lives of Indians...

That's not all, there was more to come from his sharp quiver. In that same book he also commented on Jinnah. Jinnah may not have been liked by many, perhaps by a very few outside those fanatically devoted to him in Pakistan. Whether Nirad Chaudhuri belonged to those few is difficult to say, but Nirad wrote thus about him:

> Jinnah is the only man who came out with success and honour from the ignoble end of the British Empire in India. He never made a secret of what he wanted, never prevaricated, never compromised, and yet succeeded in inflicting unmitigated defeat on the British Government and the Indian National Congress.

Jinnah had aimed high, to some it seemed impossibly high, yet he was the distinct winner. He had stayed the course; he was clear about his objective, and was ready to employ the most ruthless means. It was as if his ambition and determination validated these lines by Robert Browning: *Ah, but a man's reach should exceed his grasp. / Or what's a heaven for?*

But did he really come out of it unscathed, or was it that his passion outstripped what was moral? To some, it seems so. Had it been otherwise, six decades and more of independent history should have anaesthetized the hurt of partition. Unfortunately it hasn't and Pakistan's bitterness with itself, and all that surrounds it, lingers.

Moreover, despite all the determination he had shown in obtaining Pakistan, the fact is that post-partition he did prevaricate. Take for example his famous statement on 11 August 1947 in the Pakistan Constituent Assembly. The message of it continues to baffle people even now; some in India rise at regular intervals to acclaim it as a testimony to the secular credentials of Jinnah. Indeed that speech remains a paradox—for the historians as also for interpreters of the man. Pakistan was created on the basis of religion. Yet, three days before it was to get a separate and independent status on the basis of religion, Jinnah was telling the Constituent Assembly:

> Hindus will cease to be Hindus and Muslims will cease to be Muslims, not in the religious sense because that is the personal faith of each individual, but in the political sense as citizens of the state.

Was Jinnah seriously suggesting that Muslims will also cease to be Muslims? After all, how could he reconcile this statement with the fact that Pakistan, the land of the pure, was created for Muslims? Moreover, the word Pakistan suggests that non-Muslims are impure, so did they really have a place in Jinnah's land of the pure?

Shariful Mujahid, once the director of the Quaid-i-Azam Academy and a biographer of Jinnah called it, 'a serious lapse on his [Jinnah's] part'.

Stanley Wolpert, in his biography of Jinnah, portrays it as a surreal experience:

> What was he talking about? Had he simply forgotten where he was? Had the cyclone of events so disoriented him that he was arguing the opposition's brief? Was he pleading for a united India on the eve of Pakistan?

Saad Khairi in his book *Jinnah Reinterpreted* has an explanation for Jinnah's reference to Hindus in the 11 August speech. He maintains that 'the presence of non-Muslims was an essential part of Jinnah's Pakistan. Their presence was in fact a guarantee of safety for Muslims left behind in India.'

This, if true, was a sad reflection of the real intent. Were the minorities to be kept in Pakistan as hostages to ensure good behaviour by India towards its minorities? Whatever it was, he was soon to change that position radically. This second statement made by Jinnah in December 1947 has not received the attention that it deserves.

A meeting of the All India Muslim League's Council (there were two chapters of the Muslim League after the partition, one in India and the other in Pakistan, which still called itself 'All India') was held in Karachi on 14–15 December 1947. Jinnah was the governor general of Pakistan and the life-president of the League. In that latter capacity, he had said at the meeting:

> Let it be clear that Pakistan is going to be a Muslim State based on Islamic ideals. It is not going to be an ecclesiastical State... The whole world, even UNO, has characterised Pakistan as a Muslim State.[1]

That should clarify matters. Jinnah states here clearly that 'Pakistan is going to be a Muslim state...' It was obvious then that Muslims will not cease to be Muslims, and for good measure he also brings in the UN and the wider world as evidence in support. So where does that place the 11 August statement?

We started by talking of prevarication. Let's, therefore, for a moment go back again to the All India Muslim League's Council meeting in Karachi of 14–15 December 1947. A member of the Council asked Jinnah if he would once again be prepared to take over the leadership of the Muslims of India in their present hour of trial. Jinnah replied that:

> he was quite willing to do so if the Council gave its verdict in favour of such a proposal... If called upon he was ready to leave Pakistan and share the difficulties of Muslims in the Indian Union and to lead them.

Did Jinnah really mean to do so? If this is read in conjunction with his appeal to the Indian high commissioner, Sri Prakasa, he may have been serious about his desire to return to Bombay. Would he then have taken up the leadership of the Muslims in India all over again? And to what end? On the other hand, if he was really serious about the atmosphere of violence in both the countries then, why did he not make the type of strenuous efforts that Indian leaders were making to stop its spiral? It is a matter of recorded history that the violence in Pakistan against the minorities was greater, more systematic and lasted over a longer period. It is also a fact that the violence in India started later and in reaction to the atrocities that had commenced as early as March 1947 in west Punjab.

It is just that the Pakistani version was heard more by the outside world; its establishment was aggressive in its complaints while the

[1]Jinnah at the All India Muslim League meeting in Karachi, December 1947.

Indians were shy of scenes. Moreover, Pakistan was smaller. In the eyes of the Western world, Pakistan was a newly emerged nation that needed the crutch of sympathy. India, for them, was an ancient civilization and a settled state. It was mature and large enough to take care of itself. It may have been an unfair conclusion but it is a universal truth, historically proven and repeatedly acknowledged, that in a contest it is the underdog who gets the accommodating nod.

*

Jinnah was an intelligent man. There is no doubt about that. He was also a skilful negotiator who held his cards very close to his chest till the very last minute. Above all, he was one of those rare people who shift the boundaries of destiny and alter history. His masterstroke was the idea of Pakistan. But having come up with the idea, was he its master? For public purposes he had expressed his dissatisfaction that he had been given a moth-eaten Pakistan, meaning perhaps that the heaven offered to him was shackled to hell.

His minimum demand, the one that may have satisfied him, was parity with India. He may even have achieved it had he got Junagadh, Hyderabad and Jammu and Kashmir. But that in reality was not a minimum but a maximum position, one that would have guaranteed him absolute satisfaction; not merely because he could then get a very big Pakistan, but also because he would have had the great satisfaction of showing down Nehru and cutting India down to a size nearly equal to Pakistan.

It's a pity though that no one questioned Jinnah effectively enough to ask, why Pakistan, what was the historical basis for his demand, and why was it that only a minority of Muslims migrated eventually to Pakistan, while the majority elected to stay on in India. Was Jinnah expecting success? Did he feel confident that 'Mission Pakistan' would succeed?

A clue to this is provided by Margaret Bourke-White who went to Pakistan in September 1947 to photograph that newly independent country and its leaders. Writing about her meeting with the Jinnahs, Margaret says: '"We never expected to get it so soon," Miss Fatima [Jinnah] said when I called, "We never expected to get it in our lifetime."' Writing further about Jinnah's reaction, she adds, 'If Fatima's reaction was a glow of family pride, her brother's was a fever of ecstasy. Jinnah's deep-sunk eyes were pin-points of excitement.'

It is doubtful if any media person asked him, 'What were your first thoughts when you achieved Pakistan?' It may be a safe guess to say that no one probably did, not because journalists were too timid to ask him such a question then. Though, that is also likely because of Jinnah's acerbic tongue. However, a more plausible explanation might be that the events were proceeding at a dizzying pace then, far too swiftly for anyone to have the time to pause for a syrupy question.

But Jinnah himself could not resist a parting shot as he left Delhi a final time with his sister on 7 August 1947 in the Viceroy's Dakota. According to a telegram sent to London by the British high commissioner to Pakistan (Sir Laurence Grafftey-Smith) on 19 August 1947, while leaving for Pakistan Jinnah was said to have remarked, 'I would never set foot in Hindustan.'

Yet within months Jinnah, the governor general of Pakistan, was telling the surprised Indian High Commissioner Sri Prakasa that he wanted to go back to Bombay! It is true that Jinnah was a complex man of mixed lineage. But it couldn't just be the pull of his roots, or nostalgia for friends he had left behind in Bombay or the love of the house that he had built there which made him want to return. Bombay was the city he loved; he had merely shifted to Pakistan.

However, let's suspend reason for a moment and swing back to the time when an old civilization and a newly born country were celebrating their freedom. Let's try and recall the narrative of those times and read from another of the declassified British telegrams—this time the one sent by Grafftey-Smith on 25 August. It covers the events of 15 August in Karachi when Jinnah was formally sworn in as the governor general of Pakistan.

After describing the event and the public celebrations that followed, he writes:

> I had looked for scenes of mass excitement in the streets of Karachi, and those manifestations of improvised procession and slogan characteristic of such occasions elsewhere. There was, in fact, relatively little evidence of delirious enthusiasm among the general public...[2]

He goes on to conclude:

> He [Jinnah] attended with his sister and Governor of Sind, the first part of a Dominion Day service at the Holy Trinity Church on 19th August... Had he stayed for the sermon, he would have heard the

---

[2]Despatch no. 5 of 25 August 1947 by British high commissioner in Pakistan, Laurence Grafftey-Smith; Lionel Carter, *Partition Observed: British Official Reports from South Asia,* vol. 1.

> archdeacon declare that, if St. Paul could instruct Timothy to pray for so bloody a tyrant as the Emperor Nero, how much more deserving was Mr. Jinnah of Christian intercession.[3]

Sir Terence Shone, the British high commissioner in New Delhi, was also keeping London informed of the developments. His telegram of 18 August 1947 was adulatory:

> The atmosphere of the House during Dr [Rajendra] Prasad's and Pandit Nehru's speeches (on 14–15 Aug midnight) was one of hushed solemnity... Pandit Nehru received an ovation when he rose to speak. As *The Statesman* said, his speech was no doubt the best he had ever made in the house; the occasion, the man, the matter and the manner combined to give his utterance a dignity and emotional appeal which few Indians in the house could resist.[4]
>
> The High Commissioner goes on to describe the public functions of 15 August thus: The first ceremony on morning of August 15 was swearing in of the last Viceroy as the first Governor General of India... Then they proceeded to the Council House for the next meeting of the Constituent assembly. There was a vast and animated crowd outside (estimated at 200,000)...

The day's last public ceremony was the flag-hoisting ceremony at 6 p.m., near the War Memorial for which an estimated 500,000 people had gathered in Prince's Park. Quoting from the *Hindustan Times*, Shone described that crowd's mood as a 'torrent of joy comparable to the bursting of a dam'.[5]

The British high commissioner had not finished yet. Clearly smitten by the enthusiasm of people, he adds:

> When the flag was hoisted, to a salute of thirty-one guns, a light rain fell for a few minutes—a good omen for any enterprise according to the Hindus—and a rainbow appeared. It is to be hoped that the gloomy predictions of the astrologers have thus been confounded.[6]

---

[3]Ibid.

[4]Despatch no. 86 of 18 August 1947 by British high commissioner to India, Terence Shone; Lionel Carter, *Partition Observed*, vol. 1.

[5]Ibid.

[6]Ibid.

7

Genocide and Its Consequences

Alas, the rainbow didn't last long. Multiple fires were burning in India and in Pakistan. The first big fire had been lit by Direct Action in August 1946. Those that followed were doused out from time to time largely by Bapu's efforts, but tensions continued to simmer; it was now difficult to get out of the deep, dark forest of hate that politics had pushed people into.

The rioting in West Punjab was much bigger, better organized and continued over a much longer period. It began in early March 1947. As the governor of Punjab, Sir Evan Jenkins recorded:

> What shocked non-Muslims was the savage outbreak of rioting in Rawalpindi Division and Multan District. The violence was on a scale never before seen in British India. It was characterised by sadistic and extreme violence. In the rural areas large Muslim mobs banded together from several villages to destroy, loot and kill Sikhs and Hindus. Women and children were hacked or burned alive. There were a number of cases of forced conversion and forced marriages.[1]

The British officials in Punjab had no doubt that the attacks on Sikhs and Hindus were planned and aimed at exterminating their population in that province. A personal friend of Prime Minister Attlee saw the Muslim police stand aside as Muslims massacred Sikhs. Governor Jenkins was so exasperated that he told Firoz Khan Noon, 'The League must realize that a brutal massacre had been conducted in their name.'

The Times of London carried a report as early as 17 March 1947 that 'the chief offenders were said to have been the Muslim League National Guards'. The rioting and the massacre had the desired

---

[1]Mushirul Hasan (ed.), *The Partition Omnibus.*

effect. In April 1947, the Hindu and Sikh population in Lahore was approximately 300,000. By August 1947 it had been reduced to just 10,000. They weren't all killed, but the massacres resulted in mass migration.

There was also an eerie coincidence between the arrival of the last viceroy of India and the beginning of violence. The forty-six-year-old Viscount Mountbatten of Burma arrived in New Delhi on 22 March 1947. Nehru was present along with Liaquat Ali Khan at Palam airport to greet him. Jinnah was not present—he was busy making incendiary speeches. As if on cue, the rioting in Rawalpindi and Multan started the next day, on 23 March. It left thousands of Hindus and Sikhs dead.

It was clear that the Muslim League, anticipating the partition plan, had begun to cleanse Punjab of non-Muslim minorities so that it could claim the entire province of Punjab for Pakistan. With this background, was Jinnah sincere in what he promised on 11 August not just to the Constituent Assembly but to the world? Or was that message meant only for effect, and only for the world?

Justice G.D. Khosla held the office of a judge on both sides of the border; in Pakistan before and immediately after the partition and in India thereafter. He was also a witness to the atrocities committed then and had barely escaped a rampaging mob miraculously. He has written a detailed and as accurate an account as was possible of those days and months in his book *Stern Reckoning*:

> With the riots of March 1947 began the genocide of non-Muslims. These disturbances were confined to the Muslim majority areas only and the victims were almost invariably Hindus and Sikhs. In May and June there was another flare up in Lahore. It was not till the end of July that reprisals began in the eastern districts (eastern Punjab) and the mass killings of Muslims took place between August 15 and September 30, 1947, when the arrival of large number of refugees and the tales told by them provoked the non-Muslims to retaliate.

The officers of the administration of the time maintained they were helpless; the scale and ferocity of violence took them by surprise. But was that a fair statement to make in light of what had already happened in Calcutta in August 1946, and in other parts of the country soon thereafter? Shouldn't that have served as a warning to the British administration? Organized violence of the type that began in West Punjab from March 1947 could not remain a secret for long—it takes time to collect people and a considerable amount of planning. How could bands of Pathans and Baluchis travel the long distance to Punjab armed with guns, swords and knives? Why were they not stopped en route, and why were the authorities not prepared for this? The British could not have remained ignorant that mayhem was being planned on a gigantic scale. Why then did the British not take anticipatory action of the type that was needed?

The British intelligence service in India was celebrated the world over for its proficiency and the British administration, especially its civil service, did not tire of calling itself the steel frame of India. Surely they, with the help of the army and police, could have controlled the situation. One million lives need not have been lost to violence. Even the exodus could have been regulated better and humanely. All of it was possible; and after the Direct Action of 1946 there was enough notice to prepare for it. Why then did the British fail so miserably? Why did they let the massacre of Hindus and Sikhs go on in West Punjab from March 1947 right up to the end of the year?

How is it that the Indian leadership was able to check the situation in East Punjab of independent India? The violence there was reactive to what had been happening in West Punjab over the previous six months. The massacre of Muslims in East Punjab started only in mid-August and was brought under control swiftly by the end of September by a personal appeal of Sardar Patel in Amritsar. Couldn't human lives have been saved in Pakistan as well? Had that been done, perhaps the retaliatory killings in East Punjab may never have taken place. The partition, and the parting of ways, need not have been so bitter. Had that been so, if the parting of ways had been less vengeful, the subsequent relationship of India and Pakistan may have been less acrimonious.

Why did Jinnah not live up to his promise of 11 August 1947? Besides the atrocities in Punjab, an ethnic cleansing was also taking place in other parts of Pakistan, right under the nose of Jinnah in Karachi, where 70 per cent of the population was Hindu. Could Jinnah not have stopped the violence that was going on in Pakistan against the Hindus and Sikhs? And why did the mighty British Empire, with all the forces at its command, fail to protect the lives and property of the people for so long?

Once Maulana Abul Kalam Azad (a prominent Congress leader and later a minister in the Indian government) asked Lord Mountbatten, 'Have you taken into consideration the consequences of partition?' Mountbatten replied:

> If there should be the slightest agitation, I shall adopt the sternest measures to nip the trouble in the bud... I will order the Army and the Air Force to act and I will use tanks and aeroplanes to suppress anybody who wants to create trouble.[2]

History is witness to the sequel of that brave claim by Mountbatten.

In fact he wasn't there to provide the leadership when it was most needed. At the end of August 1947, the Mountbattens went to Simla to escape the Delhi heat. Mountbatten returned leisurely to Delhi on 5 September, and his response to the rioting there was to set up an Emergency Committee. His own role in it was largely to set up a control room with maps dotted with multicoloured pins and to devise special passes for invitees to the meetings of the Emergency Committee. When the rioting continued for another three days, Sardar Patel called the Sikh leaders and asked them to appeal for an end to the violence. They duly did so and the violence stopped soon thereafter.

It was the same story in Calcutta. A year after the deadly violence of Direct Action in August 1946, Calcutta detonated again, this time in Mahatma Gandhi's presence. The Mahatma decided to go on a fast from 2 September, and the effect was immediate. As word spread through the city, groups of people began to congregate near the Mahatma. Finally, on 4 September all leaders of the city signed a pledge that there would be no further violence in the city and it was only then that Mahatma Gandhi broke his fast. As Mountbatten confessed in his letter to the Mahatma, 'In Punjab we have 55,000 soldiers and large-scale rioting on our hands. In Bengal our forces consist of one man, and there is no rioting.'

The issue was not the numbers but the attitude. Were the British really serious about a smooth transition? Or were they simply focused on making the best of a bad situation? Why, for instance, were they in a tearing rush to recall their soldiers? Britain had 11,400 soldiers in India when Mountbatten arrived. This number was set to be reduced to 4000 by the time of India's independence. It is odd that this drawdown should have taken place when serious rioting had already started. It is stranger still that the British forces should have been reduced even as 17 million people trudged across the plains of Punjab and Bengal in what was to be the biggest migration in history. One column of people contained as many as 800,000 refugees.

Sitting in England, Winston Churchill was following the events in India closely, particularly the massacre, and from that safe haven he

---

[2]Rafiq Zakaria, *The Man Who Divided India: An Insight into Jinnah's Leadership.*

gloated over what he mockingly described as the 'ferocity of the cannibals'.[3]

There is no doubt that it was horribly feral, but was this the largest genocide that ever took place in history? There have been horrible acts of mass violence before. One million Armenians were wiped out by Turks in the beginning of the twentieth century and during the Second World War, Hitler unleashed his infamous holocaust against six million Jews. The Cultural Revolution of China consumed a staggering 25 million in its cauldron. More recently, there was the genocide in Rwanda.

There have been other instances too, not just in recent years, not just in the last century, but throughout human history. Therefore, the killing of a million people in the Indian subcontinent was not the most terrible of the tragedies to visit the world. But this was one tragedy that could have been prevented because the principal instigators and their intentions were well known. There are always theories and explanations of how and why it still happened. But none that could bring back the dead or salve the wounds of the affected families. It was doubly tragic that such vile violence should have happened during Mahatma Gandhi's lifetime, or that of Khan Abdul Ghaffar Khan.

Moreover, this tragedy unfolded in slow motion and over a long period; the elemental feelings began to erupt soon after the Muslim League adopted its resolution in 1940 in Lahore. Bit by bit the proud claim that Hindus and Muslims had coexisted for centuries was punctured till the rupture resulted in partition.

Still there was a difference in the way the leadership of the two countries handled the violence in their parts. Let's turn to the reports sent by the British high commissioners from the two capitals.

The British high commissioner in Delhi, Terence Shone, wrote on 11 September 1947:

> Prime Minister has great courage...in going about...Delhi and the surrounding country, often in areas and circumstances in which it is by no means certain that even he will be able to 'put things over'. Despite the obvious strain to which he is subjected day and night...he is determined to be indefatigable...(and) of being tough with the law breakers.[4]

---

[3]Madhusree Mukerjee, *Churchill's Secret War: The British Empire and the Ravaging of India during World War II*.

[4]DO 142/420 of 11 September 1947 by Terence Shone; Lionel Carter, *Partition Observed*, vol. I.

The next day, on 12 September, the British high commissioner in Karachi, Grafftey-Smith, sent this report to London:

> The lack of Hindu and Sikh community's faith in the ability of the Government to put into practice its good intentions for their protection is evidenced by a resolution passed by the Sind Minorities Association calling for practical action and not words only.[5]

This resolution was passed by the Sindh Minorities Association a full month after Jinnah's oft-quoted speech of 11 August in the National Assembly.

*

The violence in Pakistan and some parts of Afghanistan (because there was rioting there too against Hindus and Sikhs) and in sections of India resulted in ethnic cleansing. How much of it was planned and what portion of it was triggered by a spontaneous desire for revenge is a matter of debate. Only a 'Truth Commission' can deliver a verdict on it. A related question, more academic in nature, which is often asked and remains a doubt, is this: whether the bitterness of partition continues to linger. Is it responsible for the intractable position that the representatives of the two countries take, specially the representatives belonging to areas badly affected by rioting?

It is also said that if Punjabi diplomats from both sides were to be relieved of the responsibility for bilateral relations, the situation may be a lot better. This assertion is a matter of contention; after all, the Indian prime ministers, I.K. Gujral and Manmohan Singh belonged to Punjab. Both migrated from Pakistan to India; they had witnessed and heard accounts of the most horrible atrocities on the families of their relatives and friends. Yet both were sworn in their words and action to promoting peace with Pakistan and to accommodating Pakistan and its demands to the greatest possible extent. Nawaz Sharif is from Punjab, and despite allegations linking him to the Bombay blasts and the Kargil war, he is said to be in favour of better relations between the two countries.[6]

A third and more speculative thought is the effect that the bitterness, hate and suspicion generated by the process of partition and its

---

[5]DO 142/419 of 12 September 1947, British high commissioner to Pakistan, Grafftey-Smith; Lionel Carter, *Partition Observed*, vol. I.

[6]For the link to the Kargil war, see Shuja Nawaz, *Crossed Swords: Pakistan, its Army and the Wars Within*.

violence continues to have on the judgement, decisions and actions of people. It will be churlish to say, yes, the after-effects are visible. Yet, can it be denied that both sides are quick to anger at the slightest provocation? The wound may have healed but the mark remains on the Indo-Pak body politic. Every time it is scratched raw by some incident or the other, bitterness erupts all over again, wiping out the little progress that may have been made towards tranquillity in relations. This may continue to be the case for many more years to come because while the partition was destructive, it was not definitive.

As Pandit Nehru wrote in November 1957 in one of his occasional letters to chief ministers:

> Our world is a haunted one in which every country has its own special ghost to carry. For India it is Pakistan. No Government in that country had any policy except of fear and hatred of India and till that ceases the future is dark.[7]

There is no doubt that it was a testing time for the new nation and its leadership. But it is in turbulent times that great leaders emerge. Had the leadership in Pakistan acted, as Gandhi, Nehru and Patel had done in India to control the riots, they could have forged the national character too in the process. Their leadership could have inspired people with personal example and instilled right values that are so essential to nation-building.

Ideally speaking, it was a time to apply the healing touch and to concentrate energies on reconciliation and development. But Jinnah died in September 1948 and Liaquat Ali Khan was killed three years later in October 1951. The first military coup took place in 1958, but an unsuccessful one had taken place in 1949. The violence that continues to grip the Pakistani nation and its society may be traced back to the temperament that was formed during those early days.

There was a third party in the picture too. The British presence, it was argued, would provide administrative guidance and a calming influence in that interim period before the two nations were left entirely to their own devices. That at least was how it should have been. But did Britain and its personnel provide the healing touch? Could they restrain the feral feelings and keep emotions bottled up? Did they have the physical wherewithal to do so?

In theory, that was certainly possible. They still controlled the armed forces of the two countries. The leaders of both the countries

---

[7]Jawaharlal Nehru, *Letters to Chief Ministers.*

turned directly or indirectly to the British remnants for guidance. Mountbatten was the governor general of India, Field Marshal Claude Auchinleck was the supreme commander of the armed forces of both India and Pakistan, and the defence forces of the two countries were headed by British officers. India and Pakistan were dependent upon Britain for their arms requirement as also their food supplies, besides many other essential imports. Moreover, the Western powers were guided by British advice on policy matters related to the subcontinent. All these factors, combined with the inexperience of the two governments, made them look to Britain for advice and help in vital matters related to governance, especially bilateral relations. So, Britain could and did influence the decision-making process in some vital ways.

India itself was not without influence on Pakistan. It controlled the water lifeline of Pakistan; the six rivers of the Indus system passed from Indian soil into Pakistan. Had India turned nasty, it could have squeezed that lifeline at will. There were provocations enough for it to do so, but it chose not to follow that bullying path. Would Pakistan have acted in a similar fashion had the roles been reversed and if Pakistan, instead of India, controlled the flow of the six Indus system rivers?

India also held the purse-strings. The foreign exchange reserves were in its custody, and it reserved the right to apportion just the precise share to Pakistan at a time of its choosing. Therefore it could substantially affect the economic stability of Pakistan by delaying the release of monies. Pakistan's behaviour was such that India need not have been generous in giving more than a fair share of foreign exchange to it.

Nor was there any particular reason for India to have been prompt in passing on to Pakistan its share of defence stores. A firmer India would have held back these supplies because Pakistan was engaged then in pushing its soldiers and tribals into Kashmir.

Now, in retrospect, the question is asked whether India did well in acting so righteously. Was it the right policy to adopt? Should India have sacrificed its interests to benefit Pakistan? The argument is often made that given Pakistan's hostile behaviour, India should have catered to its interests first. By sacrificing them, its generosity was not gratefully acknowledged, but interpreted as a sign of weakness, an act of appeasement, encouraging Pakistan to seek greater and further concessions on every subsequent occasion. Undeterred, India has consistently adopted the carrot as the negotiating strategy in the hope that it might eventually have the hoped-for effect. It is also said that India's approach remains sentimental, while Pakistan's moves are calculated.

Some analysts assert that it is difficult to take a definitive position one way or the other on a complex issue like this. Both sides of the argument have some merit, and many pitfalls. One should also take into account the temper of those times and the conviction of the Indian leadership that India must be large-hearted in dealing with Pakistan.

Mountbatten and his British team, too, adopted a similar approach: that all efforts must be made by India to calm matters down. Sometimes, they brought pressure to bear on Pakistan in a similar fashion. But that was in the nature of preventing the fire from spreading. On most critical issues, however, the British policy leaned in favour of Pakistan; the shape and extent of those contours were decided in London. Mountbatten and his aides followed them scrupulously.

The British policy calculations were guided by geostrategic considerations. By August 1947 the British authorities, including the chiefs of staff, had come to the conclusion that their principal strategic interests in the subcontinent would best be served through Pakistan. The facilities of Karachi port were essential for keeping a watch on trade passing through the Indian Ocean; the hoped-for British air-bases in the NWFP would be a guarantee of stability in Afghanistan and in the Gulf region. They were also of the view that good relations with Pakistan were essential to maintain Britain's relations with the Muslim world in a benevolent state.

The question that must be asked, but has rarely been addressed adequately, is this: why did Britain continue to play a version of the 'great game' even after independence?

Would it have been better for India and Pakistan if they were told that from 15 August onwards they should manage their bilateral relations as best as they possibly could and sort out their differences as they thought fit? There is no doubt that those were dangerous times not just for people but for the leaders as well; both countries had inherited a terrible cauldron of hatred, and passions were raw and red hot. Whether or not the British contributed towards stirring the pot is not the issue here. The fact is that the British decided to stay on, based on the premise that their presence was essential to provide stability and ensure a smooth transition. Yet, they failed in that objective.

Had the British left lock, stock and barrel would the situation have got any worse? Perhaps India and Pakistan may have managed the mess better, or they might have failed miserably. Either way they would have had the satisfaction of having tried. Left to their own devices, and finally rid of the 'divide and rule' policy of the British, their native passivity may have led to a more benign future for both India and Pakistan.

Alas, they were condemned to a fractious beginning. And it was to start in a state where the poet had asserted that 'if there is a heaven on earth, it is here, it is here'.

Placid Kashmir was soon set to become the first tinderbox between India and Pakistan. The fire lit then continues to burn.

8

The Kashmir Issue

If a relationship between two countries is complicated, diplomats call it multifaceted. That ability to see a silver lining in very dark clouds is what diplomacy is about. But even the most stoic of diplomats is likely to get exasperated with a relationship as complex, and as crisis-prone, as that between India and Pakistan. Take, for instance, the period immediately after the partition. The two countries were at each other's throats; their leaders were sniping constantly in face-to-face meetings and through letters, telegrams and press statements. The accusations were mostly based on rumours and word of mouth in the absence of a settled administrative system in both India and Pakistan. That anger, based on half-facts, allowed reality to break free of its moorings and take on fantastical shapes. All this while blood continued to spill in India and Pakistan.

The need of the time was for people of both countries to live with the idea of acceptance of the other. Instead, violence prevailed and both Indians and Pakistanis remained in a state of sulk. It was a quarrelsome beginning coated with anger and hatred. This was hardly the moment to light another fire. Yet this is precisely what was done.

Pakistan's aggression in Kashmir was not due to irrationality. It was a carefully calculated strategy to catch India off guard and to keep it off-balance. Jinnah and his generals believed that with stealth and speed their Kashmir operation would be over in a matter of days. They were also confident that Britain would not obstruct this plan. In support of this argument, it is said that the British officers had known of the Pakistani plans from the time the first batch of tribals was pushed into trucks and sent off to Kashmir.

The British attitude was to wink and pretend that the Pakistani trespasses had not taken place, which influenced other powers too. Since the British had been the colonial rulers of the subcontinent for over two centuries, the wider Western world deferred to their views on matters relating to India and Pakistan. On the Kashmir issue in particular, Britain was keen that its view should prevail and this British role was in no small degree responsible for perpetuating the Kashmir problem.

A fair amount of blame must be apportioned to India. It could have been quicker off the ground in securing its interests. H.V. Hodson writes in *The Great Divide*, 'Kashmir was deliberately omitted from a committee of States' representatives called by the pre-independence States Department (of India) to discuss terms of accession, though Hyderabad was included.'

Why was Kashmir omitted and why was it done as a matter of deliberate policy? Isn't it possible that Pakistan may have interpreted this omission as an encouragement to it? Pakistan did not waste any time. The principal routes for supply of food and fuel to Kashmir were from Pakistan. Conscious of this fact, and in view of the approaching winter, it started squeezing Kashmir from September 1947 onwards, starving it of essential supplies—yet keeping enough going to make people realize how critically dependent they were on it. But even while clamping down on the food supplies Pakistan had planned carefully to send one set of vehicles into Jammu and Kashmir.

On 22 October 1947 nearly 250 trucks crossed into Jammu and Kashmir along the Jhelum Valley Road. They were carrying nearly 5000 Afridi and Mehsud tribesmen and regular Pakistani soldiers on leave. Major General Akbar Khan of the Pakistani army was their leader and they hoped to conquer the entire area in a matter of four days. They may well have succeeded in doing so because there was hardly a force worth the name to resist their advance. The vacillating maharaja had fled to Jammu and the Jammu and Kashmir army, such as it was, was hardly a match for the invaders.

The Pakistanis were so confident of their success that in anticipation, Jinnah reached Lahore on 26 October so that he could fly to Srinagar at short notice on the 27th. He had hoped to install a puppet government there, which could then announce Jammu and Kashmir's accession to Pakistan.

Unfortunately for Pakistani calculations, the tribals got distracted; loot, rape and pillage of the Kashmiri population occupied them sufficiently to stymie their progress. Even then, New Delhi was slow to react. It had been receiving reports from around the first week of October that something serious was afoot, and that batches of tribals had started infiltrating the region, leading finally to the major infiltration of 22 October. The maharaja had been sending repeated, and increasingly urgent, messages to India with an appeal for help in matters of arms supply. The Indian Cabinet was willing to respond and wanted to rush these supplies, but it was held back by its British governor general.

This was a bizarre situation where a British national continued to exercise a veto over the Indian Cabinet. But this odd situation was inflicted on itself by the government of independent India. While the Cabinet Committee was headed by Prime Minister Nehru, the Defence Committee of the Cabinet was headed by Mountbatten. It was the Defence Committee which took all the decisions regarding the movement of arms and troops. In that powerful capacity Mountbatten, supported by the British officers who were occupying the posts of the commander-in-chief and the defence chiefs, kept stalling the proposal for arms supply on the plea that the maharaja should first sign the instrument of accession.

Strangely though, no such inhibition prevented the Pakistanis from marching in to occupy Kashmir; neither the British commander-in-chief of India and Pakistan nor the British chief of the Pakistani army raised any objection.

It was only from 25 October that events in Kashmir began to be viewed in Delhi with the alarm and the urgency that they required. Still, the British chief of the Indian army, General Rob Lockhart, with the support of Mountbatten, was reluctant to commit Indian troops till the maharaja had signed the instrument of accession. This was finally done when V.P. Menon, secretary of the States' Ministry, flew to Srinagar on 25 October to assess the gravity of the situation and a second time on 26 October to Jammu to obtain the instrument of accession to India from the maharaja. During his second visit, Menon discovered that the raiders had crossed Baramulla and were marching towards Srinagar.

Even at that critical juncture when every hour counted, General Lockhart asked at the Defence Committee meeting, 'Was Kashmir of vital importance to India?' Both Nehru and Patel asserted that 'Kashmir was vital to India's very existence'.[1]

This wasn't all; there is other evidence to suggest that General Lockhart was not favourably inclined. He had purposely not shared vital military information with the Indian leadership. To cite one instance, General Douglas Gracey, the chief of the Pakistani army, had informed Lockhart in a telephonic conversation in early October

---

[1]C. Dasgupta, *War and Diplomacy in Kashmir, 1947–48.*

that well-armed tribals were gathering near the Rawalpindi area. Had that information been available to the Indian Cabinet, the course of subsequent events may have been different.

It was Lockhart again who had opposed sending military supplies to Kashmir till it had acceded to India. No wonder then that Lockhart had to resign within six months of taking over as the Indian army chief. A month earlier, the office of the supreme commander of Indian and Pakistani forces, had been wound down because Sardar Patel suspected Auchinleck of partiality towards Pakistan in the division of military stores between India and Pakistan. Patel also accused him of 'throttling the initiative of Headquarters Indian Army and acting as advanced outpost of Pakistan'.[2]

Had Lockhart not adopted delaying tactics in the despatch of arms to the maharaja's army and then the Indian troops to Kashmir, perhaps the tribals may have been stopped at the point of ingress itself. Had that been done, if the entire state of Jammu and Kashmir belonged to India, the Indian borders would have stretched up to Afghanistan, and Indian access to the Central Asian land mass may well have revived the silk route, this second time through the far more lucrative gas and oil pipelines. But more importantly, the contestation, the acrimony and the wars over Kashmir may not have taken place. And India need not have spent phenomenal amounts on keeping troops in Jammu and Kashmir. Pakistan, too, may have concentrated more on its economy.

Pakistan had started putting pressure on Kashmir from the end of September 1947. Coincidentally, on 28 September, Auchinleck issued 'Stand Down' orders to the British officers in the Indian and Pakistani armies. Was the close timing of the two initiatives a mere coincidence, or part of a considered move? This message to the British army chiefs in the two dominions explained that 'Stand Down' was the code word to be used by Auchinleck in case fighting broke out between the two countries. By this order, the British officers were to take no part in any of the hostilities.

Jinnah tried to flout the order soon after India airlifted its troops into Kashmir. He had not expected India to mount a defence of Kashmir quickly and effectively, given the difficult terrain and the logistical problems of carrying arms and equipment over a long distance. But the airlift of soldiers and equipment which started from Delhi on the morning of 27 October went on non-stop. India

---

[2]Ibid.

requisitioned and pressed private planes into service to airlift the troops. The scale of this operation, and India's determination, alarmed Jinnah sufficiently to order General Gracey to march the Pakistani army into Jammu and Kashmir. These new troops were to be in addition to the regulars in civilian clothes and the infiltrators who were already inside Kashmir.

Gracey refused to carry out the order given by Jinnah as it was in violation of the 'Stand Down' instructions. Still, the matter was serious enough for him to ring up Auchinleck in Delhi at 1 a.m.

Auchinleck flew in the next morning to Lahore to meet Jinnah. There, he informed Jinnah that after its accession, Kashmir had become a part of India and that a military violation of what was Indian territory would have terrible consequences. He added that under the 'Stand Down' instructions, all British officers would be withdrawn if the Pakistani army was to be sent into Jammu and Kashmir. Jinnah reluctantly withdrew his orders.[3] But this deference to the 'Stand Down' orders was only temporary; British troops would soon actively support the Pakistani soldiers in this conflict.

On 1 November 1947, Mountbatten flew to Pakistan to meet Jinnah. It was suggested to Jinnah that the main thing was to stop the fighting and he was asked for his suggestion on how it could be done. Jinnah replied that both sides should withdraw immediately and simultaneously. When Mountbatten asked him how the tribesmen were to be called off, he said all he had to do was to give them an order to come out, and if they did not comply he would send large forces.[4] He added that if Mountbatten was prepared to fly with him to Srinagar, he would guarantee that the business would be settled in twenty-four hours!

Mountbatten records that he was surprised at the degree of control he (Jinnah) seemed to exercise over the raiders.

Before meeting Jinnah, Mountbatten had extracted a promise from Nehru that a plebiscite exercise would be conducted under UN auspices. When Mountbatten put that suggestion to Jinnah, he refused point-blank. On being asked why he was opposed to a plebiscite, Jinnah replied that with Indian troops in occupation of Kashmir, and

---

[3]Field Marshal Claude Auchinleck to UK chiefs of staff, the supreme commander of armed forces in India and Pakistan (till 30 November 1947), Telegram no. 1114 of 28 October 1947; Lionel Carter, *Partition Observed*, vol. I.

[4]Shone's Telegram no. 1184 of 4 November 1947; Lionel Carter, *Partition Observed*, vol. II.

with the National Conference under Sheikh Abdullah in power, such propaganda and pressure would result in the average Muslim losing the courage to vote for Pakistan.

But the idea of plebiscite would not go away. This time Nehru went public. In a radio broadcast on 2 November he said, 'We are prepared when peace and law and order have been established to have a referendum held under international auspices like the United Nations.'

There was more to come from this theatre of unbelievable turns. In a telegram of 10 November 1947, the British high commissioner in Delhi recorded a conversation between chief of staff of Mountbatten, Lord Hastings Ismay, Pakistani secretary general, Mohammad Ali and V.P. Menon. With regard to a plebiscite, Ali would not touch the idea of involving the UN. He said, 'Surely it was clear that Kashmir would go to Pakistan so why this fuss about a plebiscite.'[5] This telegram goes on to mention, 'Menon said that he entirely agreed that Kashmir would go to Pakistan but emphasised that in view of what had passed a formal plebiscite was essential.'

One could argue that this is what the British high commissioner reported to London, and it may or may not have been entirely faithful to what transpired, or that he may have misheard Menon. Well, one can't rule out that possibility, but the amazing thing is that Menon, who was schooled in the tradition of Patel and who had assiduously pursued the accession of Kashmir and other Indian princely states to India, should so casually have talked of plebiscite, and where Kashmir might or might not have gone, even as the Pakistani secretary general was opposed to the idea of a plebiscite.

A bare ten days before this conversation, Jinnah, too, had reacted negatively to the idea of a plebiscite in his conversation with Mountbatten. But soon after that Pakistan's military position began to weaken in Kashmir, and in this changed military scenario they saw an advantage in pursuing the option of plebiscite. Since then, Pakistan has followed the plebiscite line consistently.

India, in contrast, tends to be flexible, even generous. Sometimes it seems that when all is going in India's favour it bends over to please Pakistan, and concede to its demands. In this particular case, the secretary general of foreign affairs, G.S. Bajpai, retrieved the situation somewhat, but just about. In his telegram of 18 November, Shone, the

---

[5]Telegram no. 1218 of 10 November 1947 by Shone; Lionel Carter, *Partition Observed*, vol. II, n. 29, p. 679.

British high commissioner, reported that Bajpai told him 'there was need for a round table between the parties involved and that no one else could help'.[6]

But a breach had been made and Pakistan was going to keep putting all the diplomatic pressure that it could for a plebiscite and Britain was going to be its ally in that quest. There was yet another factor in consideration for Britain: the situation regarding the Palestine issue was turning grave. The Muslim world felt that the Anglo-American combine had been less than fair to the Palestinians. In that background, Britain did not want to add one more grouse to the litany of grudges the Muslim world had against it. Therefore, to appease the Muslim world, Britain decided that it had to steadily increase pressure on India in favour of internationalizing the Kashmir issue and to make it agree to a plebiscite.

The first step in this direction was a suggestion by Prime Minister Attlee (conveyed through telegram nos. 1354 and 404 of 20 November to the two high commissioners) to Pandit Nehru and Liaquat Ali Khan that the International Court of Justice should both devise and administer the machinery for consulting the people of Kashmir. Not just that. Attlee made another demand of Nehru in this amazing missive, asking that any further movement of troops into Kashmir should be made in consultation with Pakistan! Attlee had, of course, rather conveniently forgotten that the Pakistani army and the tribals had not extended the courtesy of a prior consultation with India before their infiltration into Kashmir.

Around this time, visits by British officials to the two countries became frequent; they were undertaken with the intention of assessing the situation and steering it in the direction that London desired. High Commissioner Shone sent with his letter of 27 November two notes recorded by the British official Paul Grey after his meetings with Liaquat Ali Khan and Pandit Nehru. The conversations were along the expected lines—the principal objective of Grey's visit seemed to be to press Nehru to show maximum accommodation towards Pakistan.

In his report on these meetings Grey also found the time to mention:

> ...could not the messages from H.M.G. in the U.K. over Kashmir etc., be drafted in different terms to Liaqat and Nehru? They ring

[6]Mushirul Hasan, (ed.), *The Partition Omnibus.*

> quite differently in the preparatory school atmosphere of Karachi to what they do in the Oxford or Cambridge Union atmosphere of New Delhi.[7]

Meanwhile, the military tide was turning further in India's favour with the capture of Baramulla and Uri. Nehru visited the Kashmir valley on 15 November and seeing the desolation that tribals had reduced Baramulla to, he said, 'You have had a unique experience. I have had a taste of what Pakistan means.' Sardar Patel was more forthright when on another occasion he said, 'In the world of today, only those who have guts can make their voices felt.'[8]

The military conflict continued as did the diplomatic parleys. When Pakistan sensed that its military plans were not proceeding as it had anticipated, it was more willing to negotiate. But the moment its forces seemed to be on the verge of a breakthrough it would harden its stand.

This is what happened during the negotiations that started in Delhi on 27 November. The chill in the room was palpable—both Nehru and Liaquat had reason to resent the other. Mountbatten attempted to steer the discussions towards a possible solution by suggesting the broad outlines that could include a plebiscite under UN supervision, the formation of an interim government by Sheikh Abdullah and the withdrawal of tribals from Jammu and Kashmir, besides the withdrawal of the bulk of the Indian forces.

This was the starting point of the discussions; arguments, squabbling and shouting followed. Towards the end, however, tensions had eased sufficiently to veer the two antagonists towards discussing joint defence plans against external aggression!

Nothing concrete followed. The mood in Delhi changed radically in the first week of December as the tribals decimated Mirpur town. They had also stepped up attacks on Poonch and were poised to raid Jammu. There were reports of large-scale violence and the abduction of women for sale. It alarmed Nehru sufficiently for him to write to Liaquat Ali Khan:

> During the last few days while we were supposed to be discussing possible terms for a settlement, these concentrations [of raiders] have been encouraged and additional raiders have been sent into

---

[7]Enclosure to DO no. 133/69 of 27 November 1947 by Terence Shone; Lionel Carter *Partition Observed*, vol. II.

[8]Mushirul Hasan, (ed.), *The Partition Omnibus*.

> Kashmir who have massacred thousands of personnel there... This you will appreciate might involve long-term consequences.[9]

Yet, within a week Nehru was in Lahore. On 8 December he read out his charges against Pakistani complicity in the entire operation—that arms were being supplied by the NWFP government to the infiltrators, and that Pakistani soldiers were involved in raids. He also spoke of the atrocities committed by them.

Liaquat had his counter-argument ready, saying that the atrocities were not one-sided, there was no official involvement by Pakistan, the raiders were carrying their own arms and some arms may have come from Afghanistan and the Soviet Union. Finally, he added that Pakistan had hardly any power to stop the tribals unless it went to war against them.

This is precisely the pattern Pakistan has followed ever since, denying all involvement and stonewalling all charges with a straight face. On each such occasion India has shown magnanimity of spirit and hoped that the next time things might be different. They seldom are, so sometimes in frustration it goes into a sulk and decides to suspend dialogue.

Pakistanis have invariably had their way. They do not concede an inch; if they see a negotiation opening to their advantage they stick their foot in and keep pressing till the door has opened wide to their satisfaction. Each time India tires of staring at the dead-end in bilateral relations and blinks first to restart talks. Once again, India finds itself back at square one.

The fundamental point here is not so much the extent of success in Pakistani aggression, but its confidence that in the end India will climb down. Take, for instance, the matter of a plebiscite. The British governor general and his army brass had insisted that India should obtain the instrument of accession before sending its army into Kashmir. If that letter of accession was the litmus test for Kashmir to become a part of India, then where was the need for a plebiscite? The issue was Pakistani aggression, but India diluted the gravity of Pakistan's aggression by getting sidetracked and submitting to British coercion.

Coming back to the meeting in Lahore, Mountbatten's agenda was to get the two sides to make a reference to the UN. When he saw the talks collapsing, he leaned on Nehru to make a concession; hence the

---

[9]C. Dasgupta, *War and Diplomacy in Kashmir, 1947–48.*

proposal to hold a plebiscite under the UN's auspices. Nehru was persuaded, but Liaquat refused to go along because the invading forces were marching forward.

And Jinnah had other ideas, confident that his tried-and-tested tactics would work this time too.

*

The creation of Pakistan came about because Jinnah had ingratiated himself with the British masters while Gandhi, Nehru and other Congress leaders were spinning cotton in jail. In the Gandhian way, means and ends had to be in synchronization. Jinnah's methods were grounded in practice; the end result was the aim and the sole measure of success. He had obtained Pakistan from Britain and now hoped to get a favourable deal on Kashmir from a Commonwealth headed by Britain.

Jinnah didn't hope to get much through the UN route because it was a diffused body. The Soviet Union, even China and the vast number of the developing nations held Nehru in awe. To them, Nehru was the preserver in contrast to the destructive role played by Jinnah.

As a lawyer, Jinnah's calculations guided him away from giving a judgemental role to the UN. On an equally practical note he knew that Sheikh Abdullah was a leader of the masses and a plebiscite was bound to go in favour of India. An additional complicating factor for Pakistan was the public mood in Jammu and Kashmir against the atrocities committed by the invading Pakistanis. Given such a background, the people of Kashmir could hardly be expected to cast their vote in favour of Pakistan in an impartial plebiscite supervised by the UN. The likelihood that the plebiscite would go against Pakistan was the cause of shrewd Jinnah's reservations.

The British high commissioner in Pakistan, Graffety-Smith, refers in a telegram of 10 December to his meeting with Jinnah. In reply to his query as to whether a ceasefire in Kashmir would be followed by an early plebiscite, Jinnah said that India had no intention of relaxing her effective grip on Kashmir. He added that the only practical solution was for the two governors general to intervene.

What Jinnah was suggesting was in effect that Mountbatten and he should decide the fate of Kashmir, cutting the Indian leadership entirely out of the picture!

Both on the diplomatic and the military fronts, Pakistan was adopting guerrilla tactics to keep India and its leadership off-balance.

Sheikh Abdullah had probably read this strategy early on and he suggested to Nehru in November 1947 that the war should be carried into Pakistan. But Nehru demurred. It was only in mid-December that his views underwent a radical change.

This change came about due to a combination of factors. He had approached his meetings with Liaquat Ali Khan in good faith but Liaquat prevaricated and hedged. Meanwhile, reports about the Pakistani army's involvement in Kashmir operations were multiplying. The British army's role in India had also left the Indian leadership wondering if the British generals were delaying matters on purpose; this led to the premature parting of ways with Army Chief Lockhart and the Commander-in-Chief Field Marshal Auchinleck. Domestic public opinion too was building up steadily against the soft handling by Nehru of the situation in Kashmir. Moreover, the news of the precarious military situation was adding to the anger of people.

It should be remembered that all this was happening in the background of an extremely bitter population, which had only recently suffered from a most brutal partition. Nehru may have been an idealist and a pacifist who wanted to live in peace with Pakistan, but he also realized that a military setback would be a huge blow to his image and a great morale deflator for newly independent India. As if on cue, and in another turn of fortunes in the battlefield, the possibility of a setback appeared real and stark by mid-December. A major Indian defeat in Uri and Naushera seemed a clear possibility.

It was in this grim setting that Nehru proposed to his Cabinet that India should proceed on two parallel lines of action:

1. Reference to the UN.
2. Complete military preparations to meet any possible contingency. If grave danger threatens us in Kashmir or elsewhere on West Punjab frontier then we must not hesitate to march through Pakistan territory towards the bases where the infiltrators were being trained.[10]

In December 1947 Nehru spoke rather often about a reference to the UN concerning aggression by Pakistan and India's possible right of action in Pakistani territory to attack the bases of the raiders there. Yet all through Nehru also kept hoping that Pakistan would see reason and that Britain would act as an honest broker and persuade Pakistan

---

[10]Telegram no. 1513 of 28 December 1947 from the British high commissioner from Delhi.

against prolonging the conflict. Pakistan, on the other hand, rarely shared its real intent with Nehru and not wholly with the British.

Despite that, Britain's anxieties were Pakistan related. It almost seemed as if it didn't mind the Pakistani aggression in Kashmir. On the other hand, the British officers in Delhi did not hesitate to stymie Indian initiatives. That was also the reason why British military generals in India adopted dilatory tactics by suggesting the formation of committees on every major issue. A committee was bound to debate endlessly, even as India wanted to take extraordinary action immediately. The British were also trying all along to internationalize the issue and embroil India in a reference to the UN Security Council. The question that remains is this: why did Nehru not see through this? And why did he turn to Attlee so often? Surely, independence also entailed a responsibility on the Indian leadership to take independent action. Yet, Nehru sent this telegram to Attlee at the end of December (one of his many missives to Attlee on Kashmir):

> Unless Pakistan takes immediate steps to stop all forms of aid to the attackers who are operating from bases in Pakistan...our only hope of dealing with them effectively would lie in striking at them at their bases. This would involve our entering Pakistan territory. Such a step would be justified in International Law as we are entitled to take it in self-defence.[11]

Nehru then goes to say that while he is making a reference to the UN Security Council, India reserves the right to take military action. Was Nehru ill-advised by his aides into sending such a letter or did he fall into a trap set by the British? It is worth noting that Mountbatten, on instructions from London, had been urging Nehru to make a reference to the UN, and to write to Attlee for his advice.

Naturally, then, Attlee had anticipated Nehru's approach and was ready with his reply:

> I am gravely disturbed by your assumption that India would be within her rights in international Law if she were to send forces in to Pakistan in self-defence... I can assure you that it would gravely prejudice India's case before UNO, if after having appealed to the Security Council, she were to take unilateral action of this kind.[12]

And on the hypothetical possibility of India carrying the attack into Pakistan, Attlee added almost insultingly, 'I think you are very

---

[11]Jawaharlal Nehru, *Selected Works of Jawaharlal Nehru*, vol. 4.

[12]India Office Records, London, File L/WS/1/1140.

optimistic in concluding that your proposed military action would bring about a speedy solution.'[13]

There is no historical record of Nehru's reaction to this rap on the knuckles. The other question is whether, beyond momentary outrage, India has learnt a lesson from this unfortunate episode. It doesn't seem so. The basic script has remained unchanged over the years. Pakistan keeps twisting India's tail at will and India, very properly, appeals to the international community to ask Pakistan to behave. The unfortunate part of this exercise is that every time India turns to its interlocutors with complaints, it is advised to exercise restraint.

But Mountbatten was conscious that at some stage, historical records of the period would be re-examined and from that distance the verdict of history would be clinical. There the fact that the British were far from impartial, and that they had sided with Pakistan, would come out in stark relief. Therefore, to set the record straight over his role, Mountbatten wrote in an aide memoire of 25 February 1948 to the British government that:

> ...had the Indian troops not been sent to Kashmir, after the Instrument of Accession had been signed, the European inhabitants of the city would probably have been massacred, and the Government of India might have fallen...giving way to an extremist Government with the likelihood of an inter-Dominion war.

The continuing aggression by Pakistan in Kashmir and the consistent pressure by Britain finally led India to make the formal approach to the UN Security Council. This was done on 1 January 1948. Basically, India had requested the Security Council to ask Pakistan to prevent its military and civil officials from participating in or assisting in the invasion of Jammu and Kashmir, call upon its nationals to refrain from taking part in fighting, and deny invaders access to and use of its territory, military and other supplies. India reserved for itself the right to appropriate military action depending upon the situation. The idea in simple terms was that this new world body should ask Pakistan to withdraw its invaders from Kashmir and vacate aggression.

It is possible that Nehru truly believed in the efficacy of the UN, in the impartiality of its decisions and in its ability to order the aggressor to actually withdraw. Nehru's approach to the UN was heavily influenced by his vision of an ideal world.

But Britain had a different agenda. Since a victory on the

---

[13]Ibid.

battleground was now out of the question for Pakistan, Britain wanted to internationalize the issue and then put its diplomatic skills at work to achieve an outcome that suited its long-term interests. With that reference by India to the UN, Britain's purpose had been served. Thereafter Philip Noel-Baker, the British secretary general for the Commonwealth and Britain's chief delegate to the UN on the Kashmir issue, frustrated every move by India and was openly and stridently pro-Pakistan in his actions, statements and in behind-the-scenes lobbying with the Western delegations at the UN.

Noel-Baker's principal objective was to ensure that the Security Council considered not the aggression by Pakistan, but the issue of the plebiscite. His bias was so blatant that it invited a rebuke from Attlee:

> ...all the concessions are being asked from India, while Pakistan concedes little or nothing. The attitude seems to be that it is India which is at fault whereas the complaint was rightly lodged against Pakistan.[14]

But even this reprimand did not have any effect on Noel-Baker. Why was he so brazenly against India and so obvious in his pro-Pakistan tilt? Was it a personal issue, did some Indian delegate spite him, or was he beholden to Pakistan for some reason? Whatever the motivation for his prejudice, the fact is that his actions may have prolonged the war in Kashmir. Yet, a few years later this man was given the Nobel Peace prize!

It was this sympathy and support which emboldened Pakistan further.

Unfortunately, India had not prepared its case convincingly. On 15 January 1948, the UN Security Council met to hear Gopalaswami Ayyangar, the chief Indian delegate, and Zafarullah Khan, his Pakistani counterpart. Ayyangar presented a legalistic elaboration of India's request to the UN. When it was Pakistan's turn, Zafarullah devastated India in a five-and-a-half hour passionate statement, accusing India of genocide of Muslims in East Punjab and of denying Pakistan its claim over Kashmir.

With things going its way in the international arena, Pakistan felt confident enough to send regular army battalions into Kashmir in March 1948. But India kept dithering on the issue of crossing the border in Punjab to attack the camps for tribal raiders. Squeezed thus

---

[14]Public Records Office, London, Attlee to Noel Baker, 4 April 1948, F 0800/470.

on military and diplomatic sides as well, India's options were limited to defensive action by its forces.

On the bilateral front, bitterness against Pakistani leaders was exceptionally high among the people and their leaders alike. In a letter of 16 June 1948 to the Indian high commissioner in Pakistan, Sri Prakasa, Prime Minister Jawaharlal Nehru wrote:

> Zafrullah Khan and others wanted to come without Liaquat Ali Khan but we told them not to. I have an intense dislike for Zafrullah which has increased since his utterances at the U.N. Security Council... I have today received a telegram from Liaquat Ali inviting me to come to Karachi for discussions in ten days' time. I am not sending an answer just yet but I have absolutely no intention of going to Karachi. I might at a pinch go to Lahore but even that is very doubtful. It seems to me that these Prime Ministers conferences which we had agreed upon are likely to fade away after Mountbatten goes, unless of course there is a radical change in the situation which is doubtful.[15]

Mountbatten, too, was greatly disenchanted, especially with Jinnah. In that same letter, Nehru reflects this:

> Mountbatten had decided to go direct from Delhi to the Persian Gulf on his way to England without stopping at Karachi. He wanted to avoid landing at Karachi even for refueling chiefly because of Jinnah who might very well have been discourteous.[16]

Meanwhile, at the UN, matters began to move towards finality. On 13 August 1948 the United Nations Commission for India and Pakistan (UNCIP) presented a resolution that called for a ceasefire and stated that the future status of Jammu and Kashmir would be decided in accordance with the will of the people. However, there was a catch to it that is often lost sight of.

The terms of the truce required that Pakistan should withdraw its forces from the state. India would also begin to withdraw the bulk of its forces from the state after the (Pakistani) raiders had withdrawn and the Pakistani troops had commenced their withdrawal. Pending acceptance of the conditions for a final settlement, India would maintain on its side of the line existing at the time of ceasefire, a minimum force to assist in the maintenance of law and order.

India sought a clarification and confirmation from the UNCIP that

---

[15]A.S. Bhasin, *India–Pakistan Relations, 1947–2007.*

[16]Ibid.

a recurrence of aggression in Kashmir must be prevented and that India would have to maintain sufficient forces in the state to meet the threat of external aggression as well as of internal disorder; the sovereignty of the state extended to its entire territory and that there could be no recognition of the so-called 'Azad Kashmir government'. It also wanted confirmation that the Commission did not recognize Pakistan's claim to have any part in a plebiscite, should it be decided to seek a solution of the future of the state by means of one. On receiving satisfactory clarifications on these points, India accepted the resolution on 25 August 1948.

But India's troubles were not over yet. The British in India were following the lead given to them from London; and it was clearly in favour of Pakistan. The chief of the Indian army, General Roy Bucher, passed on vital Indian army operations plans regularly to his counterpart in Pakistan, General Douglas Gracey. It was on the basis of the information passed on by General Bucher that India would not open a front in Punjab that Pakistan diverted a brigade-level force which it had kept in reserve for the defence of West Punjab, to Kashmir. Bucher also ensured that the desire of Major General K.S. Thimayya, the commander of the 19th Infantry division in Jammu and Kashmir in 1948 and later, the army chief, and other Indian officers to switch from a cautious military approach to offensive action was not authorized by the Indian Cabinet.

Pakistan, on the other hand, was busy hatching yet another conspiracy in league with Britain. A part of the reason for this was its apprehension that the Indian army might soon head towards the Jhelum river boundary in the Mirpur area. That would give it control of the Chenab and Jhelum irrigation system on which Pakistan's agriculture was critically dependent. Fearing this, Pakistan took the view that Britain had now to take an even more active role to help it. Taking a cue from British colonial practices, Pakistan decided to make it an offer that it could not refuse.

It was with this motivation that Pakistan sent Major General Walter Cawthorn, the deputy chief of the Pakistani army, to London to explore the possibility of a Pakistan–UK defence pact. In London he met a very receptive Noel-Baker on 18 September and told him that Pakistan was greatly alarmed by the world situation and the danger posed by communism. Pakistan, he added, was prepared to play its part in the collective defence against Russian aggression.

In effect it was a repeat of the tactics adopted by Jinnah before the SecondWorld War. While the Congress party refused to cooperate in the war effort, Jinnah had volunteered the services of the Muslim League.

Cawthorn's mission was successful. Liaquat Ali Khan followed him to London and during the Commonwealth Prime Ministers' Conference, he met Nehru on the side and adopted an inflexible attitude on Kashmir. Separately, and unknown to Nehru, he was stitching up a closer alliance with Britain. Liaquat met Ernest Bevin, who was the foreign secretary from 1945 to 1951, and Noel-Baker where they decided that it was time to take the Kashmir question back to the UN.

Britain didn't just stop there. Later, at the end of October 1948, it hinted to Pakistan through military channels that it would allow British officers to remain with Pakistani forces in the event of an aggression against Pakistan by India and that the UN would be inclined to impose sanctions if India attacked Pakistan.

By 15 December 1948, the situation had turned in India's favour along the Mendhar–Kotli road. But on the diplomatic front, Pakistan was continuing to outmanoeuvre India. To aid the Pakistani military efforts, British officers led by Major General Loftus Tottenham began to take direct part in 'Operation Venus' which was a major offensive launched in the Naushera area. Their participation in the offensive was in direct violation of the 'Stand Down' orders. Nehru protested against this aggression, but the British were in no mood to listen.

'Operation Venus' and the participation of the British officers in it, with the real risk of reverses for India, once again turned Nehru's thoughts towards launching a counteroffensive and taking the fight into Pakistan. But as was typical with him, Nehru mixed his moral dilemmas with the conduct of war.

In the midst of war, where every day was critical, Nehru wanted to follow the proper procedure and consult the British governor general and the British chief of the Indian army on every major military step. Nor was he shy of sharing his concerns with the British prime minister, and sometimes with the Pakistani prime minister too. All that this transparency, and these consultations by Nehru, achieved was to alert the Pakistani side to Nehru's moves and plans. It allowed them to think of countermoves and to block him diplomatically and militarily. It is doubtful if this effort by Nehru was reciprocated with sincerity at any stage by Pakistan. There is very little evidence to suggest that it was so.

In fact, had there been an honest attempt at good relations, the conflict in Kashmir would not have arisen at all. It was actually a time when both countries should have put their fullest energies in alleviating the human tragedy of the partition. The other, more fundamental, issue concerns a basic contradiction in Pakistan's stand. Pakistan's case on Kashmir rested on the argument that the majority of Kashmiris were Muslims. But if, as Jinnah insisted in his 11 August 1947 speech, religion was no business of a state, what then was the basis of Pakistan's claim on Kashmir?

Yet, Nehru did not deviate from his chosen path. As in the past, once more he decided to put on record an important military move that he was contemplating. He wrote to General Bucher, the British chief of the Indian army, 'If Pakistan is foolish enough to indulge in any attack on us, we shall counter it even by crossing Pakistan territory towards Wazirabad or Sialkot.'[17]

As on previous occasions, this latest threat by Nehru was to remain a matter of record only. However, the British got into the act quickly. Even as Pakistan continued to carry out its attack, Nehru's hand was held back by his British advisers, just as they had done a year earlier to Pakistan's advantage. Had Nehru overruled them, and if the Indian army had carried out the offensive into West Punjab, Pakistan would have had to withdraw its forces from Kashmir. But that was not to be.

Britain wasn't just content by staying India's hand in the battlefield. It was actively engaged in blocking India on the global front too. For that it wooed the US actively to its viewpoint, advancing bizarre arguments such as the possibility of Pakistan moving over to the Soviet camp if the Western world did not give it support and satisfaction on the Kashmir issue.

Meanwhile, the Indian army and air force had started their offensive in Kashmir. In fact, the situation on the military front began to turn so grim for Pakistan that Liaquat Ali Khan made a desperate telephone call on 17 November 1948 to Attlee seeking Britain's support for a call for a ceasefire by the UN Security Council. Britain, in turn, began to press the US to convene a Security Council meeting immediately. But the US wasn't convinced of the Pakistani case as projected by Britain. It felt that there were considerable difficulties there in the absence of an overall political settlement and in light of India's claim to Jammu and Kashmir.

---

[17]Jawaharlal Nehru, *Selected Works of Jawaharlal Nehru*, vol. 9.

The chief US delegate to the UN then, John Foster Dulles, reported to Washington on 23 November 1948 that, 'the present UK approach to the Kashmir problem appears extremely pro-Pakistan'.[18]

Consequently, Pakistan and the UK did not get crucial American support. Around this time the UNCIP finalized its additional proposals, supplementing those of the 13 August 1948 resolution. The additional clauses in it included the appointment of a plebiscite administrator, the size of Indian forces in Jammu and Kashmir, the stationing and size of Indian troops in the territory vacated by the tribesmen and other Pakistani nationals.

The passage of time and the fog of words have together blurred people's memory on the issue, but it is important to note that the terms of plebiscite were outlined in very general terms; they were not a compulsion on India. The Indian claim over Jammu and Kashmir was recognized through the clause that Pakistan should vacate the territory occupied by it and the fact that the Indian forces alone were to be stationed in the entire territory of Jammu and Kashmir, including in the portion vacated by Pakistan.

That vacation by Pakistan never happened, nullifying the very idea of a plebiscite. But Pakistan continues to selectively interpret the supplementary UNCIP proposals, which were accepted by both India and Pakistan on 25 December 1948.

The ceasefire came into effect on 1 January 1949. But the issue hasn't gone away, largely because India has adopted a defensive posture, befuddling its position. Pakistan, in contrast, aggressively maintains that Kashmir belongs to it. That's it, period. Therefore, the message that Pakistan has been giving to the world is clear and absolute. It acts to perfection the part of the aggrieved party appealing to the good sense of the world to right a wrong committed against it.

Alas, India swamps the listener with verbiage. Its articulation of its position is flooded with needless details and lacks the force of conviction.

A remark made by Chou En-lai in August 1968 to the visiting Pakistani foreign minister, Arshad Hussain and quoted by Sultan Khan in *Memories and Reflections of a Pakistani Diplomat*, is illustrative: 'Our experience of talks with India has not been encouraging. How can we negotiate with them when they quote from their scriptures to support their claims over borders?'

---

[18]Michael Shane Smith, *Windows of Opportunity and Military Escalation: Bringing Diplomatic Factors Back In.*

Or, as Australian diplomat Walter Crocker writes in his book *Nehru: A Contemporary's Estimate*:

> Foreigners in Delhi (in 1950s and 60s) used to be told by officials and ministers...that Kashmir, the whole of Kashmir, had legally acceded to India and its accession was irrevocable, so there was no need and no case for a plebiscite; indeed, it was added, the portion of Kashmir occupied by Pakistan was held by aggression and that portion should also rightly be under India.

Implied in this remark is a sense of puzzlement. The foreigner wonders that if this is so, then why does India hold talks over Jammu and Kashmir with Pakistan. Is it to ask Pakistan to vacate the territory illegally occupied by it? Or is it to accede to the Pakistani demand for more Indian territory? Millions of words spoken in the UN and in the Security Council have also befogged the truth. Just to give one statistic: the Security Council had held 124 meetings on the Kashmir issue by 1964.

While the West has all along exaggerated Pakistan's innocence, Indian leaders, particularly Nehru, have not helped the Indian case by their defensive, almost apologetic, posture. Only Krishna Menon was firm and forthright during the Security Council debates and more than equal to his Pakistani counterpart. Only he summed it up pithily when in a Security Council debate in 1956 on the Kashmir issue he thundered, 'Sovereignty is not negotiable.'

In that 1957 letter of his to chief ministers, Nehru had explained why Pakistan would remain in an antagonistic position to India. But he had not spelt out the contours of the Indian response, which ought to be both adequate and deterrent. Some Indian leaders have sought to achieve that elusive combination. Only one configured it successfully. But the nostalgia for Indira Gandhi and her firmness is selective, need based and influenced by the dominant political mood of the day.

Finally, one must ritualistically ask the question: 'Will the Kashmir issue ever be resolved?'

Perhaps the passage of time, and sheer ennui over the hopelessness of a decisive move by either side, might lead to a 'Stand Down'—the term that the British had first thought of, hopefully, but half-heartedly.

9
Sharing Rivers

If Pakistan was in Africa, it would be a big power. The reality is that it is in Asia, and it is next to India. And it is much smaller. So it has to squiggle and shout and constantly punch above its weight. It also conjures up new tricks and new laments every so often to trap India and to extract yet another concession out of it.

The story of the Indus waters is one such instance. But let us first put the issue of shared waters in perspective.

From ancient times water has been considered critical for human survival. The Vedas recognized it as such; water is one of the five life-sustaining elements in the Hindu scriptures. Leonardo da Vinci went a step further and called water 'the driving force of all nature'. Rome's Piazza Navona celebrates the magnificence of water in the form of a grand Renaissance-era sculpture, 'The Fountain of Four Rivers' by Gian Lorenzo Bernini. In recent times Yoko Ono put it plainly, saying, 'Every drop in the ocean counts.' Yet like the air we breathe we tend to take water for granted; that it will be available forever at the turn of a tap. Alas, that assurance is only for the privileged; this is not the case for the vast masses living in less fortunate circumstances. Water does not trickle out of their community taps, except occasionally and minimally.

It is true that the last all-out war over water was fought 4500 years ago between the Mesopotamian city states of Lagash and Umma. But the absence of big wars has not meant amity, even the agreements over water have not worked generally. Between AD 805 and 1984, governments have signed more than 3600 agreements on sharing of waters. Many of these became disputed almost immediately thereafter. In the twentieth century itself water sharing, or rather the lack of it, has led to forty-two violent conflicts, short of war, in the world.

One reason for the misunderstandings and acrimony over water is the absence of a legal framework. Despite efforts by the UN and other international bodies, the world has yet to come up with an acceptable formula of how shared waters should be divided when a river flows through two or more states.

In 1997, a UN convention came close to resolving the issue by declaring that international waterways should be divided reasonably and equitably without causing undue harm to any of the states concerned. It seemed a reasonable enough proposition, one that could have given at least a basis to start with, but China, Turkey and Burundi refused to sign that agreement. In any case China, the countries of Central Asia and many other upper riparian states have national laws declaring absolute sovereignty over their waters, thus putting this national assertion in direct conflict with any international understanding on sharing of waters equitably. This lack of an agreed international law on the most vital of natural resources is one major reason why nearly 300 rivers, including the Danube, the Nile, the Colorado and the Rio Grande, are all subject to major disputes between nations.

Asia has even more reasons for multiple disputes. It is the least water-blessed continent, being the driest in the world. The fresh-water availability is less than half of the global annual average of 8200 cubic metres per inhabitant. India fares particularly badly on this scale; its citizens get less than 1700 cubic metres of water annually.

In a calculation that takes in all available water resources, Asia has less than one-fourth of those available in North America and only about one-third of Europe's. This disparity is going to increase because Asia has the fastest growing demand for water due to its industrialization and population growth. Moreover, Asia has vastly increased its agricultural production in recent decades, doubling its cropland between 1960 and 2000, adding further to the stress on availability of water.

About 70 per cent of the 302 million hectares of irrigated land in the world is in Asia. Within Asia, just three regions, South Asia, Southeast Asia and China account for 50 per cent of the global irrigated land. No wonder then that the largest number of dams should be in Asia—China alone has more than half of the 50,000 dams in the world.

The water requirements in Asia are set to increase even more in the coming years not just because of the greater agricultural needs but also because as the manufacturing hub of the world it will need more water for its power plants and industries. And unlike the Western world, the Asian population shows no sign of moderation in its growth; the younger population will simply be thirsting for more water. Unfortunately for them, they may have to be content with less water. Environmental degradation and depleting glaciers are reducing the size of rivers steadily; this is also shrinking lakes to smaller sizes.

That's why upstream countries are zealously guarding their water resources. The result is that though there are fifty-seven transnational rivers in Asia, only four of them have treaties covering water sharing or institutional cooperation. Of these four treaties (Mekong, Jordan, Ganges and Indus), two have been signed by India. To put it in other terms, fifty-three of the fifty-seven transnational rivers in Asia have no agreement governing the equitable distribution of their waters for the simple reason that the upstream countries consider the waters that originate in their territory as their national treasure, and they consider control over them their sovereign right.

China refuses to enter into an agreement with any of its neighbours on the equitable use of waters of the rivers that flow out of its territory into other states. In contrast, India has signed water-sharing agreements with both of its downstream neighbours, Pakistan and Bangladesh. The Indus waters agreement signed by it with Pakistan is the most generous agreement ever in history signed by an upper riparian state.

Can we afford to be generous with our water? Do we have enough for our people and our use? Have we catered to our expanding needs and future requirements?

The answer to all this is a clear 'no' if one goes by the grim projections of a BBC television series on water. Its promotional clips show a young Indian man driven to drinking water from a toilet because that's how acute the water situation in India is projected to be in the years to come. But why wait for the future? Shades of it are happening right now. There are villages in Maharashtra where people consider themselves lucky if they get a bucket of water once in a month from the municipal water supply truck. Andhra Pradesh has areas that are drought-prone; farmers in this region take the ultimate recourse to suicide. Tamil Nadu and Karnataka are engaged in a bitter water feud. Jammu and Kashmir, through which much of the Indus system waters flow, is starved of water to the extent of 40 per cent.

The picture gets grimmer still when we consider a few statistics.

India is one of the most water-stressed countries in the world. Its per capita storage capacity (the amount of water that can be stored as a proportion of the average river run-off) is just fifty days. This number subsumes wide variations—from 220 days in the Krishna to only two days in the Brahmaputra–Barak basin. The comparative figures for the Colorado river basin and the Murray–Darling basin are 900 days. Let's consider just one more fact—Bihar and Bengal have the lowest per capita length of rivers and canals at only four centimetres.

Obviously, then, faith, fatalism and an occasional shower are often the life-sustainers for people and their agriculture in parts of India. But even God might tire if India does not help itself and devise its own solutions.

Sadly, the problems are going to increase in times to come. States in India will bicker constantly over how much, and how frequently, they could draw water from their and other states' rivers. One possible solution to this could be a north–south grid of rivers. But a sustainable grid would need assured sources of water. There is hardly a trickle that India gets from the six Indus system rivers and given China's plans to build multiple-use mega dams on the Brahmaputra, the availability of its waters in the Northeast may not remain as plentiful as it has been so far.

China has already constructed some run of the river dams on the Brahmaputra river. Now it plans to build a mega dam on it at Metog that will be bigger than the 18,300 MW Three Gorges dam. (India's biggest Tehri Dam is just 2000 MW in comparison). If China also diverts the Brahmaputra waters, as it wishes to reportedly, the impact on the downstream environment will be huge. It will disturb the rainfall pattern, reduce river water flow into India, affect fisheries in the Brahmaputra river in India and the marine life in the Bay of Bengal. It will also mean that the Brahmaputra would not be able to contribute significantly to the Indian river grid when it comes up. Even as China builds dams and carries out irrigation works on the Brahmaputra it refuses to consult India.

China is also constructing a dam in the Gilgit–Baltistan region and carrying out other works of a strategic nature in Pakistan-occupied Kashmir (POK). Though India's claim extends to the entire Jammu and Kashmir region, including the area occupied by Pakistan, it has not effectively protested against China's building activities in POK.

The question then arises that if the rest of the world is busy protecting its interests, what was it that compelled us to go in the opposite direction? Why did we sacrifice our interests? Why did we elect to condemn our present and future generations with an unequal treaty?

The short answer to this question is that the Americans bullied Nehru into an iniquitous deal on the Indus waters. It is even more remarkable that it should have happened in an era when nations were increasingly assertive about their sovereignty and conscious of preserving their national rights.

At first, it seemed that water might not be an issue between India and Pakistan. There was an elaborate canal system that ran through Punjab. Since the proposed Indo-Pak boundary was going to cut through this system of rivers and canals, Cyril Radcliffe suggested in July 1947 at the meeting of the Boundary Commission in Lahore that there should be joint management of the vast network of canals. This should have been the obvious and fair way of settling a complex issue. But Jinnah replied caustically that 'he would rather have deserts in Pakistan than fertile fields watered by the courtesy of the Hindus'.

To this Nehru responded, 'What India did with India's rivers was India's affair.'[1]

That is how it should have been; India should have treated its waters as principally its affair.

Had the roles been reversed and if Pakistan was the upper riparian area, it would have seen to it that it maintained absolute sovereignty over the flow of waters through its territory. Indeed in defiance of all international laws, Pakistan has denied India transit rights for exports and imports through its territory to Iran and the landlocked Afghanistan.

But India views issues through a benign prism and its resolve is not immutable. Circumstances and external forces crucially make it take a view contrary to what only a little while earlier it had presumed to be in its best interest. It is odd that it should be so weak of resolve when it comes to matters of its national interest, even though it prides itself in promising permanence of policies and ensuring security of investment to all foreigners. Should such assurance not extend to its own citizens on a matter as vital as the availability of water?

Where the Indus waters are concerned, its generosity was going to impose a heavy cost on India.

Let's now consider the external environment then. The international equations post-Second World War were changing. The East–West confrontation was becoming steadily shriller; the world was getting rapidly divided into us versus them camps. In those early years of the 1950s, Pakistan decided to cast its lot with the American-led Western

---

[1]Ian Talbot and Gurharpal Singh, *The Partition of India.*

alliance. It became a founding member of the Baghdad Pact. Moreover President Eisenhower and President Ayub Khan were military men and had empathy for each other. But the US needed India as well. If it wanted Pakistan as a military ally, it regarded India as a model of non-communist development. It, therefore, considered it necessary to resolve the two principal issues of friction between them: Kashmir and water.

Meanwhile, by the autumn of 1947, Jinnah had climbed down from his previous stand of not needing 'Hindu' water. India and Pakistan decided to have a 'standstill agreement' that allowed a specified water flow into Pakistan up to 1 April 1948. On that date, India stopped the water flow from two canals into Pakistan because the 'standstill' agreement between the two countries had expired. One reason for this was to affirm its sovereign rights over waters that flowed through India. Incidentally, according to the bilateral agreement between them, Pakistan was to deposit an amount specified by the prime minister of India for flow of waters to it through the Central Bari Doab and Dipalpur canals. That it was never done is a different matter.

India restored the water supply that it had cut off on 1 April 1948, after repeated Pakistani entreaties. While Pakistan was continuing its aggression in Kashmir, India responded positively to its appeal for large-heartedness on water flow as a bigger neighbour. It was a tactic that Pakistan has successfully employed ever since.

Once the water supply was restored, Pakistan became obstructionist. It began looking for opportunities to object to any works by India to better its irrigation works in the areas that were to be settled by the refugees who came in from Pakistan. India's plans to build the Rajasthan canal were immediately objected to by Pakistan and this eventually led to the US and the World Bank taking active interest in the issue. As later events would show, the World Bank, under prodding from Washington, was hardly the model of an honest broker.

In 1954 it proposed that the three main eastern rivers (the Sutlej, Beas and Ravi) be reserved for India's exclusive use while the three western rivers (the Indus, Chenab and Jhelum) should be for Pakistan's use. On the face of it, this seemed a fair solution by dividing three rivers each. But the fact was that the western rivers carried far more water than the eastern rivers, and India's population (therefore its needs too) was seven times larger than that of Pakistan. President Ayub Khan admits in his book, *Friends not Masters,* that the 'Pakistani approach was tantamount to asking for the moon'.

Pakistan was emboldened to ask for the moon because the US had begun favouring it. As with the British calculations during the Kashmir crisis, the US had come to the view that Pakistan was to be its ally in South Asia.

Even as discussions on the water issue carried on, the US State Department proposed a 'Basket Solution' to the secretary of state, John Foster Dulles. It involved the settlement of Kashmir along the ceasefire line, and a resolution of the water issue in favour of Pakistan. The US would serve to speed up the settlement on these two issues by acting as a mediator. Dulles recommended this approach to President Eisenhower who reacted positively and wrote letters to Prime Minister Nehru and President Iskander Mirza offering his good offices as an intermediary.

Pakistan reacted enthusiastically. As an American ally, it hoped to benefit from that goodwill. Nehru was not at all keen about the prospect of this presidential intervention. As he was to explain to Eisenhower subsequently, 'If third parties intervene, even though that intervention proceeds from goodwill…the aggressor country and the country against whom aggression has taken place are put on the same level, both pleading before that third party.'[2]

There was also a more fundamental problem with the American package. Even though it claimed that there would be concessions by both sides, what the American formula actually entailed was concessions by India on both the Kashmir and water issues.

By 1959, the US had decided that the 'Basket Solution' was not going to work. It then decided to work instead on the 'water issue' first. India's financial difficulties provided the US a platform to put pressure on Nehru. What persuasion could not achieve was easily obtained through financial influence. The foreign exchange requirements of the Second Five Year Plan plus the financial strain of importing food due to drought-like conditions made India turn to the US and the World Bank for loans.

James Langley, the American ambassador in Pakistan, was quick to sense an opportunity there for settling the water issue. He suggested to Washington:

> Both Pakistan and India are edging closer and closer to bankruptcy and India in particular is in financial terms becoming more desperate daily. The USA is thus in a position to put conditions on loans to make Nehru more amenable to a settlement with Pakistan. Persuasion

---

[2]*Foreign Relations of US (FRUS)*, vol. xv, doc. 43, pp. 117–19, 7 June 1958.

> alone has failed, and will continue to fail unless some facts of international life are impressed upon Nehru. Financial pressure could serve that purpose.[3]

Pakistan realized that this might be its big chance to get favourable terms for itself, and exploited this opening to the maximum. At times it threatened to take the water issue to the Security Council, sending the Americans into a panic. Consequently, the World Bank negotiator Sir William Iliff, who had always remained in close consultation with the Americans, came up with the Indus Waters Treaty of 1960, which was and remains extremely favourable to Pakistan.

That wasn't all. As a part of this agreement the US and its allies paid nearly US$1 billion to Pakistan to construct dams on the Indus system rivers. Moreover, a nearly bankrupt India was made to cough up £62 million for Pakistan to improve its canals, even as it continued to deny India its right to construct works over the waters that flow through its territory.

One among many fundamental flaws of the Indus treaty was that it divided the rivers without taking the volume of water into account. Experts recognize the unfairness of this treaty, but the public at large remains ignorant of it. However, this might change as water scarcity, and Pakistan's obstructive tactics to any hydrological use of its waters by India, becomes a matter of debate within India. No treaty in the world can bind a state, especially if it is against its interests. Moreover, India has not even utilized the facilities given to it under this treaty. Thus:

- India is allowed 13.43 maf (million acre feet) of the three western rivers' waters but uses only 7.9 maf.
- India is allowed to tap all 33 maf of the three eastern rivers but allows 3 maf to flow into Pakistan.
- India can store up to 3.5 maf from western rivers. It hasn't touched a drop yet.

More worryingly, India has not taken up the issue of changed circumstances. Over the last sixty years its population has expanded, agricultural needs have increased vastly and the region's manufacturing sector has grown. All these need and demand vastly more water than was allowed in 1960.

Moreover, can a treaty entered into under pressure be termed a

---

[3]Telegram by Ambassador James Langley to William Rountree, 2 September 1958, *FRUS*, vol. xv, doc. 52.

fair treaty, especially one which is so blatantly biased? Let's also consider a final twist of the knife.

Pakistan completed its canal works and built dams on the Indus water system thanks to the money provided by the US and India. India never raised any objection to these works. Nor has India objected, in the manner it should, to the construction of a major dam in POK by China.

Yet, Pakistan does not miss an opportunity to raise objections to any work that might improve the hydrological potential of India. To date, it has objected to and delayed ten hydroelectric projects. Where, following Pakistani objections, India has agreed to reduce the specifications it has virtually resulted in the crippling of that project through silting. Had Pakistan been in India's position, it would have sought financial compensation for the delays that have been caused by these objections. But India prefers to take a benign view even as its citizens (including those in Jammu and Kashmir) and its economy suffer due to the opportunity lost.

Let us digress a bit for a word about Pakistan's financial acumen. The World Bank negotiator Iliff felt embarrassed squeezing money out of India because it was then in dire financial straits. Even though it was to be given to a very hostile Pakistan, Nehru agreed to give Pakistan £62 million, which must have been a rather large sum of money (probably equal to US$2 billion now).

Pakistan did not hesitate at all in accepting this large sum from India. Rather it kept increasing its demands for the money that was to come from the US. Though in May 1958 it had agreed to the Iliff estimate of US$660 million for construction of waterworks, it kept increasing that estimate every few months till it finally settled for US$1033 million just in time to sign the Indus waters agreement (in Karachi on 19 September 1960). But even then it did not agree to the terms of the eastern rivers' settlement till it had received firm assurances that the money promised would actually be given to it!

It must also be added that even as the US was forcing India to accept a treaty that involved a huge sacrifice, the US itself was extremely niggardly in its treatment of its lower riparian, Mexico.

The Indus waters agreement has held out since 1960.

India could have, but it did not switch off the water supply when it was a victim of armed aggression by Pakistan (leading to wars) on at least three occasions. Nor has it reacted to Pakistan's provocative behaviour over what is its right under the terms of the treaty. All this has been done at a considerable cost to it, as it has meant denial of water to its own citizens.

The fact that this was an iniquitous treaty signed under pressure rankles the Indian people. Moreover, the pressure of new needs, new demands and a growing population may force India to revise the treaty one day.

It has been done by other countries. Turkey is one major example of it. The world knows the Euphrates and Tigris as two historically important rivers that flow from Turkey to Syria and Iraq. Despite ancient agreements, supplemented by those it had entered into in the twentieth century, Turkey reneged on them. Basically, the Turkish change of attitude began with the realization that it needed more waters for its domestic use. In the 1960s, it decided to build twenty-two high dams and nineteen hydropower plants on the Euphrates and Tigris rivers. These were designed to generate 27 billion kWh of electricity and irrigate 1.7 million hectares of farmland. It may not be wide off the mark to say that these works on the two rivers transformed Turkey; they contributed significantly to its economic development and prosperity.

Simultaneously, these Turkish plans resulted in reducing the electricity generation capacity of Syria and Iraq and the waters that flow there. To take just the case of the Euphrates, the water flow from Turkey into Syria reduced from 30.3 billion cubic metres to only 8.48 billion cubic metres. But Turkey's priority and sole concern was the needs of its people. They had a sovereign claim over waters that flowed first through its territory and according to Turkey, its people were suffering from the historical injustice of the treaties. Moreover, new needs and a growing population had changed the water requirements of its people. In sum, its principal concern was its people, rather than the goodwill for, or worries about, the people of Syria and Iraq.

Like Turkey, it will be perfectly logical if India were to unilaterally abrogate the Indus treaty. Nor would it be without precedent if like China and many other states it were to declare sovereign rights over waters that flow through its territory. Even if the treaty is not abrogated, its Article XII provides that it 'may from time to time be modified…' The feeling that the people of Jammu and Kashmir are suffering because of the treaty has been steady amongst the people there over the years. On 3 March 2003 the Jammu and Kashmir Legislative Assembly passed a unanimous resolution calling for a review of the treaty.

The alternative to taking unilateral action is, of course, the proverbial Indian patience—stay put, do nothing. But then, that carries the risk that at some future date the pot might just boil over because of the iniquitous treatment and because of the tremendous shortfall in water availability to the Indian people.

The increasing stridency of statements from Pakistan is not a promising sign that Pakistan worries about the Indian pot or its simmer. India has not utilized even a fraction of the Indus system waters to produce energy, yet even the hint of a dam construction activity leads to high-pitched Pakistani propaganda against it, calling the activity a threat to their existence, and a conspiracy to divert or misuse precious waters that are theirs. Former Pakistani army chief General Kayani cited water to justify his 'India-centric' military stance. The Lashkar-e-Taiba (LeT) threatens that 'water must flow, or blood would flow'. An editorial in *Nawaiwaqt* demanded that, 'Pakistan should convey to India that a war is possible on the issue of water and this time war will be a nuclear one.'

Rarely though has a critical eye been cast inwards on the gross water mismanagement in Pakistan and the grudge of Sindh and other states that Punjab diverts waters from the Indus river system that should rightly go to the downstream provinces of Pakistan.

Pakistani politicians have themselves given vastly varying statements, occasioned perhaps by the audience they were addressing and the political need of the moment. Former Prime Minister Yousaf Raza Gillani claimed to the *Financial Times* in March 2010 that Pakistan had a bumper wheat crop: 'There is so much surplus that we have had to have new storage constructed for our strategic reserves. We have surplus rice, a bumper crop, people are getting good price for cotton.'

A few weeks later Foreign Minister Shah Mehmood Qureshi asserted, 'It [water] is not being stolen in India. It's being wasted in Pakistan.'

Yet, a year earlier President Asif Ali Zardari had found it politically convenient to raise the water temperature. Writing in the *Washington Post* of 28 January 2009 he maintained, 'The water crisis in Pakistan is directly linked to relations with India...'

Clearly, Pakistan's principal preoccupation is its requirements. No Pakistani leader or opinion-maker has ever expressed concern about the water needs in India. India, on the other hand, did not take an India-centric approach. In fact, its attitude at the talks leading to the Indus Waters Treaty was guided by Nehru's desire to 'purchase peace' with Pakistan. Riyaz Punjabi, former vice-chancellor of the University of Kashmir, writes that 'the treaty could not buy peace, as the 1965 war demonstrated, but in the bargain the genuine economic interests of J&K state were surrendered'.[4]

Niranjan Gulhati, India's chief negotiator at the Indus Waters Treaty talks, has this to say:

> None of us had, at that time, any real idea of the quantum of future developments in the upper reaches of the western rivers. Nor did we have any idea of the irrigation from the Indus in Ladakh. As regards hydro-electric development we felt that, being a non-consumptive use, it was not covered by the Bank proposal which dealt only with irrigation uses.[5]

Obviously, then, India miscalculated technically too. Take the case of the Wullar Lake. A century ago it measured 217 square kilometres. Today it has shrunk to 86 square kilometres. The increased water requirements of nearby towns are as much to blame for this state of a once majestic lake as the fact that the feed of fresh water into it from the traditional river sources is no longer available to it in the required quantity.

To make matters worse Pakistan drags India to international arbitration the moment it learns of a hydel project being planned on any of the Indus system rivers. Though it lost the case on the Baglihar project, it has burdened India with arbitration procedures on ten other projects. By dragging India to costly and time-consuming litigation it ensures at least a long delay in the implementation of these projects, besides adding to the irritant value of the entire enterprise. India has never calculated the cost of opportunity lost because of this delay, or the adverse impact on the people and economy of Jammu and Kashmir due to Pakistan's intransigence.

Meanwhile, Pakistan continues with mega projects in the area of Jammu and Kashmir occupied by it. After the Tarbela and Mangla dams, Pakistan now has plans to build the multi-purpose Diamer Bhasha dam in the Gilgit–Baltistan area of POK. Besides the illegality of construction in an area that India claims belongs to it, there is also the seismological concern.

The epicentre of the earthquake in 2005 that measured 7.6 on the Richter scale and killed 90,000 people lies very close to the site of the dam. Any disturbance here is bound to have an impact in Jammu and

---

[4]Riyaz Punjabi, 'Indus Waters Treaty, Human Security vs Military Security,' *Journal of Peace Studies*.

[5]K. Warikoo, *Indus Waters Treaty: View from Kashmir*.

Kashmir as it did during the earthquake of 2005. The chances of this happening are considerable because between 1927 and 2001 this area has recorded 863 earthquakes; that means an average of about eleven earthquakes a year.

Pakistan does not feel it necessary to consult or inform India on any of the projects that it undertakes on the waters of the Indus treaty rivers, even when the development is in contested areas, and in the case of the Bhasha dam in a quake-prone area where convulsions could directly affect India.

India, on the other hand, finds itself bound hopelessly by the Indus treaty knots. As with Kashmir, Nehru's idealism and India's financial situation led it to accept an unequal treaty on the Indus system waters. Still, having done so, it could have abrogated it as Turkey had done, or like China it could have declared sovereign rights over waters flowing in its territory. Instead it has chosen to follow the line that Pakistan draws from time to time. But, as seems likely, Pakistan might up the ante for domestic or other reasons in the years to come and adopt a confrontational and aggressive posture on the issue of water.

India will not be without options then; but it will need to stand firm on whatever resolve it makes. As a first it must seek the revision of a treaty that gives it only 20 per cent of the Indus treaty waters and allocates Pakistan 80 per cent share of it. Second, it must register its protest over any construction activity that Pakistan might plan in POK; it should approach aid-givers like the World Bank and Asian Development Bank urging them not to extend aid/loans for such projects. Moreover, it must consider whether it should keep delaying its projects by agreeing to costly and time-consuming arbitration procedures.

It is either that, or a continuing sacrifice of interests of people in Jammu and Kashmir. It will, of course, be ideal if reason leads to a reasonable solution, and debate is not overtaken by action. Sadly, the potential for action is great because Pakistan is unlikely to concede even a drop of water to India. Rather, it has been systematically giving out calls that it needs yet more water from the Indus system rivers. Jihadis too have taken the cue from the Pakistani government's campaign and started echoing the line that Pakistan is being deprived by India of water that belongs to it!

Thus far India and Pakistan have fought three wars over Kashmir and one over Bangladesh. Water could well become the next addition to that list.

10

'His Men Kill My Boys'

Benazir looked visibly pleased when she came to the Karachi International Airport to see off the former Indian Prime Minister V.P. Singh. His attendance at the South Asian Association for Regional Cooperation (SAARC) opposition leaders conference in Karachi in September 1992 was a great morale booster for her. The conference of opposition leaders was her idea; it was the first of its kind and it had gone off well. Its declaration was a voice in support for democracies in the SAARC region.

V.P. Singh was a great crowd-puller; his secular credentials and his reputation as a leader who had taken on Rajiv Gandhi were formidable assets in his favour. The Pakistani media could not get enough of him, mobbing him and hanging on to his every word. All this was a tonic for Benazir. That and the fact that every opposition leader from SAARC had turned up to attend her conference, the news coverage in Pakistani media, and glowing references to her by the assembled leaders had put her on a solid comeback trail domestically.

Nawaz Sharif was Pakistan's prime minister then. Prior to V.P. Singh's arrival in Karachi, he had sent a message inviting V.P. Singh to Islamabad after the conference. But when the declaration of the opposition leaders came out it was taken amiss by Sharif's advisers. A perfectly innocuous appeal for the preservation and promotion of democracy was taken as an attack on Nawaz Sharif and his government. The reaction of the Pakistani government was swift; the invitation to V.P. Singh was withdrawn abruptly. It pained V.P. Singh that an unnecessary affront had been taken where none was intended. But such is the nature of the murky intelligence world in Pakistan that misrepresentations and rumours suffice to prejudice governments.

When he left for Delhi, I had gone with him to the airport. Benazir came separately to meet us at the airport lounge. 'Do you know who I met on the way here?' she asked.

'Who?' both of us enquired encouragingly.

'It was the Karachi area commander, a lieutenant general.' She added, 'I asked him if he would like to come and shake hands with a former prime minister of India. He said no, he wouldn't because "his men kill my boys."'

Benazir chuckled and left it at that. But I kept wondering if an Indian general would say the same thing. I doubt it and in case someone were to say it as an exception, he will be criticized as a hardliner and for being unreasonable. Not just the Indian general, but even an average Indian is hardly likely to think in these terms. The fact is that over the years Pakistan barely figures in the daily imagination of Indians, except episodically for the wrong reasons.

Since I was conditioned by such an Indian experience, the Pakistani general's logic continued to elude me; the killings are not one-sided, soldiers from both sides fire their guns when ordered. It is a job that their chosen profession tasks them to perform. Soldiers from one side or the other cannot be held accountable for doing their professional duties. Why, then, should hatred be carried to such a personal extreme? Was it because the feeling was deeply ingrained? Was it this that led repeatedly to a call for arms? The more I pondered over it the more it seemed to me that the general's statement was not an off-the-cuff, impulsive reaction. It was the result of a more complex syndrome; an indication too that people underestimate the obsession with India in the daily life of Pakistan.

One explanation for this could be the state within the state in Pakistan. Post-partition, Pakistan has been governed either by dictators or by politicians who are authoritarian in their behaviour. In both cases the rulers have derived comfort by relying on intelligence sources. This in turn has resulted in the weakening of institutions and bureaucracy. Normally, it is the institutions which fill the gap between the rulers and the governed, but in their absence, Pakistani rulers rely on intelligence agencies who provide the feedback that they would like the ruler to hear.

There is ample evidence of prejudice against India in the Pakistani establishment, especially its security and intelligence set-up. The Foreign Office is mostly a willing accomplice; the odd, occasional voice in favour of peace at the political level is heard but not tolerated.

It is certainly not the case that the entire Pakistani nation is hostile. In fact, as in other parts of the world, there are sections of Pakistani society who are liberal and curious about people they were partitioned away from. But the liberal voice is faint in Pakistan, and increasingly hesitant. It is either drowned out in the passion of the moment, or elects to remain mute for fear of being branded pro-India. Sometimes, it seemed that even Field Marshal Ayub Khan, the all-powerful first military dictator of Pakistan, was a victim of this syndrome. He acted with circumspection when Bhutto was around.

Why was the all-powerful field marshal wary of Zulfikar Bhutto? There is no doubt that Bhutto was charismatic and a gifted speaker. He was also one of the richest landlords in Pakistan, and entertained those in power lavishly. Politically, he had established a loyal and powerful band of supporters around him. But was it enough to make the field marshal wary?

Lest there be any doubt that Ayub Khan was a great friend of India, let's clarify that though he was in the military service in pre-partition India with Hindu, Sikh and Christian officers, this burly Pathan's knowledge of Indian society was not based on a deep study. Take, for instance, this note sent by him on 6 October 1967 to the governors of East and West Pakistan and the ministers for defence, foreign affairs and information and broadcasting:

> The dominant classes in this [Indian] society are the Brahmins and Banias. These are the classes which have exploited the people of the subcontinent for centuries... The fact that we have found salvation in Pakistan does not mean that the domination and exploitation of people in India by the Brahmins and Banias has ceased. This is a point which gets lost in general criticism of Hinduism and Hindu society. There are deep schisms in Indian society. These schisms, differences and distinctions should be made use of in our approach to India. We must make the broad masses of India conscious of their Brahmin–Bania axis...[1]

What Ayub Khan was suggesting contained the seeds of a campaign to divide Indian society; the support to the Khalistani movement falls in this category. This note also betrays an unfortunate misreading of India at the highest levels in Pakistan.

Let's get back to Zulfikar Ali Bhutto. How was this son of a Hindu mother and a Shia father so completely able to dominate a Sunni majority Pakistan from the time he got his first ministerial post in 1958 till the time he was condemned to his prison cell in September 1977? This, incidentally, was the period when India had to fight three wars: one with China (in 1962) and two with Pakistan (1965 and 1971).

---

[1]Baxter Craig (ed.), *Diaries of Field Marshal Mohammad Ayub Khan*.

India and Pakistan also signed three of the most important agreements during this period—the Indus Waters Treaty (1960), the Tashkent Agreement (1965) and the Simla Agreement (1972). Zulfikar Bhutto was a central figure in each of the wars as well as the agreements.

One way or the other, while in power, during his incarceration in prison and in the manner of his trial and execution, he managed to affect Pakistan and its people in most fundamental ways. Throughout this period of nearly two decades he was either a close confidant of the dictator of the day or dictator-like himself. His and indeed the example of many other civilian leaders, who preceded or followed him, raises the valid enquiry of whether there is a substantial difference between Pakistan's civilian regimes and its military ones.

Perhaps there is very little, because democracy in Pakistan is constantly threatened by the extremist, religious, military and negative economic forces. In the absence of a large middle class there is hardly an effective body that can monitor or check a government's performance for society, leading thereby to too much 'state' and too little 'society'. Consequently, military dictators, the feudal class and the very rich are the 'state'. They get the best positions in the government, grab the biggest contracts, and take the largest bank loans which they do not pay back. That monopoly has been challenged in recent years by the religious and the extremist shades. But so far, and especially during Zulfikar Bhutto's twenty years in government, the army and the feudal class had a cosy relationship—and Bhutto was comfortable riding both horses.

Still, the judgement of history may not be generous in his favour. Its considered verdict might be that if Jinnah was the creator of Pakistan, Zulfikar Bhutto was its destroyer; not completely, but substantially. Did Bhutto have great loyalty to anyone else except his daughter Benazir and to his own self-interest? There is some evidence to suggest that he wasn't exactly reverential, even towards Jinnah. A letter he wrote from Geneva in April 1958 to the first president of Pakistan, Iskander Mirza, is illustrative:

> I would like to take this opportunity to reassure you of my imperishable and devoted loyalty to you... I feel that your services to Pakistan are indispensable. When the history of our Country is written by objective historians, your name will be placed even before that of Mr. Jinnah. Sir, I say this because I mean it and not because you are the President of my Country.[2]

[2]A.G. Noorani, 'Bhutto's Treachery', *Frontline*.

There is no doubt that Bhutto had great charisma. He was a leader of men, a demagogue and a forceful personality as well and could ooze charm when he wished. Bhutto was loved by the masses but greatly feared by his rivals—even Field Marshal Ayub Khan did not wish to contradict him. Had it been otherwise, he would have given peace with India a try, like any Pathan would.

But wily Bhutto had other ideas and luck seemed to side with him. His appointment as the water and power minister came just around the time when negotiations for the Indus Waters Treaty were getting into the final phase. The American pressure and the World Bank's financial clout were responsible for getting India to agree, but as the water and power minister he could and did take all the credit for getting Pakistan a highly favourable Indus Waters Treaty. By then he had also become one of the closest advisers of Ayub Khan. A Machiavellian genius, Bhutto provided articulation and an intellectual veneer to the straight-thinking soldier who happened to have become a dictator.

Bhutto was a rising star of Pakistani politics during the waning years of Nehru's political life. This shift was also reflected in the more reserved style of interlocution between the leaders of the two countries.

In the early years of independence, Nehru and Liaquat Ali Khan exchanged letters and telegrams regularly. Some of them were extremely detailed and copious, covering largely the same ground on issues like Kashmir, the treatment of minorities, claims and counter-claims. Many of these missives were acrimonious, reflecting the tensions of the day. Reading them, even now at this dispassionate distance in time, one wonders why this high degree of acrimony did not turn into an all-out war, far bigger than the localized one in Kashmir. One reason for this was the mutual regard since they had once worked together and known each other in pre-partition India.

This changed when Ayub Khan took over in 1958. He was not a politician and hardly an intellectual match for Nehru. Moreover, Ayub Khan was being constantly goaded by Bhutto to seek more and yet more from Nehru. Steadily, their meetings became infrequent and the exchange of letters was rare and formal. Still, Nehru gave generously when it came to settling the Indus water issue. It was his expectation that after the extremely liberal terms that India had agreed to, Pakistan would reciprocate with credible symbols of friendship. At first it seemed that this might be the case and actual bonhomie may begin to prevail. But Nehru had reckoned without the guile of Bhutto, or the fact that the concession on the Indus waters had whetted Pakistan's appetite for more.

Within a year, Pakistan raised the pitch on Kashmir much to the bewilderment of the Indian government. But the professional diplomats knew that it was coming. In his letter of 6 September 1961 to India's high commissioner in Pakistan, Rajeshwar Dayal, the foreign secretary of the time, M.J. Desai wrote:

> Frankly, all the agreeable noises that Pakistan makes have one major objective, namely, to get us to change our stand on Kashmir. Once we get entangled and take tentative positions, they would reopen the whole matter and try to get what they could not in spite of their efforts in the Security Council, their Defence Pacts and alliances.[3]

That's exactly what India did; it took tentative, almost apologetic positions and got entangled.

Pakistan suffered from no such ambiguity. It never does as far as India is concerned. As Imran Khan once said, in an Indo-Pak cricket match during his playing days, every ball was critical because national prestige was on the line. He added that if Pakistani cricketers were at the point of losing a match in Lahore, then the two umpires stepped in!

As in cricket so in negotiations—Pakistan must win every deal. It chooses a line and keeps repeating it till India gets tired, or concedes out of a false hope that yet another concession by it might pave the way for better relations with Pakistan.

From the very beginning Pakistan was clear about the objectives it was going to pursue vis-à-vis India or Hindustan as Pakistani representatives insisted on calling it. It was a deliberate slight aimed at Nehru's secular vision for India. Naturally, this riled him as it was meant to. This insistence on Pakistan's part was symbolic of a mindset. Moreover, from early on the matrix that Pakistan followed was self-interest. This principle applied most notably in dealings with India, but the US, too, was treated as a readily available milch cow.

Margaret Bourke-White, the *Life* magazine photographer, wrote of an interview where Jinnah told her, 'America needs Pakistan more than Pakistan needs America… Pakistan is the pivot of the world…on which the future position of the world revolves.' With these words Jinnah had set the foundation of a future transactional relationship with the US.

Bourke-White attributed the interest of Pakistan's early leaders in

---

[3]Avtar Singh Bhasin, *India–Pakistan Relations, 1947–2007.*

foreign affairs to a bankruptcy of ideas in building the new state. Pakistan, according to her, had a policy of profiting from the disputes of others. She could have also added that two paradoxical themes were going to dominate Pakistan's foreign policy. The sense of internal weakness would drive successive governments to seek outside support to compensate for that weakness. However, this goal was to prove elusive. Second, its foreign policy was often to be conducted with little regard for domestic ramifications.

The effect of the first syndrome mentioned above was addictive; once Pakistan got hooked to external aid, it couldn't do without it. This dependence would keep eroding the nation's self-esteem. The constant search for external means to solve internal problems would also mean that self-reliance was not going to be Pakistan's mantra, and that it had elected to stand on foreign crutches. It was on account of the second aspect that Pakistan got into Catch-22-like complications. Because of the IOUs (I Owe Yous) that invariably accompany aid, Pakistan was obliged to undertake commitments that it might not have accepted otherwise. Moreover, the strategic alliances that it entered into led to external interventions where it did not have a direct interest. Its strategic partnership with the US, and its alliance with the Gulf Arabs, was not a natural fit. Culturally, historically and ethnically, its people would have been more comfortable in their near neighbourhood and the government less prone to adventurism. But Pakistan opted for the comfort of ready money.

External financing, as distinct from foreign investment, poured in steadily from the US and the oil-rich Gulf states because of Pakistan's alliances. But this approach compounded Pakistan's structural problems, which in turn, retarded the country's economic progress. However, Pakistan's rulers were satisfied with temporary palliatives. As a result, despite billions of dollars in aid, there is no US-aided hospital or university in Pakistan. The cash transfers dissipate after they have served their immediate purpose.

From the very beginning, Pakistan had decided that the US would be the great power patron of choice for it. In September–October 1953 General Ayub Khan, then the army chief, invited himself to the US. There in his meetings he sought a deal where Pakistan for the right price was willing to serve as the West's eastern anchor.

When that alliance with the West came through in the form of the Southeast Asia Treaty Organization (SEATO) and Central Eastern Treaty Organization (CENTO), Ayub Khan was its most significant gainer. It also provided an increased role for the army which was already riding a wave of popularity for its gains in Kashmir (1947–48), and for its help in settling the refugees during and after the partition. Now it had emerged as a major reason for American interest in Pakistan and General Ayub was the cause of that tilt. This American acknowledgement of Ayub Khan was to bring about the first dictatorship in Pakistan.

In his military mind, Ayub Khan was quite clear about Pakistan's policy priorities; India was Pakistan's eternal enemy and Islam was a national unifier. He was egged on towards this, especially the first objective, by Bhutto. On the wider external front, too, matters were moving most satisfactorily. By 1961, Pakistan was making successful moves towards China and its relations with the Islamic world were warmly fraternal. The UK had already provided immense support to it in the UN on the Kashmir issue. Now, the US too was its firm ally.

Or so Ayub Khan thought till he went to meet President Kennedy in July 1961. Ayub Khan pressed his case from the very beginning, telling Kennedy that:

> ...80% of the Indian army on borders was deployed in Kashmir against Pakistan and only 20% against the Chinese borders and from this it was clear that to Indians the Chinese problem was just an aberration, Pakistan was its enemy no. 1 and India wanted to neutralise all of Pakistan. If India resolved the Kashmir problem it would mean it wanted to live in peace with Pakistan.[4]

After making it clear that the US did not want India to collapse, Kennedy asked Ayub what he thought might be acceptable to both Nehru and him on Kashmir. Ayub replied with soldierly logic, 'Nehru has shown no disposition to yield anything beyond the cease-fire line in Kashmir. Pakistan would have no objection to India taking Jammu.'[5]

In contrast to this aggressive advocacy of Pakistan's case with the US, India's support came largely from the Soviet Union and tenuously from the debating chambers of the non-aligned countries.

If any proof of India's vulnerability was needed it came through in the debacle of 1962. India had been humiliated militarily, and for all its claims of leadership of the developing world Nehru found himself practically friendless when it came to getting meaningful support against the Chinese aggression.

India's humiliation in the war and its considerable efforts at seeking

---

[4]*FRUS*, 1961–63, vol. xix, South Asia, doc. 30.

[5]Ibid.

support internationally were noted carefully by Ayub and Bhutto. Thus encouraged, they felt if China could batter India, so could Pakistan. Ayub was convinced of it and he boasted rather often that one Pakistani soldier was equal to five, even ten, Indian soldiers in the battlefield.

11

Crossing the Line

The year 1962 marked the dividing line. After India's humiliating defeat in war with China, Pakistan's hostility towards India increased steadily. So did its propaganda on the Kashmir issue. It lobbied its cause actively with its allies and friends in the international fora and in their capitals.

It also set about cementing its relationship with China. By the beginning of 1963 it had achieved that objective—from then on the the Pakistan–China relationship was set to soar higher than the mountains.

Therefore both diplomatically and militarily, the time seemed propitious for Pakistan to pursue its objective in Kashmir. India was demoralized, its military vulnerable and internationally it was without powerful allies. Pakistan scored heavily on all these counts. Moreover, its success in the Indus waters deal had convinced Pakistan that if American pressure had worked on India, then so could it on the Kashmir issue. That, and Pakistan's own military strength, could ensure a settlement favourable to it. All indications therefore pointed to the realization that it was the right time to increase pressure.

The first step of course was to exhaust the diplomatic option by engaging with India. On its part Pakistan wanted to be seen by the international community as reasonable. Accordingly, Nehru and Ayub Khan agreed on 29 November 1962 (a bare month after the Chinese debacle) to talks to resolve Kashmir and other related matters. Six rounds of discussions followed between Zulfikar Bhutto, who had become the foreign minister of Pakistan, and Sardar Swaran Singh, then India's railway minister.

Even as the first round of talks was going on, Pakistan was committing itself to a deal with China. This is what Nehru stated in the Lok Sabha on 13 August 1963 regarding the Indo-Pak talks and Pakistan's deal with China:

> ...From the very beginning, the Pakistan Government took various steps which came in the way of a settlement. On the eve of the first round of talks in Rawalpindi, Pakistan announced its so-called 'agreement in principle' with China on Kashmir's border with Sinkiang. The timing of this statement was apparently intended to provoke India to refuse to start the talks the next morning.
>
> We felt that this was a bad augury for the future of the talks. Nevertheless, because of our earnest desire to arrive at some settlement, we decided to continue with the talks.
>
> When the Pakistan Delegation shifted from a futile discussion of plebiscite to the consideration of a possible political settlement, they began to put forward astonishing proposals. Pakistan claimed the catchment areas and the watersheds of the three western rivers, the Chenab, the Jhelum and the Indus, in Jammu and Kashmir, on the ground that these rivers had been allotted to Pakistan under the Indus Waters Treaty. Our delegation pointed out that the Indus Waters Treaty protected Pakistan's interests fully and gave her no ground to claim any territory in Jammu and Kashmir on the basis of the use and development of waters. If every lower riparian claimed the territory of the upper riparian on the pretext of its water requirements, the maps of many countries in the world would have to be drastically revised. By that argument, the lower riparian might even claim Tibet because the Indus and the Brahmaputra start in Tibet.
>
> No less absurd was another of Pakistan's claims to Jammu and Kashmir, namely, that they must have the State to protect their Grand Trunk Road and their railway line, the security of which, our delegation was told, was essential to ensure, what Pakistan called, its 'defence in depth'.
>
> Finally, Pakistan claimed Kashmir on the basis of its Muslim majority. This was a vicious communal approach repugnant to the entire spirit animating our national struggle for independence, and contrary to our Constitution and to our whole attitude to the problem of relationship between the State and the individual.
>
> Pakistan's objective was obviously not a rational and realistic solution of the problem. They were just out to claim the entire State of Jammu and Kashmir, leaving to India, as it happened, in a forgotten moment of generosity, an insignificant area in the extreme south, roughly coinciding with the district of Kathua.[1]

It must have been deeply disappointing for Nehru to have invested so much faith and hope in the process of dialogue. That attempt by itself is unobjectionable. But as his statement in Parliament shows, he felt

---

[1]J.C. Aggarwal and S.P. Agrawal, *Modern History of Jammu and Kashmir: Ancient Times to Shimla Agreement.*

deeply disappointed. He was a statesman enough to realize that in negotiating with Pakistan, 'faith and hope' are an idealist's prayer. Alas, Nehru was an idealist.

Bhutto was deliberately provocative all through the talks, wanting them to fail. He could then goad Ayub Khan in the direction of a war. Bhutto was convinced that after the shock of 1962, India was simply incapable of resisting the Pakistani might. Once the Pakistani army had vanquished the Indian forces, that victory would transform Bhutto into the greatest leader ever in Pakistan, bigger than even Jinnah.

That was the fundamental difference between the leaders of India and Pakistan. Their approach to bilateral relations and even to nation-building was poles apart. India had uniquely used democracy as a tool for nation-building. It had also hoped to follow the same broad principle in its relations with its estranged sibling.

But Pakistan was in a hurry. It was pursuing its own unique project of enlarging and consolidating its new state. The path it had chosen was muscular with no patience for elaborate rituals of a democratic process. Like the older democracies of Europe, where nation-building preceded democracy by at least 200 years and where they used war as an instrument of nation-building, Pakistan too wanted to get on with the job of building a mighty nation first. As with his personal career, Bhutto wanted to put Pakistan on a fast track. Democracy and its ideals could wait.

But other Pakistani leaders were wary of him. They did not exhibit any great level of confidence in his goodness. As Ayub Khan recorded in his diary, Said Hassan, Pakistan's Permanent Representative at the UN in 1960–61, told him:

> When Bhutto visited New York for the UN session he met US Secretary of State, Christian Herter and volunteered to spy for USA on all delegations to UN.
>
> At the same session Khrushchev abused Bhutto and told him that if Pakistan looked towards India or Afghanistan, the Soviet Union would take its eye out. Bhutto told Khrushchev not to get angry. Pakistan was ready to quit all (western) pacts.

Yet, this man was to so seminally guide Pakistan's destiny in the 1960s and for much of the 1970s. Is it possible that if the Pakistani delegation at the six rounds of talks with India had been led by someone other than Bhutto, the shape of Indo-Pak relations may have been different?

There are hardly any quotable instances where a Pakistani leader has genuinely tried to meet India halfway. Perhaps Benazir came close to that with her open and liberal outlook. So if she, instead of her father, had been the leader of the Pakistani delegation in 1963, the Indo-Pak script may have read differently. Or at the very least the war of 1965 may not have taken place.

Even Ayub Khan may have led the talks more constructively. Despite his naïve notions about the exploitative ways of the Hindu Brahmin and Bania combine, Ayub Khan was not vicious. Bhutto, on the other hand, was made of entirely different stuff. In October 1963, he visited Washington and London. In his meetings there with ministers he had impressed both the Americans and the British leaders as a bright young politician who presented his case with legal acumen. His uniform refrain all through was that Pakistan had a genuine claim to Kashmir, that India had provoked China into the 1962 war, that Pakistan was right in forging better relations with China, and that the US and the UK should stop arms shipments to India.

The modest arms supplies by the US and the UK to India were in response to Chinese aggression, and it had been made clear to India that they were not to be used against Pakistan. All this was explained to Bhutto but his aim was different; he had come to Washington and London to put a scare that the West was upsetting a military ally like Pakistan in favour of India. Moreover, by these pressure tactics he wanted to build a case in favour of Pakistan in anticipation of a future conflict. As he admitted during one of his meetings in London, Pakistan had already sent some troops across the ceasefire line into Kashmir.

His final meeting in London was at 10 Downing Street on 17 October 1963 with R.A Butler, the first secretary of state. There he lashed out at Nehru, 'Nehru was neither young nor vigorous.' Bhutto said, before continuing:

> Indians had mishandled the whole Chinese situation. Pakistan had a similar problem but had always taken a firm line with the Chinese and had resisted incursions where they had been made. The Indians had adopted quite a different attitude and had allowed the Chinese to build roads, barracks and so forth in the disputed territory which the Chinese then assumed was theirs. Then when Mr. Nehru and Mr. Krishna Menon had said that they would throw China out of the disputed territory, and had attempted to do so, the Chinese had counter attacked.[2]

---

[2]DO 196/120. Record of a conversation at 10 Downing Street at 4 p.m. on 17 October 1963 between the UK's first secretary of state, R.A. Butler, and Pakistan's minister of external affairs, Z.A. Bhutto. Roedad Khan (ed.), *The British Papers: Secret & Confidential: India, Pakistan and Bangladesh Documents, 1958–1969*.

Though Bhutto met a large number of ministers in the UK and US during this trip in October 1963, he did not reveal that during that precise period his colleagues were finalizing the schedule for visits to Pakistan in December 1963 by Chinese Premier Chou En-lai and Foreign Minister Chen Yi.

If Bhutto was duplicitous, Ayub Khan made a more favourable impression on the British leadership despite a minor storm in the British press linking him with Christine Keeler.[3] The British high commissioner in Pakistan wrote this pen sketch on 9 April 1964 for his secretary of state for Commonwealth affairs:

> At heart the President is a decent, upright man with some sterling qualities... So are his limitations... He is particularly scornful of, and antipathetic to intellectuals (hence in part his dislike of Mr. Nehru and his incompatibility with the Bengalis)... It is a tragedy that for first hand advice about other nations than this [Pakistan] he should have to rely so largely on the officials of the Pakistan Foreign Ministry. These men seem to specialise, particularly where India is concerned, in taking up a narrow, petty and destructive approach... Unfortunately the advice which has been reaching the President both from the professional India haters in the Pakistan Foreign Office and also from his fellow Muslim Leaguers is to the same effect, 'Distrust India and say loudly why all Pakistanis should do so. Thus by rendering articulate the inmost feelings of your people, you will be putting yourself at their head.'[4]

At that time, in the middle of 1964, Pakistan was showing signs of relative prosperity and economic development. But as the British high commissioner apprehended:

> all of it could be spoilt by miscalculations in the external field. The scene is already depressingly overshadowed by strains in the relationship with India, towards which the Pakistan Government's insensitivity and impatience have contributed.

This is exactly what happened.

---

[3]DO 196/5, letter of 19 June 1963 by Iftikhar Ali, high commissioner for Pakistan in the UK. Roedad Khan (ed.), *The British Papers: Secret & Confidential: India, Pakistan and Bangladesh Documents, 1958–1969.*

[4]Letter of 9 April 1964 by British high commissioner in Pakistan, Morris Lames. Roedad Khan (ed.), *The British Papers: Secret & Confidential: India Pakistan and Bangladesh Documents, 1958–1969.*

12
Conflict

Six weeks later, on 27 May 1964, Pandit Jawaharlal Nehru died. His successor, the diminutive Lal Bahadur Shastri was a humble man of modest origins. In the beginning even his Cabinet colleagues just about treated him as the first among equals. An interesting exchange between Sir Paul Gore-Booth, the British high commissioner in India, who called on President Ayub on 23 February 1965 during his farewell visit, is illustrative.

Ayub Khan mentioned to Gore-Booth that:

> he had reminded Mr. Shastri when they met that little men sometimes compensate for their small stature by showing off a special power of decision; he had encouraged Mr. Shastri, who had observed that he was not a Nehru, to do just this.[1]

Meanwhile, within Pakistan, Zulfikar Ali Bhutto began to chip away steadily at Ayub Khan's public standing. Though young, he was already positioning himself to succeed Ayub. Towards that goal he needed a dramatic achievement on the foreign policy front, which he could clearly claim as his. Bhutto chose carefully, and began to assert himself on issues relating to the US, India and China. With the US, relations became a lot more steady after Lyndon Johnson took over from an India-inclined Kennedy.

Still, the US was preoccupied with its ordeal in Vietnam and continued to be sore with Pakistan that though an ally it had refused to provide troops for the Vietnam War. It was also uncomfortable with the growing warmth between China and Pakistan. However,

---

[1]Telegram no. 317 of 23 February 1965 from High Commissioner Morris James. Roedad Khan (ed.), *The British Papers: Secret & Confidential: India Pakistan and Bangladesh Documents, 1958–1969.*

Pakistan was important enough for it to continue to provide substantial aid and two squadrons of F-104 fighter aircraft.

Pakistan's and Bhutto's principal agenda with India was the unfinished business of Kashmir. Towards this end, Bhutto had gathered around him like-minded senior officers from the Foreign Office and the army. Leading this pack he rationalized that the time was just right for a grab-and-run operation on Kashmir. Nehru was dead and Shastri appeared to be tentative as a leader, while India itself was yet to recover from the shock of the 1962 war.

In contrast, Pakistan was stable and prosperous economically; militarily, it had twice the strength of the army it had had at the time of independence. With so many factors working in its favour, time was of the essence. Since India was arming at an alarming rate, and was being helped in this by the US, the UK and the Soviet Union, it would not be long before it became militarily far superior to Pakistan.

Ayub Khan himself needed a major success on the external front to refurbish his reputation internally. He had been bruised in a vicious political battle during the January 1965 elections in Pakistan. His opponent, Fatima Jinnah, had drawn large crowds, scaring Ayub Khan enough during the election campaign to launch personal attacks on her, referring to the unnatural state of Fatima's relationship with Jinnah. She, in turn, attacked him on corruption and the huge riches Ayub's sons had acquired, particularly Gohar Ayub Khan. Ayub Khan won that election but he had been challenged; hence his anxiety for a decisive gain on the foreign policy front.

Both Ayub Khan and Bhutto had Kashmir in view; each for his own reason felt that a victory there was bound to bring immense success domestically. But an unexpected turn drew their attention elsewhere first. Events in the Rann of Kutch started unfolding rapidly in February 1965.

This desolate area of about 23,000 square kilometres separates India's Gujarat from Sindh in Pakistan. Prior to 1913 there had been claims and counterclaims between the Bombay Presidency and the princely state of Kutch. In 1913, an agreement was reached between the two, which was also endorsed by the then Government of India in its letter of 11 November 1913. By this agreement, the boundary between Kutch and Sindh was the:

> green line from the mouth of Sir Creek to the blue dotted line drawn on an agreed map. From there it should follow the blue dotted line East until it joins the Sind boundary as marked in purple on the map.

It was also agreed that as the Sir Creek changed its course from time to time, the western boundary of the area should be the centre of the navigable channel of the Sir Creek.

The land in the Rann of Kutch was full of marshes and sanddunes. Pakistan had a network of roads and even an airport close to the border, and fearing that the tactical advantage lay with Pakistan, India stepped up its construction activities in the area. By March 1965, aggressive patrolling by both sides led to skirmishes and India decided to evict Pakistani paramilitary troops from Kanjarkot, a fort that was about 1400 metres inside the Indian border. The two armies engaged indecisively in the first major military battle on 8 and 9 April, followed by a larger battle in which the Pakistani army attacked Indian positions in what came to be called the battle of Bets. By the end of it, Chand Bet and Biar Bet were in Pakistani control and Kanjarkot was with India.

The stage was now set for the British Prime Minister Harold Wilson to swing into action. He suggested ceasefire by both sides (it came into effect on 30 June), talks between the two adversaries and a return to the status quo on ground pending a decision by an international tribunal. India nominated Ales Bebler, a Yugoslav jurist. Pakistan made its choice shrewdly by nominating Nasrollah Entezam, former foreign minister of friendly Iran. The UN secretary general nominated a Swede as the presiding judge.

The presiding judge went largely by the opinion of the Iranian judge, who was clearly inclined to take Pakistan's side. As C.S. Jha, the then foreign secretary of India, records; 'The award was not in conformity with the agreement that it would be based solely on facts and evidence; it was close to a political award based on equity and distributive justice.'[2]

The verdict of the Kutch tribunal was given on 19 February 1968 and it resulted in a gain of 802 square kilometres of territory for Pakistan, which included Kanjarkot and Chand Bet.

India had found itself friendless in 1962, now it had been outwitted on the legal-diplomatic front. In both cases India had lost territory. Soon, yet another war was to follow.

After the defeat by the Chinese in 1962, and the less-than-impressive performance by its army in the battle of Bets in March–June 1965, Ayub and Bhutto were of the view that the morale of the Indian army was bound to be low. Writing about it, civil servant and writer Altaf Gauhar felt, 'Ayub's judgement did get impaired in one respect. His

[2]C.S. Jha, *From Bandung to Tashkent: Glimpses of Indian Foreign Policy*.

old prejudice that the Hindu has no stomach for a fight turned into belief...which had a decisive effect on the course of events.'[3]

After the battle of Bets, Pakistan started preparing for incursions into Kashmir. It was encouraged by an assessment that the valley was ripe for revolt. Externally too, raising the heat on Indo-Pak issues had won gains for Pakistan. Above all, the changeover from Nehru to Shastri suited Pakistan; Shastri was seen as meek and timid, hardly the type who could stand up boldly against a military challenge. Moreover, he had yet to establish a personal equation with any of the major leaders of the world.

Given this favourable combination, Pakistani strategists set in motion 'Operation Gibraltar'. The objective of this grandly named plan was to capture the Srinagar radio station besides the airport and set up a revolutionary council, which would announce the liberation of Jammu and Kashmir. There was also to be an additional operation, equally boastfully titled as 'Grand Slam', the aim of which was to attack the Poonch and Akhnoor sectors.

'Operation Gibraltar' had been conceived by the Foreign Office and the ISI with the full support of Bhutto and Foreign Secretary Aziz Ahmed. Ayub Khan gave his consent reluctantly. The plan was based on a fundamental assumption that the Kashmiri population would welcome and give full support to the Pakistani infiltrators. Accordingly by 5 August, heavily armed commandos in civilian dress began surfacing in different parts of the valley. Jinnah had employed the same tactics in 1947–48; then too army commandos in civilian dress had infiltrated along with the tribals. All along Pakistan had flatly denied that its soldiers were involved.

As in 1947–48, this time too, the Pakistani infiltrators received a hostile reception from the local population. Some of the commandos were captured quickly and under interrogation Captain Ghulam Hussain of the 8th JK Battalion and Captain Mohammad Sajjad of the 18th AK Battalion revealed the military plans of the infiltrators to their Indian captors. Still, the Pakistani infiltrators inflicted considerable damage and kept a large Indian force engaged.

The full details of the infiltration did not reach Delhi till 7 August 1965. It was then that the gravity of the situation became clear to the Indian authorities, as did the danger. The heavily armed infiltrators had sneaked into Jammu and Kashmir in batches of six to twelve people. As in 1947, some of them managed to reach close to Srinagar

[3]Victoria Schofield, *Kashmir in Conflict*.

airport, and in a case of history repeating itself, additional forces had to be flown in from other parts of India to save the airport.

When India protested against this invasion, Pakistan said it had nothing to do with the infiltrators, and that if there was any trouble it was because of an internal movement by the 'freedom fighters' of Kashmir!

Shastri was coming under increasing public pressure to retaliate and on 16 August a crowd of over a lakh marched to Parliament House demanding that the government should take firm action against Pakistan. The Indian counteroffensive started soon thereafter.

Indian forces attacked Pakistani positions in the Kargil sector and in Tithwal and Uri–Poonch. By 28 August the Indian forces were successfully poised in Haji Pir as well, this high feature being of particular strategic importance.

These new developments took the Pakistani army by surprise. General Muhammad Musa, Pakistan's army chief during the 1965 war, egged on by Bhutto, had begun pressing Ayub Khan in late August for approval to launch 'Grand Slam'. But Ayub had retired to Swat where he kept postponing a decision on the issue; he was worried over the setbacks that 'Operation Gibraltar' had received. But he came under persistent pressure from Bhutto to give the army the go-ahead for 'Operation Grand Slam'. Finally, on 29 August he sent a signed instruction to Bhutto and the army chief telling them to 'take such action that will defreeze the Kashmir problem, weaken Indian resolve and bring her to the conference table without provoking a general war'.[4]

Field Marshal Ayub Khan did not think that India would escalate the situation to a full war because of his confidence that, 'the Hindu morale would not stand more than a couple of hard blows at the right time and place'.[5]

'Grand Slam' came into full play on 1 September with heavy artillery providing covering fire and armoured units leading the advance towards Chamb. But in its enthusiasm for heroics, one of the Pakistani units made the mistake of crossing a small section of the international frontier between Sialkot and Jammu. It was precisely this 'Rubicon' that Nehru had agonized over in 1947 and 1948. The British, too, had put tremendous pressure on him asking him not to cross the international border and spare himself the international odium that was bound to follow.

---

[4]Brian Cloughley (ed.), *A History of the Pakistani Army, Wars and Insurrections.*

[5]Farooq Bajwa, *From Kutch to Tashkent: The Indo-Pakistan War of 1965.*

Now a Pakistani unit had crossed the border and changed the terms of conflict. Thereafter, it was war. Pakistan had given Shastri sufficient provocation through 'Operation Gibraltar' first and then 'Grand Slam'. By crossing the international border they had given him the excuse to retaliate. This was just the opening that he needed.

Boldly, Shastri decided to cross the international border in retaliation. Ayub Khan had once advised Shastri that his short size should not cramp his ability to take courageous decisions, but even Ayub Khan could not have imagined this dare in Shastri's leap.

On 6 September, two columns of the Indian army marched towards Lahore, which lay just about 20 kilometres away from the international border. This took the Pakistani army by complete surprise; they had not anticipated that the Indians would take such a major step.

Talking of the Pakistani reaction to this advance, the British High Commissioner Morrice James wrote:

> Their [Pakistani] troops had not been alerted and were asleep in their barracks. Some of them left with their weapons for the front line in their pyjamas for want of time to put on their battle dress.[6]

Simultaneously, another Indian column began to march towards Sialkot.

The decision to cross the international border was significant in many ways. In purely military terms it was an effective response to the Pakistani pressure in the Chamb–Akhnoor sector; psychologically, it signalled that India was no longer content with a defensive posture; it was also a clear statement to Pakistan and the rest of the world that an attack on Kashmir was an attack on India. Finally, it also shattered the image built by Pakistan of a pacific and docile India and its gutless army.

The situation was turning in favour of India while Pakistan was beginning to run short on ammunition. By 7 September Ayub Khan was disheartened enough to hint at a ceasefire. The British, still with a colonial mindset, were quick to condemn the Indian attack across the border.

The Chinese were making encouraging noises without actually coming to the aid of Pakistan in any concrete manner. On 4 September, Chinese foreign minister, Chen Yi met Bhutto in Karachi and stated support for Pakistani action in repelling what he termed as 'aggression

---

[6]Roedad Khan (ed.), *The British Papers: Secret & Confidential: India Pakistan and Bangladesh Documents, 1958–1969.*

in Kashmir'. This was followed by Chinese threats in the form of an ultimatum accusing India of building military works on the Chinese–Sikkim frontier...and warning India of the consequences. The US viewed it seriously enough to warn China that in case it intervened in the war, it in turn would assist India.

Pakistan had hoped that under its secret agreement of 1959 with the US, it would get American arms support against India. But its interpretation of the agreement was flawed. It had not taken into account the fact that the basic prerequisite of an aggression being committed against Pakistan was missing in this case. Here, Pakistan had started the aggression against India.

Finally, when Pakistan's grand plans seemed irretrievably punctured, Ayub Khan made a secret air dash across the Himalayas to Beijing and met Chou En-lai on 19 September. Chou En-lai offered him support on the understanding that Pakistan should be prepared for a long war in which cities like Lahore may be lost to India. Ayub Khan was not ready to take such a huge risk and came back, disappointed, to Pakistan, retracing the same route over the Himalayas. Ayub Khan was tired and depressed. He was also disenchanted with Bhutto's reckless adventurism and was open to a sensible way out. By the third week of September, Pakistan had also run down its stock of ammunition with no hope of early replenishment because of the embargo imposed by the US and the UK on both Pakistan and India.

On 20 September, the UN Security Council passed a stern resolution demanding that a ceasefire come into effect within two days. India could have carried on with the war. It was far better placed in terms of war stocks and had exhausted only 14 per cent of its frontline ammunition by 22 September. But when Shastri asked army chief, General J.N. Chaudhary whether India could win a spectacular victory if the war was prolonged by a few days, the reply given by the general was hedged by ifs and buts.

Midway through the war, and before deciding to cross the border, Shastri had set the following objectives on 3 September 1965 for India's defence chiefs:[7]

a. Defeat Pakistani attempts to seize Kashmir by force and make it abundantly clear that Pakistan would never be allowed to wrest Kashmir from India,
b. Destroy the offensive powers of Pakistan's armed forces,
c. Occupy only the minimum Pakistani territory necessary to

---

[7]C.S. Jha, *From Bandung to Tashkent: Glimpses of Indian Foreign Policy*.

achieve these purposes, which would be vacated after the satisfactory conclusion of the war.

Though the junior officers and soldiers from both sides fought well, the same by and large could not be said about the battlefield brilliance of the generals. Nor did either of the two countries fulfil their war objectives. Even in terms of territorial gains, it was an almost a draw.

Inevitably then, both sides accepted the UN demand for ceasefire, which came into effect on the morning of 23 September. But as Shastri said in his radio broadcast to the nation:

> Even after accepting the ceasefire, Pakistan has behaved in a most untrustworthy and atrocious manner by deliberately bombing the civilian population of Amritsar and by shooting down an unarmed plane carrying the Gujarat Chief Minister.

On the external front, if the US was relieved that the war had not been extended, the Soviet Union viewed the developments as its chance to play the peacemaker. In the one-month period between 18 August and 18 September, Soviet Prime Minister Alexei Kosygin wrote three letters to Ayub Khan and Shastri offering the Soviet Union's good offices in negotiating a peaceful settlement of differences between the two countries. In his third letter, Kosygin offered to host the talks in Tashkent. The only nation unhappy with this offer was China.

As Sultan Khan, Pakistan's ambassador then to China, records, 'China felt concerned that [by accepting the Soviet offer] Pakistan was moving into the Soviet orbit and contributing to China's isolation.'[8]

Speaking of the general reaction in the Soviet Union to the war, India's ambassador in Moscow, T.N. Kaul, wrote on 28 September 28 to Foreign Secretary C.S. Jha:

> They cannot, however, understand why we cannot deal with the infiltrators on our side of the ceasefire line... Some people have even asked me why we cannot send guerrillas across the ceasefire line and why only Pakistan can do so. I have, of course, replied that we do not wish to provoke a conflict or a conflagration with Pakistan. But this argument does not seem to carry much conviction with outsiders...[9]

Kaul's lament has been shared by succeeding generations of Indians; why is it that we cannot deal with the infiltrators with deterrent firmness, and why can't we send guerrillas into Pakistan?

---

[8]Sultan M. Khan, *Memories and Reflections of a Pakistani Diplomat*.

[9]Avtar Singh Bhasin (ed.), *India–Pakistan Relations, 1947–2007: A Documentary Study*.

Meanwhile, Ayub Khan continued to procrastinate. He took nearly two months to accept Kosygin's offer; his hesitation was on account of a feeling that the Soviet Union might not be a honest broker, and that it could lean in favour of India. Even after accepting the Soviet proposal on 11 November, he wanted to make one more attempt to persuade the British and American leadership to settle the Kashmir issue, preferably before the Tashkent meeting.

Clearly, Ayub Khan's advisers wanted him to try and claw back on the diplomatic front what could not be achieved through the 'Operation Gibraltar' and 'Operation Grand Slam'. He set off on this mission in December. At Ayub Khan's first stop in London, British Prime Minister Harold Wilson told him bluntly, 'China was the greatest danger in the region because it was far more expansionist than Soviet Union or India.'[10]

This wasn't the sort of message that he had hoped to hear from Wilson; after all, the UK had been quick to condemn India when its forces had first crossed the international border. But times had changed, and Indian protestations with Britain had worked. Wilson concluded the meeting by saying, 'We cannot hurry the Kashmir issue, though we realise the conflict is driving India and Pakistan to orbits we fear.'[11]

Ayub Khan's next port of call was Washington, where he turned emotional and urged President Lyndon Johnson, 'If India could not comply with the UN resolutions then arbitration by an independent body was the only peaceful way to settle the dispute.'[12]

The US president had little to say about Kashmir but a lot about Vietnam. He added significantly that he was praying for the success of the Tashkent meeting. Then he gave President Ayub Khan some unsolicited advice:

> I know you rely on Bhutto like I rely on Dean Rusk and like Eisenhower relied on Dulles, but you can't rely on him that way...this man (Bhutto) is damn dangerous as far as you are concerned and you are my friend and I can give you this warning and I know whereof I speak.[13]

Bhutto, the instigator of the 1965 war, was already making moves to dissociate his name from the disappointment of its result.

---

[10]Altaf Gauhar, *Ayub Khan: Pakistan's First Military Ruler.*

[11]Ibid.

[12]Ibid.

[13]*FRUS*, 1964–68, vol. xxv, South Asia, Department of State, Washington.

13

Death in Tashkent

Tashkent was the capital of the Soviet province of Uzbekistan. Beyond that it had nothing greatly remarkable to recommend itself as a venue for a historic meeting. If you think hard and look closely, you might observe that a stream of water gurgles through narrow canals in the city. That's it—there are no grand madrasas or magnificent palaces in Tashkent.

This is what bureaucratic sloth does to a city; Tashkent is as colourless as its bureaucrats. Yet, the summit had to be held there because it was the capital. That's what the bureaucratic rule book said. So, why take a chance and experiment? In any case this was serious business the visitors from India and Pakistan were expected to discuss and negotiate all the time. They would hardly get the time to roam in the city.

Still, the setting matters. Had the Soviets let their imagination soar, they would have hosted the summit in the glorious setting of Samarkand. Once it was the seat of Tamerlane's empire, and it was here that magnificent madrasas, mosques and palaces stood. It was this city that the Lebanese writer Amin Maalouf described as 'the most beautiful face the earth has ever turned towards the sun'. Or, they could have chosen the magnificent Bukhara as the host city. Instead, the Soviets opted for dour Tashkent, the capital of Uzbekistan. It was to bitterly cold Tashkent that the aircraft from India and Pakistan were headed on 3 January 1966.

The Indian position for the Tashkent summit was finalized through two memoranda: one dealing with strategy and tactics, the other listing out the numerous problems between the two countries, other than Kashmir. By early December Shastri approved the plan, which basically consisted of the maximum and minimum acceptable positions from the Indian standpoint.

C.S. Jha has described it thus:

> The ideal position would have been the conclusion of a treaty of friendship and peace which in addition to withdrawal of armed forces from each other's territory occupied during the hostilities, would pledge each country to perpetual friendship and abjuration of war... The second best position was a joint communiqué which, while not being a treaty, could incorporate the substance of such a treaty. The minimum desirable objective was implementation of the ceasefire resolution of the UN, disengagement of forces, restoration of territory of each other...occupied during war.[1]

Now, in retrospect, one could term all these positions as snatching defeat from the jaws of victory.

Every one of the three options that Indians had listed for their internal discussion recommended the return of the strategically important territory captured during the war. It is true that Pakistan had taken more Indian territory in terms of area. But that was largely barren, non-strategic land whereas the features captured by India, like the Haji Pir pass, were hugely vital. While the Indian strategists were content with aiming for idealistic paper treaties, the Pakistani objective was clear—grab diplomatically what was lost militarily. Once again, India was going to be the loser in the process.

It is often said that Indian and Pakistani negotiators pride themselves over their ability to quibble over commas and full stops to stall negotiations in international fora. Still, seven days should have been enough to discuss every punctuation mark in the relationship, or the lack of it. Otherwise the debate could have gone on endlessly. It was with this in view that on arrival, Shastri informed all concerned that 10 January was the last day of the trilateral talks because on the morning of 11 January he was scheduled to be in Kabul.

The Soviet, as also the American, objectives were clear from the beginning. A week before the start of the Tashkent Conference, Foreign Minister Swaran Singh was told in Moscow that peace between India and Pakistan had to be established on the basis of the UN Security Council resolution of 20 September which demanded the 'withdrawal of all armed personnel to positions held prior to August 5, 1965'.

It is true that in the days prior to leaving for Tashkent, Shastri had responded to strong public sentiment against withdrawal from the strategic Haji Pir pass by saying that 'if Haji Pir were to be given back

[1]C.S. Jha, *From Bandung to Tashkent: Glimpses of Indian Foreign Policy*.

to Pakistan some other prime minister would do it'.[2] They were brave words indeed, and in an inadvertently prophetic way the physical handing over of Haji Pir to Pakistan was going to happen under a new prime minister.

Shastri may have stood firm publicly on the issue, but he had made up his mind already on what exactly was to be done. As we know, he had told his defence chiefs on 3 September 1965: 'Occupy only the minimum Pakistani territory necessary...which would be vacated after the satisfactory conclusion of the war.'[3]

On 5 January 1966, in a meeting with Kosygin in Tashkent, Shastri agreed to return to status quo as on 5 August. Encouraged by this, Kosygin felt confident that a successful early conclusion of the Tashkent summit was now in sight. Ayub Khan too seemed amenable when Kosygin took the proposal to him. But soon Bhutto took charge of the discussions and Kosygin found him to be 'a really obstructive person...a destroyer of all ideas'.[4]

However, efforts were continued to reconcile the differences between the two delegations, and there were one-to-one meetings too between Ayub Khan and Shastri. Often, the two leaders preferred a mix of Hindi and Urdu at these meetings.

C.S. Jha records that:

> Ayub used honeyed words to affirm his desire to live in peace with India, whom he termed as elder brother... He [Ayub] said he was getting old; it was his one ambition in life to see a solution of the Kashmir question before he retired from political life... Shastri was firm in his reply and asked a blunt question, What do you expect me to do? Do you realistically expect any government in India to surrender Kashmir?[5]

By 9 January the negotiating process had reached a dead end. All that remained was for the two delegations to pack their bags and head home. But a final effort by the Soviets, and the apprehension that the lack of their ability to reach an agreement, might lead to escalation in tensions again, made Ayub Khan and Shastri agree to the draft which essentially amounted to the disengagement of troops.

Zulfikar Ali Bhutto, however, was unhappy. Anxious to sabotage an agreement somehow, he suddenly demanded that the entire

---

[2]Ibid.

[3]Ibid.

[4]Ibid.

[5]Ibid.

paragraph committing the two countries to 'discourage hostile propaganda against each other' be deleted.

By then Kosygin had tired of his obstructionism. Kosygin turned to him and asked sternly: 'How do two countries that agree to make peace and maintain good-neighbourly relations also proclaim that they would carry on hostile propaganda against each other?'[6]

The agreement that was signed in the afternoon of 10 January wasn't well received in both the countries. Indians felt that the sacrifice of Indian soldiers had gone in vain; people failed to understand why Haji Pir was being returned. When Shastri rang up home to find out the public reaction to the accord, he was told by his daughter that there was a huge feeling of disappointment.

The news that the agreement to withdraw, especially from Haji Pir, was not well received in India must have been anticipated by Shastri. He was a grassroots politician, and knew the pulse of his people. Why then did he go against their consensus on a subject as emotive as dealings with Pakistan, and on an issue where it was common knowledge that Haji Pir had been taken after considerable loss of Indian lives? Moreover, as this feature dominated the Indian positions, once it was returned to them Pakistanis would continue to inflict losses on Indian forces.

It wasn't an easy decision for Shastri to make. He had agonized over it for many days, but in the end the hope that it might bring peace swayed him. It was this, and a combination of circumstances, that made Shastri concede after holding out for seven days.

First, there was the Security Council resolution that clearly demanded withdrawal to the pre-war positions. Second, the US, the UK and the Soviet Union felt strongly that this was the only way to lessen tensions. Third, China had started making aggressive moves on the border in November–December 1965. Fourth, there were worries about food security and considerable pressure to devalue the rupee. Above all, Shastri was gentle to the core; there is no doubt that he had displayed steely resolve in ordering that the battle be taken across the international border, but he was also realistic enough to advise his generals that having taken territory and taught a lesson to Pakistanis, they should not prolong the humiliation. Hence his decision as early as 3 September that conquered territories should be returned.

But Haji Pir was different; its capture was a strategic prize and the issue of its return emotive in India.

---

[6]Ibid.

On the evening of 10 January, after signing the agreement and after leaving the celebratory party, Shastri retired to his dacha. Others carried on till much later. Later that night Shastri suffered a heart attack and died. Ever since, conspiracy theories have abounded. Some blame the Soviets, others allege a Pakistani hand in poisoning Shastri's food. But nothing in the official records, and this writer has trawled through almost every paper available, suggests anything unnatural, except for Bhutto's reaction to the news that Shastri had died.

At the guesthouse where the Pakistani delegation was staying, the news of Shastri's death was greeted with uproarious joy. Disturbed by the noise, Bhutto opened his door, saw senior members of the delegation in a boisterous mood, and demanded of his foreign secretary: 'What is this, Aziz?'

Aziz Ahmed replied: 'Sir, the bastard is dead.'

Bhutto asked, 'Which one?'

14
Ayub and Bhutto

The first time I met Benazir Bhutto, Zulfikar Ali Bhutto had fixed us in an unblinking stare. To me, his look appeared to be hostile. It is quite possible that when Benazir was alone in that room his gaze turned benign because he doted on his daughter.

No. 70 Clifton is the address to be in in Karachi. It has always been so ever since Bhutto got his first Cabinet post in 1958. But there was no shortage of people at the Bhutto home even before that. When Zulfikar's father Shahnawaz first built the house in 1954, it was palatial in style and filled with fine furniture. Zulfikar added his touch by stocking the library with a vast collection of books on Napoleon.

The little drawing room that we were sitting in, for there were many other sitting areas, was remarkable for its portraits: Benazir's brothers Shahnawaz and Murtaza on two sides and Zulfikar in the middle, dominating them all.

Benazir needlessly adjusted the dupatta on her head. The dupatta was in deference to the people of Pakistan, otherwise Westernized Benazir was a leader of men and confident in speech and action. Still, there was a hint of sadness in her eyes as she began to speak of her mother. 'My mother is fine now. The wounds have healed somewhat, but she has suffered a lot in her life.'

I had heard stories about Zulfikar's philandering and the pain her mother must have suffered when he brought women home even while Nusrat slept in the adjoining room. I had only been in Karachi for a few weeks when I met Benazir in the autumn of 1992, but that was sufficient time to pick up all the juicy details because rumours spread quickly in Karachi.

Benazir blinked away a slight film of wetness from her eyes as she added, 'There is a lot of suffering in people's lives behind closed doors, even for those who seem to have it all.'

I was wondering why she had opened up like that with me; after all, I was meeting her for the first time and I was an Indian. Perhaps she too became conscious of that barrier because she qualified it all by saying, 'My mother couldn't accept what they did to Shaheed Zulfikar.'

Benazir never referred to her father only by his name, maybe because that's what ordinary folks did. She would always prefix Shaheed, martyr, with it. 'My mother couldn't accept what they did to him,' she repeated, 'first the imprisonment, his mental and physical torture there, and then the murder.'

What she left unsaid was the pain Nusrat had suffered during Zulfikar's lifetime; his debauchery, his principal mistress Husna Sheikh, and his insistence that those close to him should follow his Lotharian lifestyle. Benazir was blind to all that, much like the Pakistani people for whom Zulfikar remained a hero despite his many warts.

Foreigners, however, didn't view him through tinted glasses. For them he was a flawed Lucifer. After all the warnings by the world leaders, Ayub Khan too was looking for the right time to drop Bhutto from the Cabinet. When he finally took the decision, the news was received with relief in many quarters. In November 1966 the British prime minister told Ayub Khan during his visit to London, 'I'm glad you got rid of Bhutto. He was not trustworthy.'[1]

Ayub Khan had got rid of Bhutto in the summer of 1966, but that had given Bhutto enough time to distance himself from the failures of the 1965 war. Bhutto encouraged the feeling that Ayub Khan and his military had failed the nation and that the tales of victory were just that, simply tales.

By the summer of 1966, little fires were burning all over Pakistan. Students were restive, East Pakistan was alienated and the army was itching to take over. It was only a question of time before Army Chief General Yahya Khan staged a coup against his mentor, Field Marshal Ayub Khan. All signs were ominous. The conditions in East Pakistan were even more worrisome. But was Ayub Khan perturbed? Outwardly he seemed to be absolutely in control.

The British high commissioner in Pakistan, C.S. Pickard, informed London thus about his meeting with Ayub Khan on 8 July 1966:

> The political crisis in the East and West wings…do [sic] not appear to be causing the President any loss of sleep at present… In any case he was self-confident and relaxed and more concerned with Rhodesia and Viet Nam than with his domestic problems.

---

[1]Roedad Khan (ed.), *The British Papers: Secret & Confidential: India Pakistan and Bangladesh Documents, 1958–1969.*

Though Ayub Khan had said 'never again' to another war, he authorized a frantic effort to rearm his army soon after Tashkent. During the 1965 war Turkey and Iran had supplied ammunition to Pakistan. Indonesia had supplied two submarines, some missile boats and a few MIG aircraft. But these supplies, though generous and timely, were not sufficient to replenish the stores lost in the war, especially the 200 destroyed tanks.

Since the embargo put by the US and the UK was still in place, Ayub Khan sent a delegation to Moscow in the hope that it might be more amenable to giving arms. The next stop on the list was Beijing. Though it was engaged in the convulsions of the 'cultural revolution' that had been launched in July 1966, it welcomed a purchase mission of generals from Pakistan in August 1966.

Sultan Khan, Pakistan's ambassador then to Beijing, records that Chou En-lai promised to meet all defence requirements listed by the generals. Having given that assurance he asked the basis on which the equipment requirements were calculated by Pakistan.

One of the generals responded, 'On fourteen days' reserves.'

To this Chou En-lai responded, 'What happens on the fifteenth day?'[2]

The Pakistan–China relationship gathered speed thereafter, particularly its defence relationship. The visits too increased in frequency. One such was in August 1968 when Foreign Minister Arshad Hussain visited Beijing.

India continued to preoccupy both sides, including the possibility of the next war between India and Pakistan. In response to a comment by Foreign Minister Arshad Hussain that 'Hindus worship cows, Muslims eat it', Mao Tse Tung said, 'In that case why don't you get into the stomach of the cow and grab it by the throat?'

Before Pakistan could grab India by the throat, restless Yahya Khan wanted to seize Field Marshal Ayub Khan's chair. The first attempt took place on 29 January 1968 when soldiers surrounded the Presidential palace even as Ayub Khan was having a heart attack.

Ayub Khan carried on for another fifteen months amid strikes, nationwide protests, the machinations of Bhutto and the impatience of Yahya Khan, both of whom were manoeuvring and aiming for the big job.

Meanwhile, East Pakistan continued to simmer.

But Ayub Khan had now caught the anti-India bug; he had

---

[2]Sultan M. Khan, *Memories and Reflections of a Pakistani Diplomat*.

convinced himself that exciting the popular emotions against India may be the best way to hang on to power. Once this notion took hold as a means of survival at the top, he became increasingly prejudiced. Three entries in his diary, in the months between September and November 1968, illustrate the point. In September 1968 Ayub Khan notes in his diary:

> In East Pakistan they talk about Bengali culture common to both Muslims and Hindus. How can this be true when sources of inspiration are diametrically opposed? The philosophy of Islam and Hinduism are poles apart, we too had Hindus in our part of the world [West Pakistan]. There was nothing common between them and the Muslims. Our customs, dress, method of cooking, beliefs were totally different. Even the language was spoken differently by the two communities. This same must apply in Bengal [East Pakistan]. Hinduism does not seek integration.[3]

As if that was not enough, Ayub Khan was strategizing about the next war with India. Had it not been a major concern with him, his close aide Fida Hassan wouldn't have raised the issue with Mao. In a diary inscription of October 1968 Ayub Khan records:

> My advisor Fida Hassan had a long talk with Mao Tse-Tung in Peking. He advised on how to defend Pakistan and specially the cities of Lahore and Sialkot which are bound to be attacked by the Indians in the event of war. Mao's solution is tunnel warfare... I told Fida that our aim is to destroy the enemy before it reaches these places. The Chinese keep talking of guerrilla warfare because that is their experience, besides they have space for this. Unfortunately, we lack depth in our country and besides some of our centres of population, communication links, head-works and canals lie near the border so we have to be ready to defeat the enemy as soon as he enters our territory. This is what we did the last time.

Finally, as things got steadily worse for him domestically, Ayub Khan began to think of India-bashing as a political instrument that could unite the country against India and divert people's attention away from domestic difficulties. In November 1968 Ayub Khan noted in his diary, 'I have been told...that people will react better if I appeal to their emotions as they are so emotional. Things like Kashmir and Islam appeal to them immensely.'

Once again it was back to the tried-and-tested formula: when in

---

[3]Ayub Khan, *Diaries of Field Marshal Ayub Khan, 1966–1972.*

doubt or political difficulty just whip up emotions. Populism and considerations of staying on in power substituted policy. It also seemed as if the principal lesson of an exhausting war in 1965 was the bitterness that it did not end decisively in favour of Pakistan. Ayub Khan and many of his generals were convinced that the Pakistani army was superior and that the next time the war should be definitely and decisively in favour of Pakistan. Moreover, it must be fought before India rearmed itself to a superior position.

But Bhutto, the instigator of the 1965 war, had a more immediate priority. This time it wasn't the next war with India, but his own political battle that had to take precedence; building up passions against India or finding fault with Ayub Khan for his handling of India relations was a means towards his political ends. Soon, he was going to be very busy working up people against Ayub Khan and the Tashkent agreement.

15

After Tashkent

Indians slipped back into their routine quickly. They, too, were not satisfied with the outcome at Tashkent. In fact, there was a national feeling that India had let Pakistan get away lightly with all its trespasses. Had Shastri not died, he would have faced a rather hostile reception on return. Even so, it is doubtful if he would have reneged on a document he had signed in Tashkent. It is an Indian tradition to honour a national commitment once it has been made.

But what would have happened to his standing as a leader had he returned to Delhi? There is no doubt that it would have come down a notch or two. As it is, the situation was not looking good domestically. After facing two expensive and exhausting wars, one after the other, the Indian economy wasn't exactly in the pink of health. The rupee was under strain and even as economists were advocating devaluation, the political voices in the Congress were expressing concern that such a move might not go down well with the people, making it politically risky.

Moreover, there was jostling for power within the Congress party. Would Shastri have survived that struggle? There is no clue about what he might have done, but his successor Indira Gandhi was put to the test immediately and on multiple fronts.

The first few months were particularly trying for her. The established and old leadership of the party were dismissive of her political acumen and considered her a novice who could be manipulated to their design. They did not expect her to take an active interest in the high office that had been thrust on her. Among the chattering classes outside the Congress party, the opinion-makers of society wondered if she was intellectually capable of handling the multiple challenges facing the country, from inflation to food shortages internally, and from China to Pakistan externally.

But they had miscalculated grossly. Indira Gandhi grew quickly in her job. It took her just about six months to make her mark in the Congress party. During her visits abroad, Indira Gandhi's reputation as a decisive and firm leader with a mind of her own was established quickly. It was also commonly acknowledged by foreign and Indian observers that Indira Gandhi exerted something of her father's magnetic appeal among the people of India.

There was something more, a particularly difficult moment, that the father and daughter had shared once. It was the evening of 14 August 1947; there was excitement in the Nehru household as just a few hours were left for that historic midnight appointment when India would obtain freedom. Nehru and Indira were about to sit down for dinner when the telephone rang. It was a call from someone in Lahore who wanted to convey something urgently to Nehru. The new authorities of Pakistan, he said agitatedly, had cut off the water supply to the Hindu and Sikh neighbourhoods. It was a very hot summer that August and people were desperate for water, just the smallest amount that they could drink. But the authorities were determined to deny them that minimum so that they were forced to come out of their houses. Men, women and children who went out for a glass of water were promptly massacred by Muslims.

Twenty-nine-year-old Indira Gandhi watched her father's knit eyebrows and the taut facial muscles as he listened to the voice from Lahore. Gradually, the colour drained from his face, but in practical terms there was very little that even Nehru could do. When the call finished, he sank back tiredly into his chair. How, he wondered, could he rejoice over independence when Lahore was bleeding?

At her young age, Indira was not aiming to make her mark on eternity. She was content being of help to her father, but even then she was not one of those who forgot hurt easily. When Nehru turned to look at her, she was surprised to see tears in his eyes. His handsome face was snarled with helplessness. That pain and the look of defeat on his face stayed with her, gnawing at her conscience—they could not save those Hindu and Sikh families in Lahore. She would have also felt unhappy when during her time the northern part of the Rann of Kutch had to be ceded to Pakistan. This plus the fact that the talks with Pakistan were not proceeding satisfactorily must have left a strong impression about the hopelessness of these negotiations, just as Nehru had felt once.

She must have also been quick to realize that the Indian objective in the 1965 war to remove the Pakistani threat to Kashmir had not succeeded. India could not get a guarantee that Pakistan would not use aggression across the ceasefire line again. Instead, India was faced with the tired old theme where Pakistan acted the part of an aggrieved party and insisted that negotiations must be held between India and Pakistan for a final settlement of the Kashmir issue. Alternatively, there should be a third-party involvement.

Therefore, much remained the same between the two countries. They were still deeply suspicious about every move made by the other side and deeply distrustful of each other's motives. In sum, they still growled every time the other side made a move.

In some respects, however, there were other conclusions that the outside world was beginning to draw. There was a general consensus in the capitals which mattered that over a year or so prior to 1965 Ayub Khan had allowed himself to be led astray by Bhutto. It was under his influence that he had indulged in the folly of sending infiltrators into Kashmir. But even as the world was making this assessment of Bhutto, there was no corresponding echo from Indian quarters. If the Indian leadership was wary and distrustful of Bhutto, it did not show in its policy.

The Americans and the British were also in a fix. Had they made the right choice by putting all their policy eggs for the South Asian region in the Pakistani basket? They had allowed their overwhelming fixation with communism to distort their strategic view of the region and they had placed disproportionate reliance on Pakistan to the extent of letting their relationship with the largest democracy in the world take a secondary place. Gradually, however, there was the realization that perhaps they had erred. Pakistan's nominal membership of CENTO did not provide the West with a great bastion against communism. Moreover, Pakistan had not proved to be an essential card in their relationship with the Muslim world in general, and the oil-rich Gulf in particular. Rather, the Muslim world was not enthused by Pakistani efforts at posing as the defender of the faith.

On the other hand, India might have been a more effective counter to the Soviets and the Chinese. It is true that there was an ideological purdah between India and the West. But neither made any serious effort to bridge this gap. Had they tried, and if Nehru's soaring idealism had not come in the way, this new 'Great Game' may have shaped differently.

Another conclusion that some quarters drew was that, regardless of what happened to the superpowers and their rival interests, relations between India and Pakistan were going to remain rocky. The three deplorable weeks of fighting in 1965 had shown Pakistan's inability to get what it wanted by force. And temporarily at least, it was the Soviet Union rather than the US which played the peacemaker. But at the end of the Tashkent talks it, too, had tired of the endless debates and acrimony between the two sides. After that frustrating experience, the Soviet Union was no longer interested in offering its good offices.

But that was in so far as mediation was concerned. Otherwise, from the age of the Great Game, Russia had always had a special interest in looking south and in reaching the warm waters of the Indian Ocean. That 'game' was played particularly vigorously in the nineteenth and the early part of the twentieth century. This time, in the second half of the twentieth century, the Soviet Union was reaching out to India as an ally. India had its own reasons to respond positively; the fear of China was one of them. Therefore, in the months and years after the 1965 war, India and the Soviet Union twined themselves strategically into a close embrace.

Parallel to this development, but in no way directly related to it, the Chinese hug of Pakistan became tighter still. And to the long-lasting gratefulness of the US, it was Pakistan which was going to show Kissinger first and later Nixon the way to China.

Ordinarily, a frustrating war that led nowhere should have discouraged any future attempt at adventurism. But the international developments were such that the two superpowers, each for its own reason, ended up arming and unwittingly encouraging the two protagonists. The lines had been drawn and Indira Gandhi was to play a stellar part in the drama that was beginning to unfold in the second half of the 1960s.

This complex melange was to lead ultimately to the Bangladesh war in 1971.

*

Pakistan was on the brink in 1968. One could easily add 'once again' to that because Pakistan has a habit of looking over the cliff. Some foreigners have ascribed these frequent lurches towards instability to the wild and volatile nature of its people. They also say that Pakistan's warlike people draw sustenance from strife. Their easy excitability and quick recourse to violence betrays some impatience with permanence. Therefore a hesitant regime, one which fails to deliver, can easily be overthrown. A change, any change, is better than stagnation; that at least is the hope.

Was Ayub Khan's government heading towards such a precipice?

The fact is that his government had barely managed to hang in there through the year of 1968. People were disenchanted and did not expect Ayub Khan to provide a decisive leadership any longer. In early 1969, Ayub Khan confided to his family members that the time had come for him to quit.

Ayub Khan had done well by his country for much of his tenure; in the initial years he had brought stability, an economic upturn, an alliance with the US and a steadily developing relationship with China. But by 1968, economic conditions were worsening and unrest in the country, especially among the youth, was growing.

There were many reasons for this alarming turn against the government. Ayub Khan was an autocrat who was living in a political vacuum by allowing himself to be surrounded by sycophants. He was obstinate and overbearing; this made it difficult for an honest opinion to reach him. The state of Emergency which was declared during the war with India was still in force, not to defend the country, but to put thousands of people in prison without trial.

The allegations against his family were many and substantial—from land-grabbing to money-making deals. If Ayub Khan was aware of it, or of the amount of corruption in the country, he did not show any sign of being concerned about it.

The economic upturn, while it lasted, placed riches in the hands of a few while workers continued to be paid subsistence-level wages. Since political activists were being put into prison at whim, the dissatisfaction of people could not find a natural outlet. As a result, they were being pushed into taking extreme positions. One manifestation of this was attacks by people on army officers and their property. These incidents reached a peak in November 1968 when reports from Abbotabad, Peshawar and Rawalpindi spoke of mob attacks on military personnel. Even the chief of air staff, Air Marshal Nur Khan, barely escaped the mob fury; he was saved by the timely intervention of the police.

Finally, in March 1969, the chief of the Pakistani army, General Yahya Khan, slithered into the Presidential palace, sending Ayub Khan into forced retirement. Once, as a devoted deputy, the same Yahya Khan had helped Ayub Khan stage a coup—this second time, Ayub was the target.

For the next two years and more Yahya Khan and his army made merry, a vast Bacchanalian feast followed. Unlike Ayub Khan, who was not particularly acclaimed for his military prowess, Yahya Khan had a soldier's mind. But he was also known to be an alcoholic and a womanizer with little inclination for the mechanics of politics. Under the circumstances, it was merely a question of time before Pakistan hurtled headlong into another crisis.

But why is it that Pakistan is crisis-prone? The answer to this puzzle must surely lie in the way it all started. As in India, so in Pakistan, the initial years were ones of bewilderment, shock and a sense of loss, yet some exhilaration too that finally the British had gone, letting the people of the two countries manage their own affairs in the best manner that they could. This is where the two differed fundamentally. In India, the idea of the 'state' was stronger than that of the individual. In Pakistan, religion became paramount, and individual interest took precedence over everything else.

In India, Nehru was determined to prove Jinnah's two-nation theory wrong. It must, therefore, have been a matter of personal satisfaction to him that the overwhelming majority of Muslims had opted to stay in India.

Though Mahatma Gandhi was killed within five months of the partition, and though he took no part in the governance or politics of independent India, his colossal moral authority informed the public debate about values and nation-building. While Nehru, Sardar Patel and others inspired right values in public life and laid much of the initial foundations of society, it was Gandhi's enormous influence that was the binding glue of unity in diversity.

Another character-building factor in those initial years was the manner of migration. Millions of Hindu and Sikh refugees had migrated, leaving flourishing businesses and properties behind in Pakistan. When they came to India they had to start life all over again. Their efforts, full of blood, sweat and tears, instilled the right values in that first generation of independent India.

People in newly created Pakistan also had their woes, but many hit the jackpot. It is a fact that in the pre-partition Pakistan part of India, the Hindu community was the most prosperous; they owned most businesses and properties in the cities. In the villages they were the moneylenders. Their sudden departure left a large number of Pakistanis debt-free almost overnight. This very mercantile reason in seeing the back of Hindus and Sikhs added to the atrocities against them. As a result those who had migrated out of India into Pakistan, and others who belonged to the areas that were now Pakistan, had a bonanza waiting for them after partition.

There was a scramble among people to grab the best house, the biggest tract of land and the best business that the migrants to India had left behind. Friends fought with friends to be the first to claim an evacuee property. Neighbours competed against each other to be the first to put a lock on the empty house next door. Sometimes members of the same family fought a bitter feud to make the first claim. This competition for unearned goodies was a fractious beginning for a new nation. Self-interest, rather than the right values, took precedence. And this syndrome wasn't just limited to the masses.

Jinnah was very ill already, and his movement outside the governor general's residence became increasingly infrequent. His principal preoccupation in the first year was to get as much of a military success in Kashmir as his forces could deliver. Otherwise, he had become withdrawn and irritable; his relations even with Prime Minister Liaquat Ali Khan were cordial at the best of times. Finally, when he went to Ziarat in Baluchistan for recuperation, it was a signal that the end was near. When he was brought back to Karachi, the ambulance carrying him broke down on its way from the airport into the city. Conspiracy theorists sometimes suggest that this delay hastened his end, but the fact is that it was only a matter of time. With Jinnah's death on 11 September 1948, an era came to an end. But as in life, so in death, he casts a larger-than-life shadow over Pakistan. He continues to be revered.

Had he been alive, it is quite possible that the fear of the fundamentalists may not have paralysed the public discourse in Pakistan in the manner it has done today. Jinnah may well have ensured that even the fundamentalists followed him and his narrative on what was right for Pakistan. Legend has it that once when he had to address an Eid congregation in Karachi, Qazi Isa suggested to Jinnah that he should recite a Quranic verse. Jinnah learnt one by heart and recited it. When he finished his address he asked the Qazi whether he had recited the verse correctly.

The Qazi exclaimed happily, 'Al-hamdu Lillah.'

'What does that mean?' Jinnah asked.

'It means Allah be praised,' the Qazi replied.

'Damn you,' Jinnah snapped, 'I did not ask you about Allah, but about me.'

'You, my Qaid, are always right,' the Qazi assured him promptly.[1]

Alas, Jinnah's successors were not held in equal esteem. His political second, and Pakistan's first prime minister Liaquat Ali Khan was killed in 1951, setting a trend that was to persist. Coups and killings

---

[1]Rafiq Zakaria, *The Man Who Divided India: An Insight into Jinnah's Leadership*.

were to become a norm rather than the exception of governmental change in Pakistan—as were dictatorships. The surprising element, however, is that of the military dictators only one, Zia ul-Haq, was a Punjabi; the rest were either Pathans or Muhajir. This is a surprising distinction in an army dominated by Punjabis.

Even otherwise, a generally quarrelsome polity ensured that if unity in diversity was the abiding theme of the Indian political ethos, quite the opposite was the case in Pakistan. In support of this argument it is asserted that if you ask an Indian settled abroad where he is from, he is bound to reply instinctively, 'India'. But if you ask a Pakistani the same question he is likely to give you the name of his locality. On a second try he will come up with the name of the city he belongs to, and in response to the next enquiry he is likely to come up with the name of the province. It is only on your persistence that he will finally tell you that he belongs to Pakistan.

The umbilical link, which is otherwise a reflex response, remains diffused even after six decades. And given the ethnic, religious and terror-related violence in recent years besides the growing differences between Punjab and the other provinces, this sense of alienation is likely to persist, perhaps even increase. A combination of these grudges and prejudices led Pakistan to the precipice in 1971.

16

On the Brink

By the mid-1950s, the first signs started to appear that all was not well and that the otherwise healthy Pakistani economy was beginning to flounder. Till then, Pakistan's per capita GDP was higher than that of India, China and most other Asian countries. It was an agriculturally rich country with a reasonable base of small and medium industries. But the next seven years, that is, till Ayub Khan took over in 1958, were a textbook example of how not to build a nation.

East and West Pakistan were an unnatural union to begin with. The neglect of the eastern wing by the central government added steadily to the feeling of alienation there. Both sides showed a lack of faith in the parliamentary system, with the result that quarrels about it started soon after the Constitution was belatedly adopted. These quarrels made it impossible to hold elections so the Constitution that had been agreed to could not be put into practice. Corruption, profiteering and hoarding—all these contributed to pushing Pakistan towards bankruptcy by 1958.

Misunderstandings between the East and West wings increased further when it was decided to introduce Urdu as the only official language of Pakistan. Nor was this a new grudge; in fact, as early as during his first visit to the eastern wing Jinnah had declared that Urdu should be the official language of Pakistan. Bengalis had sulked ever since. In contrast India had fourteen official languages to begin with.

The overbearing attitude of West Pakistani officials in East Pakistan didn't help matters either. The complete rout of the Muslim League in East Pakistan in the 1954 elections was a message that this part of Pakistan wanted more autonomy, and that it was not satisfied with the way it was being treated by the central government. Instead of heeding that warning, the central government decided to integrate all the provinces into one unit.

In a further insult to East Pakistan, a West Pakistani was sent as its governor. By this time resentment against Punjab was beginning to build up in other provinces as well because of the domination by Punjabis in government jobs and because of the excessive share of economic benefits for the Punjab province.

By 1956 the United Front in East Pakistan began to demand parity with West Pakistan in government jobs, in recruitment to the army and in allocation of foreign exchange. But the distrust of West Pakistan and the central government had reached such levels that every action by it was viewed with suspicion.

The next stage in East Pakistan's litany of complaints came in 1962 when elections to the national and the provincial assemblies were held. In the run-up to the elections, the central government thought it fit to imprison the popular leader Sheikh Mujibur Rahman on trumped-up charges. Though he continued to be in prison while elections were being held, his candidates won impressively, adding to his aura.

Sometimes it seemed that the central government was cavalierly negligent about East Pakistan's sensitivities. This came through most clearly in the 1965 war when East Pakistan was caught in a double dilemma. It sided nationalistically with the rest of Pakistan as it fought against India. But at the end of the war the East Pakistanis were left wondering if it was an essential part of Pakistan's quarrels with India. What did it have to do with West Pakistan's grudge about Kashmir? After all, during the war it was virtually out of touch with West Pakistan. The first faint cries for secession started then but even at that time the real demand was for greater autonomy.

In February 1966, Sheikh Mujibur Rahman announced his 'Six Points'. They were to become the rallying cry of East Pakistan's aspirations and the emotional outlet for the rough treatment they had received so far from the West Pakistanis. The essence of the 'Six Points' was that there should be a federal system with the federal government controlling defence and foreign affairs while the rest, including taxation, should be provincial subjects. The government's response was to send Mujib to jail again, adding further to Mujib's popularity.

In 1968, forces which were eventually to lead to a revolution began to build up. They still lacked cohesion and a long-term vision. But once again the government stepped in ham-handedly to give momentum to the movement; it arrested Mujib and his main aides on charges of conspiring for secession. Even at this stage, secession wasn't on their minds; they would have been satisfied with greater autonomy. But by arresting Mujib on the charge of secession, the government had itself planted the seed, giving the idea life and a momentum of its own. This case came to be known as the Agartala Conspiracy (so called because Sheikh Mujib was alleged by Pakistan to have met Intelligence Bureau officials in Agartala, Tripura, to conspire against Pakistan) and turned Mujib into a martyr.

Around this time, a political process had also begun to crystallize in West Pakistan. Zulfikar Ali Bhutto, at the head of the Pakistan Peoples Party (PPP), was already a phenomenon in his home province, Sindh. Now, he had caught the imagination of the youth, particularly in volatile Punjab. The Awami National Party was for long a potent force in the NWFP and the Islamic parties were regaining momentum. With all these parties vying for their attention, people now had the leadership to lead them and to articulate their anger.

In the eastern wing, Sheikh Mujib was drawing enthusiastic crowds with his appeal to Bengali nationalism. If religion was the flawed foundation of Jinnah's 'two-nation' theory, the imperialism of West Pakistan and the cultural differences with the Punjabi-dominated western wing were solid enough reasons for Bengalis to aspire for a space they could call their own. Consequently, tensions were rising steadily but the situation was still redeemable.

In a moment like this a politician would have made the effort to reach out to the people. He would have listened to them and announced concessions to salve the hurt and brought the two wings together into some sort of workable amity. But Yahya's military mind saw things in broad strokes of black and white.

As the provincial elections set for October 1970 approached, Yahya and his inner circle turned increasingly to the ISI for political assessments. The ISI's captain and major ranked officers fed them with low-level raw intelligence based on market rumours. These lacked the depth of a mature political analysis, and eventually, they turned out to be far off the mark.

On the basis of comforting reports that the ISI officers presumed their masters wanted to hear, Yahya did not anticipate a sweep in East Pakistan by Mujib, nor indeed the majority that Bhutto managed in West Pakistan.

The National Assembly elections were set for 7 December 1970. The results exceeded even the wildest expectations of the two principal parties: the Awami League won 160 of the 162 National Assembly seats from East Pakistan and the PPP won 81 out of 138 seats in West Pakistan. At the Army Headquarters General Gul Hassan decided that the time had come to prepare for a civilian government. 'Let's back Bhutto,' General Hassan decided in defiance of the people's verdict that gave a majority of seats to the Awami League. By all democratic norms Mujib's Awami League should have formed the government, but how could a Punjabi general countenance his nation being ruled by a Bengali?

Personal likes and dislikes apart, time was running out for any procrastination. The National Assembly was required to be called early so that it could discuss, debate and formulate a Constitution within 120 days of the national elections. That was the legal requirement. With that deadline in view Yahya went to Dhaka (then Dacca) to meet Mujib, and at the airport he even referred to Mujib as the future prime minister of Pakistan.

Later, on his return he announced 3 March 1971 as the date for convening the National Assembly in Dhaka. But Bhutto was not prepared to sit in the opposition benches and in a speech at Lahore's Mochi Gate on 27 February he threatened to physically harm any elected member from West Pakistan who dared to attend the National Assembly session. Some of the army generals too were not happy with the call for the Assembly session.

Eventually, Yahya postponed the Assembly session, citing Bhutto's refusal to attend it, and the heightened tensions with India as the reasons. The stage was now set for an East–West confrontation within Pakistan.

Yahya and Bhutto became frequent travellers to Dhaka in early 1971, but instead of achieving political accommodation their visits added to the Bengali complaints. The army commanders in East Pakistan multiplied the misunderstandings by conveying the worst about the mischievous intentions of the Awami League—that if they were to have the majority in the Assembly they were likely to call for the cessation of East Pakistan.

Fed constantly on such reports, and encouraged consistently by Bhutto, Yahya responded in a military way to a political problem. More troops were flown in from West Pakistan; they came in civilian clothes but were easy to spot in hostile Dhaka. Every fresh arrival of a military battalion from the western wing added to the suspicion and anger of the average Bengali. By March 1971, the average East Pakistani citizen was in a sullen mood, and the West Pakistani soldier walked in Dhaka with his hand poised over his holster. It was in this tense stand-off that the Awami League began a non-cooperation movement against the government. But instead of responding to a political movement with calm and measured administrative steps, Yahya Khan reacted swiftly—he banned the Awami League and declared martial law.

The military was now ready to launch 'Operation Searchlight'. The crackdown by the army came on 25 March 1971. It arrested Sheikh Mujib, destroyed the students' dormitory in Dhaka University, attacked newspaper offices and generally set about terrorizing people. That night, thousands were killed, drenching Dhaka in blood. According to an American assessment of the time, the pathologically anti-Hindu Pakistani army was systematically engaged in killing and driving out the Hindu population to India.

The performance of the army must have satisfied Bhutto because he returned to Karachi on 26 March to announce, 'By the grace of God, Pakistan has been saved.'

But he must have given a different version of the events to his family because Benazir writes in her book *Daughter of the East*, '...Yahya Khan ordered in the army to quell the insurrection. Alone in his hotel room, my father watched Dhaka go up in flames; sick at heart at the Generals' inevitable solution of force.'

She goes on to describe her reaction to the events from her college:

> Looting, Rape, Kidnappings, Murder. Where no one cared about Pakistan when I first arrived at Harvard, now everyone did. And the condemnation of my country was universal... Dacca (according to Western press accounts) had been burned to the ground and firing squads sent into the university to execute students, teachers, poets, novelists, doctors and lawyers... Refugees were fleeing by the thousands, so many of them strafed and killed by Pakistani planes that their bodies were being used to erect roadblocks.

Pakistan could have been saved even at this late stage; it was a bleak chance, but it was there.

Had an astute politician reached out, Bengalis may have grasped an accommodating hand. Even the international leadership was in favour of an accord, that somehow the nation be called back from the brink. Both the US and China also wanted it to be saved, but Bhutto's destiny was linked to a divided Pakistan and that was how it was going to be. Still, the US and China made the effort.

*

Both had reason to do a good turn to Pakistan; at least they felt that they owed it a big favour each. Pakistan's good offices had brought

China out of international isolation and set it on a road where, with American and Western help, it was to achieve industrial and economic greatness. Out of that gratefulness, and for other strategic reasons, China reached out and aided Pakistan in numerous ways to help it in its nuclear quest and to aid its defence sector. But it was the US which overwhelmed Pakistan with financial and armaments help.

Richard Nixon and Henry Kissinger have both been credited with great wisdom and immense diplomatic acumen. One event which has added to this perception is the *pas de deux* with China. The stealth with which it was conducted added a sense of drama to the entire exercise, and the selective media leaks inspired a degree of anticipation about what, when and how the next step might follow.

Nixon may have felt the need to reach out to China as a part of his grand design to counter the Soviet Union. But did it really help achieve his objective? Was the Soviet Union subdued as a result? Did this US–China rapprochement lead in any remarkable way to the break-up of the Soviet Union? Did China contribute significantly in this East–West struggle? None of the answers to these questions is reassuring.

On the other hand, the American initiative allowed the Chinese genie to come out of its isolation. The earlier suspicion of the world about China was henceforth to be replaced by fascination. Every inane uttering of Mao was anointed as the words of an oracle, laced with deep philosophical meaning.

Looking at the record of a perfunctory audience granted by Mao to Nixon and Kissinger (February 1972), one can't help wondering if it really was a meeting of equals. Nixon comes across as an awed, eager visitor who is keen to discuss international affairs with the master. But Mao fended off Nixon's requests and kept his interaction at a so-called philosophical level to show that his status was higher than that of the president of the United States who had taken the initiative to travel to Beijing.

It was Prime Minister Chou En-lai who engaged the visitors and talked to Nixon about matters of the world. In their meetings too, it was Chou En-lai who largely determined the pace and direction of their talks.

Nixon stooped willingly to allow himself to be conquered by the Chinese leadership. Even the otherwise status-conscious Kissinger went to Paris to meet the Chinese ambassador there on over two dozen separate occasions. That pandering, and the large-scale investment in China by the West, has elevated it to a near-equal status economically and technologically with the US. It now aims to compete with the US in the strategic sphere. Yet, the US continues to regard the truncated Russia as a greater security threat to its global interests.

Kissinger's report to Nixon of his preparatory two-day visit to China in July 1971 was adulatory. As a matter of fact his first sentences said it all: 'My…visit resulted in the most searching, sweeping and significant discussions I have ever had in government.'[1]

The twenty-seven-page Top Secret report was also peppered with gushing remarks about Chou En-lai:

> He spoke with matter of fact clarity and eloquence. He was equally at home in philosophic sweeps, historical analysis, tactical probing, light repartee… There was little wasted motion, either in his words or movements. Both reflected the brooding inner tension of a man concerned both with the revolutionary fire of the next generation and the massive daily problems of caring for 750 million people…

Kissinger summed up his assessment of Chou En-lai by concluding, 'In short Chou En-lai ranks with Charles De Gaulle as the most impressive foreign statesman I have met.'

He reached this conclusion after only a two-day stay (July 1971) in the hitherto closed Beijing, a city that very few foreigners had access to and a leadership that only a handful of Americans had met in the previous two decades. No wonder then that the Chinese should have extracted the maximum even before the meetings started; they had demanded that the talks should be constructive and as between equals. Chou En-lai reconfirmed that this position of 'equality' was indeed the basis in his first interaction with Kissinger when he said, 'The first question (between USA and China) is that of equality, or in other words, the principal of reciprocity.'[2]

Kissinger also notes the Chinese 'contempt of the Indians, hatred for Russians, and apprehension over Japanese…'[3]

Chou En-lai described the South Asian subcontinent as a prime area of turmoil under heaven. He said that this was because India had long ago under Nehru adopted an expansionist philosophy, committing aggression not only against Pakistan but against China as well. Speaking on a topical issue of the time, Chou En-lai added,

---

[1]Donald E. Davis and Eugene P. Trani, *Distorted Mirrors: Americans and their Relations with Russia and China in the 20th Century.*

[2]Ibid.

[3]Ibid.

'India is responsible for the crisis in East Pakistan…and has allowed a Bangla Desh headquarters to be set up on Indian territory.'

When Kissinger said that the US was trying very hard to discourage an Indo-Pak war, Chou En-lai said it was a good thing but added that the US might not be able to do much because it was 10,000 miles away, while China was much closer. Recalling the defeat of India in 1962, he hinted rather broadly that the same thing could happen again. The Chinese detestation of Indians came through loud and clear to Kissinger. Conversely, China's warm friendship for Pakistan as a firm and reliable friend was also made very plain to him. However, despite nodding readily in agreement about support to Pakistan, Kissinger had his doubts about the capacity of Pakistan to stay as a single unit.

In Washington, he had already made a pessimistic assessment about the long-term integrity of the country. As early as 22 February 1971, Kissinger sent a memorandum to Nixon which maintained:

> A realistic assessment would seem to recognise that there is very little material left in the fabric of the unity of Pakistan… At a minimum, it would seem imperative that, in the face of growing possibility that East and West Pakistan would split, we draw together our contingency planning on how best to protect US interests.[4]

On 28 April 1971, Kissinger sent yet another memorandum to the president. This too was written before his trip to China:

> By training and equipping a relatively small Bengali resistance force, India can keep active resistance alive and increase the chances of a prolonged guerrilla war. From all indications, the Indians intend to follow such a course.[5]

It was on this note that Nixon had recorded his famous minute, 'To all hands. Don't squeeze Yahya [Khan] at this time.'[6]

Nixon was greatly criticized in America for this symbol of a pro-Pak tilt because the nation at large was appalled by the media reports about the genocide in East Pakistan. But little did the public realize that Nixon's minute was based on a specific recommendation by Kissinger, a recommendation that was duly endorsed by the National

---

[4]Memorandum of 28 April 1971 from Henry A. Kissinger to President Richard Nixon. F.S. Aijazuddin (ed.), *The White House & Pakistan: Secret Declassified Documents, 1969–1974.*

[5]Ibid.

[6]Ibid.

Security Advisor, General Alexander Haig. Obviously, this policy went against the situation in East Pakistan, and the repeated reports of gross human rights abuses that the international media had been carrying after the 25 March crackdown in Dhaka and for months thereafter in every other city of East Pakistan.

Moreover, both the US ambassador in Pakistan, Joseph S. Farland, and Consul General Archer Blood in Dhaka had been imploring Washington to remain cognizant of the suffering and the sentiments of the Bengali people.

A precise figure is not available for the number of people killed by the Pakistani army in East Pakistan, but estimates vary from 200,000 to 3 million men, women and children. Besides the countless raped and looted by the Pakistani army, 10 million people were forced to flee and seek shelter in India. It was the worst genocide after the Second World War, and shocking in its scale.

Archer Blood and his staff were daily witnesses to it and were horrified by the experience. Their reports to the State Department in Washington described the killings in gruesome detail and urged the strongest possible intervention to try to bring the carnage to an end. Blood sent a telegram titled 'Selective Genocide' on 28 March after witnessing the genocide that was unleashed by the Pakistani army against Bengali Muslims, and Hindus in particular, in Dhaka and other metropolitan cities.

But the consulate's cables met with a 'deafening' silence from Washington. In desperation, Blood's younger staffers drew up a 'dissent cable', a Vietnam War-initiated reform in the US Foreign Service meant to allow diplomats to speak out, confidentially but frankly, against official policy. This cable of 6 April, known ironically, and memorably, as 'The Blood Telegram', accused the Nixon administration of 'moral bankruptcy' and demanded action to stop the murders 'in order to salvage our nation's position as a moral leader of the free world'.[7] Twenty members of the consulate staff signed the cable, which was like a 'roll call of honour', as Blood put it.

Washington ignored this telegram, just as it had ignored the media reports about the genocide in East Pakistan. But in doing so, the Nixon administration was acting against the mood of the Western world which was liberal and hugely pro-human rights. The Nixon–Kissinger combine had also failed to anticipate the future American policy which was going to enshrine 'Responsibility to Protect' as a

---

[7]Gary J. Bass, *The Blood Telegram: Nixon, Kissinger and a Forgotten Genocide.*

cardinal principle of its foreign policy in the early part of the twenty-first century.

Nixon, Kissinger and General Haig did not regret this gross miscalculation even after the extent of the abuses became known worldwide. Nor did they ever accept the possibility that their unquestioning support may actually have encouraged the Yahya regime to take even harsher measures in East Pakistan, steps that may have resulted in a much larger number of killings. There is no doubt that Nixon was anticipating his opening to China when he decided to tilt in favour of Pakistan. But why is it that none of the citizens' bodies, or the NGOs, which are otherwise so active in the US, questioned the American state's decision to look the other way while Bengalis were being targeted?

A candid assessment of the conditions in East Pakistan was made by a visiting World Bank team. Ironically, its report was relayed to Kissinger by the Pakistani ambassador! Soon after he returned from China via Pakistan he met Agha Hilaly, Pakistan's ambassador to the US, on 24 July 1971. In what can only be described as a self-goal, Hilaly lamented that the World Bank team members who visited East Pakistan (after the army crackdown) had made comments like, 'It [Dhaka] looked like Arnheim after the Nazi blitz,' and that 'It looked like a country after a nuclear attack.'[8] On his part Kissinger wasn't at his diplomatic best when he suggested to Hilaly that 'Pakistan has not been good at public relations'.[9]

The situation in East Pakistan continued to engage Nixon, but in a perverse way. In a meeting of the Senior Review Group at the White House on 11 August, he said the first priority (for the US) was to look at the situation above all in terms of US interests. 'The interests of the US,' he stressed, 'would not be served by a war. The new China relationship would be imperilled, probably beyond repair, and we would have a very sticky problem with the USSR.'[10]

His irritation with India came through clearly in this meeting. Some of it may have been due to accumulated prejudices over many visits to India starting from 1953. One visit in particular must have riled him deeply, and that happened in the initial years of Indira Gandhi's leadership.

---

[8]*FRUS*, 1969–76, vol. 11, doc. 104.

[9]Ibid.

[10]Sajit Gandhi (ed.), 'The Tilt: The US and the South Asia Crisis of 1971', National Security Archive.

Indira Gandhi was called sister by Yasser Arafat, Saddam Hussein and Fidel Castro and held in great esteem by many world leaders. Some called her an iron lady and within India she was known as Durga, the goddess of power. With a fine sense of style, saree-clad Indira's aura in international affairs was unique to her. She chose her words carefully, and when she spoke in a soft but clear voice, people listened. She could be extremely charming, but could whimsically switch off as well. When India's interests demanded it, she could be very patient, as she was with an extremely offensive and rude US secretary of state, Will Rogers, whom she met in the months leading up to the war with Pakistan.

In the initial years of her prime ministership, she seemed aloof, cold and complex. Sometimes critics wondered how despite her withdrawn and quiet personality, her public figure could appeal as it did to many millions of Indians. Sometimes she was rude during meetings, pointedly opening letters and signing papers when foreigners visited her in office.

In 1967, for example, when Nixon, then a private citizen, visited her, Mrs Gandhi barely concealed her boredom, and after twenty minutes of chatting she asked the foreign ministry official escorting Nixon how much longer the visit would last. The question was in Hindi, but its purport was clear to Nixon.

Nixon and Kissinger loathed India because it had adopted a neutral position in the Cold War. More unpardonably to them, it had turned to the Soviet Union to obtain weapons, which it could not get from the US, to fight Pakistan. To Nixon, the Indians were 'a slippery, treacherous people'. To Kissinger—who was a cold-blooded practitioner of realpolitik given to rages when he didn't get his way—the Indians were 'insufferably arrogant', with 'convoluted minds'.[11]

At one point on the White House tapes, Nixon remarks, 'The Indians need—what they really need is a...'—Kissinger interjects, 'They're such bastards.'[12] And then the president finishes his thought: 'a mass famine'.[13]

The third contributing factor to Nixon's jaundiced view of India may have been his obsession in building a brand-new relationship with China. Anything that came in the way of strengthening this

---

[11]Fredrik Logevall and Andrew Preston (eds.), *Nixon in the World: American Foreign Relations, 1969–1977.*

[12]*FRUS*, 1969–76, Vol. E-7, *Documents on South Asia: 1969–72*, doc. 135.

[13]Ibid.

relationship had to be viewed negatively. Therefore Nixon remarked caustically at the 11 August meeting in the White House:

> Every Ambassador that goes to India falls in love with India. Some have the same experience in Pakistan—though not as many because the Pakistanis are a different breed. The Pakistanis are straightforward—and sometimes extremely stupid. The Indians are more devious, sometimes so smart that we fall for their line.[14]

Nixon's verdict on Pakistanis may have been shaped by his interaction with the army men who were ruling the country from 1958 onwards. In so far as the Indian leadership was concerned, Nixon seemed to have little inclination to get to know them.

It is a pity that unlike the American leaders, Indian leaders do not maintain records of their conversations in office, nor do they generally pen memoirs which could give a glimpse into their interactions with other leaders and how they tackled critical issues. Besides the curiosity value, this record would be an invaluable reference for similar situations when they recur. In their absence, the dry bureaucratic record of a meeting hardly captures the atmosphere or the nuances of the moment.

Indira Gandhi gave some indication in the interview she gave to Jonathan Power of the *Washington Post*:

> Nixon would talk for a few minutes and then say, Isn't that right, Henry? From then on Henry would talk for quite a while and then Nixon would say two words and then he would say, Wouldn't you say so, Henry? I would talk with Henry rather than with Nixon.

Power quotes her further to say, 'Nixon was unwilling to accept my assessment of any situation.'[15]

Still, Indira Gandhi's meeting with Nixon in the White House on 4 November 1971 was remarkable for the assurance with which she set forward the Indian viewpoint. Though they were to meet again on the 5th, it was the meeting on 4 November 1971 which was significant.

She began by saying that many people (in India) harboured the feeling that her father had let down the country by accepting the partition along the lines ultimately reached. Yet, it generated a persistent 'hate India' campaign (in Pakistan) which resulted in the

---

[14]Memorandum of Meeting of President Nixon with Members of the Senior Review Group on 11 August 1971. F.S. Aijazuddin (ed.), *The White House & Pakistan: Secret Declassified Documents, 1969–1974.*

[15]Pupul Jayakar, *Indira Gandhi: A Biography*.

conflicts of 1947 and 1965. She added that America's arms supplies to Pakistan had become a major point of concern to the Indian people, leading her own party to attack her.

Building on this theme, she went on to differentiate the Indian political ethos from the path chosen by Pakistan: 'Following India's independence, it was the leaders of the independence movement who formed India's Government. On the other hand, in Pakistan it was the loyalist or pro-British factions who formed Pakistan's Government.' She added:

> Pakistan proceeded to imprison or exile leaders of the independence movement. Baluchistan, as well as the provinces along the northwest frontier, has a strong desire for autonomy. There has, therefore, been a long history of separatist policies in Pakistan which heretofore has not necessarily been supported in India.[16]

Then she described the atrocities being committed by the Pakistani army against the people of East Pakistan, which had resulted in a massive refugee problem for India. Though India had come under a massive social and financial strain, Yahya Khan continued to speak of a 'Holy War' against India. All this was posing a huge security threat to India, challenging its very unity. This had forced India into keeping its troops on the border and to enter into a pact with the Soviet Union.[17]

It was a cogent and forceful presentation of India's case. But Nixon was a prejudiced listener; he had already formulated his views. Indira Gandhi was aware of this, but her principal aim was to convince Nixon that she was not launching a war—and in that she succeeded fully. She also succeeded in reaching out to the Western media, whose writings about the human rights violations in East Pakistan were to become a huge pressure on the American conscience.

Around this time, the army in East Pakistan had almost complete control over the administration and policies concerning the province. Only foreign policy was being handled by Islamabad.

The skirmishes along the Indo-Pak border began in late November; sometimes the Mukti Bahini, the Bengali resistance force, along with

---

[16]Avtar Singh Bhasin (ed.), *India–Pakistan Relations, 1947–2007: A Documentary Study*.

[17]Memorandum of Conversation between President Nixon and Prime Minister Indira Gandhi at 10.30 a.m. on 4 November 1971 at the Oval Office, White House. F.S. Aijazuddin (ed.), *The White House & Pakistan: Secret Declassified Documents, 1969–1974*.

Indian troops also crossed over into East Pakistan. But the war started only on 3 December when Pakistan launched an aerial attack from the west on some Indian cities. Simultaneously, Pakistan was putting pressure on the US to honour the commitments that it had made under various treaties with Pakistan. There were many treaties and a number of provisions in them which could be interpreted favourably. Thus the South Asia Treaty of September 1954 stated that 'an armed attack in the treaty area against any party would endanger the peace and safety of other parties'.[18]

The US State Department was also conscious of its obligations of a similar nature under the Eisenhower Doctrine (Resolution on the Middle East) of May 1957 and the Baghdad Pact of July 1958.

The most specific of commitments was the bilateral US–Pakistan agreement of cooperation of 5 March 1959 by which:

> In case of aggression against Pakistan, the Government of United States…in accordance with the Constitution of the US…will take such appropriate action, including the use of armed forces, as may be mutually agreed upon and as is envisaged in the Joint Resolution to Promote Peace and Stability in the Middle East, in order to assist the Government of Pakistan at its request.[19]

This was supplemented in a note sent by the US ambassador to the foreign minister of Pakistan on 15 April 1959, '…The United States would promptly and effectively come to the assistance of Pakistan if it were subjected to armed aggression…'[20]

The question then arises about why the US did not fulfil its treaty obligations, especially the seemingly firm ones under the March 1959 agreement. After all, Pakistan did press the US for its military assistance, just as it had done during the 1965 war. The explanation was given in an internal White House memorandum of 8 December 1971.

According to this internal note, the March 1959 agreement was not absolute. The US commitment was limited by its resolution on the Middle East, which effectively limited US action to 'consultation'. In fact, the US had informed both India and Pakistan of this limiting

---

[18]SEATO Treaty, 1954; US–Pakistan Agreement, 1959; Treaties in Force: A List of Treaties & Other International Agreements of US State Department.

[19]Ibid.

[20]Leo Rose and Richard Sisson, *War and Secession: Pakistan, India, and the Creation of Bangladesh.*

clause as soon as it had signed the March agreement. Now, that limitation came in handy at a time when the US did not want to get embroiled in yet another conflict in distant lands. Moreover, as in 1965, in 1971 too, it was Pakistan which launched the aggression on 3 December whereas the March 1959 agreement had clearly specified that it would come into play 'in case of aggression against Pakistan'.

Still, the US didn't want to abandon its ally altogether. By 10 December, planes loaded with arms supplies were leaving airbases in Jordan, Saudi Arabia, Turkey and Iran for Pakistan. All this was being done with an encouraging nod from the US. Nixon had also ordered the aircraft carrier *Enterprise* and its fleet of supporting ships to the Bay of Bengal as a warning to India. But Kissinger was not satisfied with just that. He wanted something more tangible and immediate to be done for Pakistan.

To seek that something concrete and immediate, Kissinger flew in to New York on 10 December to tell the Chinese Permanent Representative to the United Nations, Huang Hua, 'When I asked for this meeting, I did so to suggest Chinese military help, to be quite honest. That's what I had in mind, not to discuss with you how to defeat Pakistan.'[21]

Even as he was making this desperate attempt for Chinese military help to Pakistan, Kissinger knew that he and the mighty American empire with its limitless resources had been trumped by the frail lady sitting in Delhi. The Indo-Soviet treaty was a big deterrent for China.

Indira Gandhi had outmanoeuvred Nixon and Kissinger on every front. In support, her team of diplomats, bureaucrats and soldiers had performed to perfection, so much so that Kissinger paid this ultimate compliment in his memoirs to L.K. Jha, the then Indian ambassador in the US: 'I was supposed to be skilful in dealing with the press. On the Pakistan–India issue Jha clearly outclassed me.'[22]

As the two nations were heading towards the declaration of a ceasefire on 17 December, Indira Gandhi decided to write to Nixon. This letter of 12 December puts in perspective the events leading up to the Indo-Pak war and India's repeated urgings for a political

---

[21]Memorandum of Conversation between Ambassador Huang Hua, Chinese permanent representative to the United Nations and ambassador to Canada and Henry Kissinger, assistant to the US President for national security affairs on Friday, 10 December 1971 at 6.05 p.m. in New York. F.S. Aijazuddin (ed.), *The White House & Pakistan: Secret Declassified Documents, 1969–1974*.

[22]Henry Kissinger, *The White House Years*.

settlement in East Pakistan. Among many others this paragraph of the letter stands out:

> We are asked what we want. We seek nothing for ourselves. We do not want any territory of what was East Pakistan and now constitutes Bangla Desh. We do not want any territory of West Pakistan. We do want lasting peace with Pakistan. But will Pakistan give up its ceaseless and yet pointless agitation of the past 24 years over Kashmir? Are they willing to give up their hate campaign posture of perpetual hostility towards India? How many times in the last 24 years have my father and I offered a pact of non-aggression to Pakistan? It is a matter of record that each time such offer was made, Pakistan rejected it out of hand.[23]

Nixon waited for the ceasefire to come into effect. The very next day he wrote a short, acerbic missive in reply to Indira Gandhi. He addressed none of the issues raised in her letter, nor did he bother to refer to the points that she had made in the paragraph quoted here. Instead, he concentrated on putting the blame on India for preferring war to negotiations. Still, the Indian victory had sobered him sufficiently to add this final paragraph:

> We recognize that India is a major Asian power and that we share the common values of genuinely democratic government. No action has been taken with a desire to damage the relationship between our two great countries. We would hope that the day may come when we can work together for the stability of Asia, and we deeply regret that the developments of the past few months in South Asia have thrust the day of stability farther into the future.[24]

That acid-tipped last sentence was a clear giveaway that 'Tricky Dick' was not in a forgiving mood. Nor was he gracious enough to sign off his letter with the minimum courtesy of 'With regards and best wishes', as Indira Gandhi had done in her letter.

---

[23]Avtar Singh Bhasin (ed.), *India–Pakistan Relations, 1947–2007: A Documentary Study*.

[24]Ibid.

17
The Split

War does not determine who is right, but who is left. The Indo-Pak war of 1971 wasn't greatly destructive; certainly not on the scale of the two world wars. Yet, it was seminal for the changes it brought into being.

First, it disproved Jinnah's two-nation theory. The cultural and societal differences proved to be too strong for the two wings to co-exist. There was also the issue of attitude; Bengalis in East Pakistan had got rid of their British masters only to find themselves under the subjugation of the masters from West Pakistan. Theirs too were the exploitative ways of the colonial times. For instance, East Pakistan's exports provided the foreign exchange revenues for West Pakistan, but the budget allocations that it got from the central government were stepmotherly. Consequently, East Pakistan remained economically deprived, just as it had been during colonial times— 90 per cent of military jobs and 80 per cent of government jobs were occupied by those from West Pakistan even though East Pakistan's population was much larger at 75 million compared to 55 million in West Pakistan. After the introduction of Urdu as the only official language, the Bengali-speaking East Pakistanis hardly stood a chance of getting government employment. Therefore, the parting of ways between them was inevitable; the only indeterminate was the timing. That, too, was provided by a series of missteps by the central government.

The massive people's verdict in favour of the Awami League in the elections and Bhutto's refusal to accept that a Bengali could lead Pakistan, leaving him in a secondary position, speeded the break-up.

The US and China counselled Yahya that he should try a political touch to deal with what was essentially a political problem. But every time Yahya thought of making the effort, Bhutto whisked him away to his country home in Larkana. There, lost in a vaporous haze, Yahya would be swayed by Bhutto's corrupting logic. He would harden his political position, and once again masterly inactivity followed. Once more Mujib and his principal aides would be locked up, inciting popular passions all over again. These protests by people provoked the army into yet another round of loot and pillage in East Pakistan. This in turn led the youth to rebel.

The rebel force of Mukti Bahini that rose as a result would ultimately reach an impressive 100,000 in numbers. They were trained and equipped in a large measure by India. Those who stayed on in East Pakistan rebelled in one way or the other against the army.

Lieutenant General A.A.K. Niazi took over as the commander of the East Pakistan forces on 10 April 1971. That was also roughly the time when the scorched earth policy was in full swing. Not content with that, Niazi wanted to exercise a hot pursuit and hunt the Mukti Bahini across the border in India. Had Niazi moved into India, he might have met an unprepared Indian army.

Around this time, Mrs Gandhi asked General Sam Manekshaw, the Indian army chief, if the army could be launched into East Pakistan. Manekshaw replied in the negative, advising against any immediate action because during the monsoon the rivers in East Pakistan became like oceans, making visibility very poor. He wanted time till after the monsoons, which would also enable him to make the necessary preparations. Even Defence Minister Jagjivan Ram tried to persuade him, 'Sam, maan bhi jaao, Sam, please do agree.'[1] But the army was not yet ready and the monsoon was hardly the time to launch a major offensive.

Mrs Gandhi turned then to the Border Security Force (BSF). It wasn't a case of impatience on her part but a reaction to Niazi's increasing attacks against the Mukti Bahini. Still, launching an attack inside East Pakistan by the BSF was both inadequate militarily and ill advised. When the BSF troops did try that once, they were surrounded by the Pakistani army and regular Indian troops had to be sent in to rescue them.

But by November 1971, both sides had completed their preparations. There were over 90,000 Pakistani troops in East Pakistan, an increase by almost 50,000 over the numbers in March 1971. India had assembled nearly eight divisions on its borders with East Pakistan, besides equipping its troops with at least one month's supply of stores and ammunition. The objectives listed by General J.F.R. Jacob, the chief of staff of the Indian army's Eastern Command were:

---

[1]Sandeep Dikshit, 'How he and his men won those wars', *The Hindu*.

- Thrust lines to be opened to isolate and bypass Pakistani forces,
- Destroy enemy's command and control capabilities and secure communications,
- Draw out Pakistani forces to the border, leaving key areas in the interior lightly defended,
- Final objective is to be Dhaka.[2]

In the meanwhile, Indira Gandhi had also signed a twenty-year Treaty of Peace, Friendship and Cooperation with the Soviet Union on 9 August, giving India much-needed support internationally and an ally who could be relied upon for the supply of defence equipment even as the Western suppliers were closing the tap. Article IX of the treaty was of crucial importance. It said:

> Each High Contracting Party undertakes to abstain from providing any assistance to any third party that engages in armed conflict with the other party. In the event of either Party being subjected to an attack or a threat thereof, the High Contracting Parties shall immediately enter into mutual consultations in order to remove such threat and to take appropriate effective measures to ensure peace and the security of their countries.[3]

It will be fair to say that the Soviet Union acted as a good friend of India.

Thus, by the end of the year, India was prepared militarily and diplomatically. However, the Pakistani generals were not in a state of readiness. It wasn't their fault because they were often relayed information indirectly, through third sources. As a result their reading of the situation varied. Thus, while the National Security Council of Pakistan warned of an Indian invasion in the east, the ISI felt as late as in June 1971 that if Pakistan could prevent the imbalance of forces from going too heavily in favour of India, then India might not go to war. As against the National Security Council's assessment warning of war, Pakistan's Military Intelligence Directorate discounted completely the possibility of a war. The Pakistani army's chief of general staff, Gul Hassan had agreed with this assessment prepared by military intelligence in June 1971.

The fault, however, wasn't in these differing assessments. It was in the empire of senses that Yahya and his confidants had elected to dip themselves into. The reality that they were living in was surreal.

---

[2]Shuja Nawaz, *Crossed Swords: Pakistan, its Army and the Wars Within.*

[3]Avtar Singh Bhasin (ed.), *India–Pakistan Relations, 1947–2007: A Documentary Study.*

Even Kissinger, who was highly partial to Yahya, was disillusioned enough by July 1971 to tell the senior review group of the White House that:

> Yahya and his group would never win any prizes for high IQ, or for the subtlety of their political comprehension...they have a real intellectual problem in understanding why East Pakistan should not be part of West Pakistan.[4]

The war that eventually started on 3 December was short, swift and one-sided. Besides high morale, better strategy and meticulous planning, Indians also enjoyed the advantage in terms of numbers. India's army of 833, 800 men was supported by 3000 artillery pieces and 1450 tanks. In contrast, the Pakistani army of 365,900 men was supported by 800 guns and 850 tanks over two fronts. The contrast was even more striking in air power. India had 625 combat and 450 transport aircraft compared to 278 bombers and fighters of Pakistan. The Indian navy, too, was better equipped with twenty-one major battleships, an aircraft carrier, four submarines and many patrol boats. Pakistan had only eight battleships, four submarines and just a handful of patrol boats.

The Indian strategic aim in East Pakistan was to draw the Pakistani army to the border and to keep them engaged with the Mukti Bahini and the BSF. Once they had committed their resources thus, the Indian army was able to isolate Pakistani defenders in their separate sectors, and with that they also managed to bypass the tough targets. Realizing that Pakistani Army Commander General Niazi was going to fortify towns and defend them in strength, General Jacob's 'war of movement' plan was to bypass intermediary towns, and use secondary routes to reach Dhaka. The rest went in a textbook fashion. The Pakistani divisions were isolated and began to function as separate units without a coherent united plan.

Thereafter, the Indian advance in East Pakistan, ably aided by Mukti Bahni's local resources, was quick. The overwhelming air superiority was immensely valuable too. Much to the dismay and anger of the Nixon–Kissinger combine, the war was over in thirteen days and a new nation had been created.

As a matter of fact the war was over within a week of it being launched, following the air attacks by Pakistan on 3 December 1971. On 9 December, A.M. Malik, the governor of East Pakistan, sent a

[4]Shuja Nawaz, *Crossed Swords: Pakistan, its Army and the Wars Within.*

message to Yahya suggesting an immediate ceasefire. Yahya replied, leaving the decision to the governor and Army Commander Niazi. When Malik called a meeting at the Governor's House on 14 December to discuss the issue, the Indian air force carried out an air strike on the Governor's House just to reinforce the point.

All that remained now was to sign on the dotted line at the ceremony of surrender. This was duly done between General Niazi and General J.S. Aurora on 16 December at 4.55 p.m. at the Race Course Ground in Dhaka.

On that day of surrender by its forces in Dhaka, the main headline in Pakistan's principal newspaper, *Dawn*, announced, 'Victory on All Fronts'.

18

The Peril of Shaking Bhutto's Hand

The people of Pakistan had been led to believe that the Pakistani army was invincible. In fact, even experienced foreign visitors were in awe of its macho army men.

US Secretary of State John Foster Dulles visited Pakistan in May 1953. On his return to Washington he told the Senate Foreign Relations Committee that Pakistan would fight communists with its bare hands—that its lancers were 6 feet 2 inches tall and sat on great big horses and were out of this world.[1]

Alas, on recommendations such as these the policies of great powers were shaped. And it was on impressions such as these that alliances were formed. No wonder then that a close ally like the US should have been disappointed with the result of the 1971 war.

Neither the mood of despondency within Pakistan nor the sorrow of an ally like the US dampened the spirits of General Yahya Khan. Pakistan may have been humiliated, but Yahya Khan wasn't ready to give up power. In fact he had wanted to promulgate a new Constitution on 17 December, but he was stopped by the resentment of middle-level officers led by Brigadier Ali. They, rather than General Gul Hassan, the army chief, were instrumental in ensuring that Yahya quit his post. The message that was ultimately conveyed on their behalf by Gul Hassan to Yahya was this: 'Yahya must announce his resignation by 8.00 p.m. on December 19.'[2]

Given the mass feeling against the army then, a takeover by another general would not have been possible. The Pakistani army's vice-chief, General Abdul Hamid, tried to promote his candidature with a group of junior officers but they rejected it out of hand. It had to be a civilian leader now.

---

[1]Bruce Riedel, *Deadly Embrace: Pakistan, America and the Future of the Global Jihad.*

[2]Shuja Nawaz, *Crossed Swords: Pakistan, its Army and the Wars Within.*

The choice fell automatically on Bhutto whose PPP had won the elections in West Pakistan. In that tense atmosphere no one had the time or the inclination to quibble about details like the need for a new election as the previous one should have been considered null and void after the break-up of Pakistan. Moreover, the mood of the country had changed and in this new framework people wanted to give democracy a fresh chance, even if they were tweaking the rules of democracy a bit.

But desperate times require desperate solutions. There was no time or desire to challenge the flow of power from a discredited president to a politically savvy and charismatic Bhutto. The generals sent a special aircraft to Rome, where Bhutto had stopped on his way back from New York waiting for the ferment at home to settle. Bhutto returned on 20 December to take over as the president and the chief martial law administrator (CMLA) of Pakistan at the age of forty-four.

One of Bhutto's early aims was to rub the already humiliated army's nose in the ground by showing the surrender ceremony on TV and by sacking many of the brighter generals, as also Brigadier Ali, who had been instrumental in bringing him to power. For a while the situation was so dismal for the army that soldiers did not dare go into bazaars in uniform; they would change into civilian clothes for fear of being humiliated by people. This suited Bhutto because it increased by that much the army's reliance on him for getting the POWs back from India.

*

Getting the POWs back wasn't the highest priority for Bhutto. His aim was to meet Indira Gandhi on equal terms.

There was a big difference though this time; there were no direct intermediaries pushing the two sides to the conference table. In the Kashmir conflict of 1947–48, the UN had got involved and after the 1965 war, the Soviets had acted as mediators. But this time India and Pakistan were going to tackle the issue directly. The other big difference was that instead of New York or Tashkent, the venue for the talks was going to be Simla.

All along Mrs Gandhi's effort was to avoid lingering bitterness with Pakistan, and for this reason she did not agree to the Bangladeshi demands for a trial by a war crimes tribunal. Nor did she agree to persistent requests that the major culprits accused of human rights violations be handed over to Bangladesh. Her objective was to get the relations back to normal. She had mentioned that clearly in her letter of 12 December to Nixon, and she did the same in a letter to the Soviet prime minister.

Sultan Khan, Pakistan's foreign secretary at the time, records that during Bhutto's meeting in March 1972 with Soviet Prime Minister Alexei Kosygin, the latter read out a letter he had received from Indira Gandhi in anticipation of the meeting:

> Please convey to Mr. Bhutto our desire to live in friendship with Pakistan. We are ready to make our contribution, and will be willing to hold negotiations without any preconditions... We wish to bury forever the senseless conflict about Jammu and Kashmir...[3]

Rarely does a victor come to the table with all cards displayed and with an assurance that there were no preconditions. Nor does a country with all ace cards agree to a minimum position on an issue like Kashmir even before the talks had started. Yet, this is exactly what Indira Gandhi was conveying through her letter.

A month later, in April 1972, Indira Gandhi's emissary D.P. Dhar travelled to Murree to meet Aziz Ahmed, Pakistan's minister of state for foreign affairs. After three days of hard bargaining they were able to recommend two documents: an agenda for the summit and an agreed set of principles that should guide the negotiators at Simla. Primarily, the aim was to carve out a new beginning that would overcome the confrontations of the past and pursue a new path towards peace and development.

In another first, India cast aside its traditional reservation and decided to accede to Pakistan's persistent demand to discuss the Kashmir issue first. But for once Pakistan baulked at the idea. Its priorities this time were different: they related to the developments following the emergence of Bangladesh as a separate nation.

In their internal preparations the Pakistani army recommended that Bhutto should tell the Indians that if they desired durable peace they should:

- Withdraw all forces from areas occupied by them,
- Return all POWs,
- Reduce the size of their armed forces to reduce the fear of aggression in Pakistan.

These were the sort of terms that a victorious army should set. That they were actually recommended by the Pakistani army was as much

---

[3]Sultan Ahmed, *The Memories and Reflections of a Pakistani Diplomat*.

an indication of their mindset as the influence of the new army chief, Tikka Khan, who had earned notoriety for atrocities in Bangladesh. It was also reflective of the aggressive stance that the Pakistani negotiators usually employ.

Still, there was an air of anticipation in India as the two leaders headed for Simla. It was due in part to the afterglow of a massive victory, and in part because of the charisma associated with Zulfikar Ali Bhutto.

Indira Gandhi knew she was dealing with a tricky customer. Before leaving for Simla, she had asked R.N. Kao, the intelligence agency Research and Analysis Wing (RAW) chief, 'Can I trust Bhutto? People tell me that if I shake hands with him, I should immediately count my fingers.'[4]

The summit in Simla was set for 28 June to 3 July 1971. Mrs Gandhi reached Simla a day in advance and was horrified to see the less-than-perfect decor of the suite that Bhutto and his daughter Benazir were to stay in. She personally chose the new furniture and curtains. The first set of curtains that were stitched that day did not meet with her perfectionist approval. Late at night, a store was opened again in Simla and tailors worked through the night to stitch the second set of curtains. This met with the approval of the gracious hostess.

Bhutto was accompanied to Simla by his favourite child Benazir who had just graduated from college. She, too, evoked great curiosity among the media and Indian people. Bhutto had tutored her in advance:

> You must not smile and give the impression you are enjoying yourself while our soldiers are still in the Indian prisoner of war camps. You must not look grim either, which people will interpret as a sign of pessimism.[5]

The meetings in Simla between the two delegations began with a fundamental difference in approach. P.N. Dhar, secretary to Indira Gandhi, records it thus:

> On Kashmir, Pakistan strongly felt that it would be more feasible to first try and settle other, less emotionally charged disputes step-by-step and to take up the Kashmir question later. This approach, they believed, would generate a friendly atmosphere and a favourable

---

[4]Inder Malhotra, 'The collapse of Shimla accord', *Indian Express*.

[5]Benazir Bhutto, *Daughter of the East*.

> public opinion for acceptance of a solution of the problem, which would necessarily have to be a compromise.
>
> India though willing to take up the issues of occupied territories and prisoners of war, was keen, in addition, to solve long-term problems, Kashmir in particular. India itself had advocated the step-by-step approach in the past but this had not yielded the desired results. This time, India was determined that the Simla Conference should not turn into a replica of the Tashkent Conference which addressed the immediate problems created by the war of 1965 without tackling the basic reasons that gave rise to it. To break this impasse, Bhutto agreed to negotiate on long-term problems, his code name for Kashmir, provided that the solution, if arrived at, was implemented gradually, in a piecemeal manner and in step with improvement in overall Indo-Pak relations.[6]

Against the background of the rigid stand taken by his officials, Bhutto sounded more reasonable. He said that he was convinced by the events of 1971 that Pakistan could not acquire Kashmir by military intervention. 'Kashmir troubles me a lot,' Bhutto said.

He added that he did not want its dark shadow looming over Indo-Pak relations. He wanted his countrymen to get over the trauma of the emergence of its eastern wing as a separate independent state as quickly as possible and concentrate on making the residual Pakistan a prosperous country. Therefore, Bhutto was personally inclined to accept the status quo as a permanent solution of the Kashmir problem.

Essentially, Bhutto was performing to a rehearsed act, where he would be the good cop and Aziz Ahmed the bad cop who could be blamed for taking a hardline position. Bhutto also said there he had to contend with the belligerence of the army back home. They, and the people of Pakistan, would not accept the status quo on Kashmir so soon after the loss in war. He needed to get back his POWs and the territories under India's occupation first. That, he said, would give him a good basis to convince his people that it was time to resolve the Kashmir issue too.

Indira Gandhi was receptive to his reasoning. She was also conscious of the Versailles syndrome where the tough terms set by the Allied powers after the First World War had triggered a feeling of revenge among the defeated Germans. Indira was keen that the settlement at Simla should not lead to another war, prompting Bhutto and Aziz Ahmed to play on that sentiment.

---

[6]P.N. Dhar, *Indira Gandhi: The Emergency and Indian Democracy*.

The Indian side put their proposal in a discreet manner by suggesting that the name of the line dividing India and Pakistan in Jammu and Kashmir be changed from the 'ceasefire line' to the 'line of control'.

Aziz Ahmed adopted a negotiating stance by objecting to the proposal. He said the proposed change of terminology would mean a change in the status of the line. Aziz Ahmed put forth this view vehemently and stated that he was not prepared to accept the change in the nomenclature of the line.

But this change was the core of the Indian solution to the Kashmir problem: the de facto line of control was to be graduated to the level of the de jure border. Since no agreement was reached on this point, negotiations were called off and the curtain came down on five days of hectic talks, which had begun with great hopes throughout the sub-continent. This was the afternoon of 2 July and the Pakistan delegation was scheduled to leave the next morning. Soon word spread that the conference had failed. Media persons rushed to announce the failure.

P.N. Dhar says that after this mammoth failure, Bhutto asked to see Mrs Gandhi: a request that was granted. There were no aides, from either side, at this meeting. After the meeting, Bhutto looked 'very pleased'. Mrs Gandhi, on her part, told her coterie that she was 'sympathetic' to Bhutto's concerns and would 'hate to appear to be dictating terms to a defeated adversary'. She agreed to withdraw troops from the territory conquered by them in West Pakistan, as soon as possible. Her justification for the Indian proposal was that neither country was losing territory, whole populations were not getting transferred, and the line of control would be an 'ethnic and linguistic frontier'. Bhutto seemed to agree with her point of view, and while not inclined to include the terms in the agreement, seemed willing to push for its implementation over time. P.N. Dhar adds that several clauses included in the agreement had to be drafted and re-drafted in a way that would provide the context in which the agreement was to be read and implemented. The most important of these was sub-clause 4 (ii), which says:

> In Jammu and Kashmir, the line of control resulting from the ceasefire of December 17, 1971 shall be respected by both sides without prejudice to the recognised position of either side. Neither side shall seek to alter it unilaterally, irrespective of mutual differences and legal interpretations. Both sides further undertake to refrain from the threat or the use of force in violation of this line.

The phrase 'without prejudice to the recognised position of either side' was a concession to Bhutto to save him from his domestic critics. But to prevent the abuse of this concession and to lay the foundation for a future settlement of the Kashmir issue, the second and third sentences had to be incorporated and the sub-clause is, therefore, to be read as a whole.[7]

This was the interpretation of the Indian delegation. And this too was how it was interpreted by observers who followed the negotiations closely.

Peter Hezelhurst, *The Times* London correspondent, in an article titled 'Concessions at Simla Summit bring hope for deal on Kashmir', described the agreement 'as a historic breakthrough in the protracted efforts to resolve the differences between the estranged Asian neighbours during the past 25 years'.

His report of 4 July 1972 mentions:

> Apparently this will mean that Pakistan has agreed to settle the Kashmir issue bilaterally with India and President Bhutto of Pakistan will not raise the dispute in the United Nations if he keeps to the spirit of the Agreement. This would appear to be an important concession to Mrs. Gandhi, the Indian Prime Minister, who has advocated bilateralism as the means of settling Kashmir and other disputes with Pakistan... The Agreement also stipulates that both parties have agreed to recognise the cease fire line in Kashmir as it stood at the conclusion of the war in December, and convert it into a line of peace.

Bhutto agreed not only to change the ceasefire line into a line of control, for which he had earlier proposed the term 'line of peace', but also agreed that the line would be gradually endowed with the 'characteristics of an international border' (his words). The transition was to take place in the following manner: after the resumption of traffic between India and Pakistan across the international border had gained momentum, movement of traffic would be allowed at specified points across the line of control. At these points of entry, immigration control and customs clearance offices would be established.

It was thought that with the gradual use of the line of control (LOC) as a de facto frontier, public opinion on both sides would be reconciled to its permanence. In the meanwhile, the opening of trade and commerce and cooperation between India and Pakistan would result in easing tensions between the two countries. When Mrs Gandhi,

[7]P.N. Dhar, *Kashmir: The Simla Solution*.

after recounting their points of agreement, finally asked Bhutto, 'Is this the understanding on which we will proceed?', he replied, '*Absolutely, aap mujh par bharosa keejiyea* (absolutely, please trust me).'[8]

Sadly, Mrs Gandhi's trust was misplaced. On reaching Pakistan, Bhutto confided to Mairaj Mohammad Khan, at one time his close political aide, 'I have made a fool of that woman.'

He could have added that twice over, because in that last-effort meeting between them on 2 July, Mrs Gandhi had told him to choose between the immediate return of the 5000 miles of captured Pakistani land or the Pakistani POWs. When he returned to their suite, Benazir asked him why he chose territory.

Bhutto replied with a twinkle in his eyes:

> Prisoners are a human problem. The magnitude is increased when there are 93000 of them. It would be inhuman for India to keep them indefinitely. And it will be a problem to keep on feeding and housing them. Territory, on the other hand, is not a human problem. Territory can be assimilated. Prisoners cannot be...[9]

And Bhutto was heartlessly right.

India's iron lady Indira Gandhi had shaken Bhutto's hand in good faith, but having shaken it she forgot to count her fingers.

Why did a formidable leader like Indira Gandhi trust a Machiavellian man like Zulfikar Bhutto? That will remain an enduring mystery because there is so little direct source material about what impelled her to change her mind about a person who was trusted by so few.

Sir Morrice James, the British high commissioner in Pakistan, had made this assessment in 1965 about Zulfikar Ali Bhutto:

> Bhutto certainly had the right qualities for reaching the heights—drive, charm, imagination, a quick and penetrating mind, zest for life, eloquence, energy, a strong constitution, a sense of humour, and a thick skin. Such a blend is rare anywhere, and Bhutto deserved his swift rise to power... But there was—how shall I put it—a rank odour of hellfire about him. It was a case of corruptio optima pessima... I sensed in him a ruthlessness and capacity for ill-doing which went far beyond what is natural... his triumphs came too easily for his own good... I judged that one day Bhutto would destroy himself... Bhutto was born to be hanged...[10]

---

[8]Ibid.

[9]Benazir Bhutto, *Daughter of the East*.

[10]Morrice James, *Pakistan Chronicle*.

A few years later, his American counterpart Farland wrote thus in a telegram of June 1971 to Kissinger, '...I do not trust him [Bhutto]. Above all Bhutto is a very sly fox as a politician and does very little without good reason.'[11]

Bhutto's personal conduct often bordered on the deceitful. Ayub Khan recorded in his diary in June 1967:

> Upto the time he became a Minister in 1958 Bhutto had been declaring before the Indian courts that he was an Indian citizen residing in Karachi. The object was to get some compensation for the property left by his parents in India. In fact he was selling his soul for about one lakh fifty thousand rupees. All this was not known to us till recently when the matter was discussed in the Indian Parliament and came out in their press.[12]

Ayub was quoting from a discussion in the Indian Parliament. Yet, with all the information that pointed to a sly, deceitful and ruthless man, Indira Gandhi had decided to gift away all the gains on the battlefront. It is doubtful if such a chance would ever come the way of an Indian leader again. On the other hand if in the next war Pakistan were to have the upper hand, its leadership would not let sentiments override the determination to rub India's nose in the ground. Cold calculation, the glee and vanity of a conqueror, rather than a trusting heart, would drive Pakistan.

Soon after he came into power in 1971, Bhutto lost no time in taking up aggressive complaints with the US, that the Soviet Union and India were working to further Balkanize Pakistan. He also made a case for the resumption of the American arms supply to Pakistan on this basis. But the US State Department saw through his ruse. In a note to President Nixon it recommended:

> In the short run neither the Soviets nor the Indians have designs on the integrity of Pakistan... Over the longer run if Pakistan is internally unstable and deeply divided, the Indians, Afghans and Soviets may be tempted to place pressures on Pakistan. In this environment we see the resolution of Pakistan's security problems primarily in political/psychological and economic terms...[13]

---

[11]F.S. Aijazuddin (ed.), *The White House & Pakistan: Secret Declassified Documents, 1969–1974.*

[12]Ayub Khan, *Friends not Masters.*

[13]F.S. Aijazuddin (ed.), *The White House & Pakistan: Secret Declassified Documents, 1969–1974.*

Now, in retrospect, it seems that this State Department note of 1971 had a prophetic tinge to it. But Bhutto was not deterred by such dire warnings, nor was he one to sit back and sulk because of a rebuff by an interlocutor. He wasn't going to give up his anti-Indian agenda easily.

Bhutto was in a large measure responsible for two costly wars against India. Both in 1965 and in 1971 he instigated and goaded the straight thinking and relatively blunt army generals into wars that were unnecessary and in 1971, destructive for Pakistan. Still, Bhutto was instinctively inclined to go on fighting against India; he had himself called for a 'thousand-year war'. Why then did he not launch a war when he was the controller of Pakistan's destiny? In fact, he was the sole controller, because from the time he took over from Yahya Khan he was the unchallenged Caesar.

There is no doubt that Bhutto would have liked to poke India in the eye, but he had to heal the internal wounds of Pakistan first.

After the 1971 war, Pakistan's economy was in a shambles; its export earnings had plummeted because the highly lucrative jute and cotton exports originating from what was once East Pakistan were no longer available for Pakistan. The rump Pakistan did not have either raw materials or any significant manufacture to export. Its foreign exchange earnings came largely from agricultural products which by themselves did not bring in significant revenues. The domestic economy was skewed because of the stranglehold of a handful of large business houses; two dozen families controlled the finance and manufacturing industry of Pakistan. Moreover, the morale of the Pakistani army had hit rock bottom; its confidence needed to be replenished almost as much as its equipment.

With all these handicaps, launching a military charge against India would have been akin to tilting at windmills. And whatever else he may have been accused of, Bhutto was no Don Quixote.

There were other problems internally. Baluchistan was restless. A revolt was going on in this troubled province against the government. This movement acquired a heroic quality when some Oxbridge-educated youth decided to join in the struggle of the Baluch nationalists. Bhutto responded to this challenge in an autocratic fashion by deploying helicopter gunships and the army. The atrocities committed there, especially against the youth, so soon after the experience in Bangladesh disgruntled a group of young army officers. Some of them had been a part of the move that resulted in the overthrow of the Yahya regime, but instead of heeding the young officers he persecuted them.

On 30 March 1973 this group of young officers was arrested as a result of a leak from within. Third degree torture of these officers followed inevitably, as did a court martial. But the interesting part of this trial concerning what came to be known as the Attock Conspiracy was the choice of the officer to head the tribunal.

Bhutto wanted a pliant officer, one who would serve his political purpose even as he conducted the trial in such a fashion as to ensure the harshest possible punishment for them. His choice fell on Major General Zia ul-Haq, who always seemed anxious to please. Bhutto would have also heard of Zia's role in Jordan, where as a part of the Pakistani military group he had served the kingdom of Jordan so loyally that he came to be known as the butcher of Palestinians in Jordan. It was a direct reaction against these atrocities that led to formation of the Black September group by the Palestinians.

Zia's conduct in that trial was to be a major factor in choosing him to replace Tikka Khan as the army chief. Bhutto superseded six senior officers in April 1976 so that Zia could get that post.

The Attock Conspiracy made Bhutto more determined to evolve a counterbalance to the army, and the Federal Security Force was his specific creation for the purpose. Bhutto was also active on multiple other security-related fronts. By March 1972 he had gathered a group of scientists to work towards manufacturing an atomic bomb for Pakistan. He reached out to Saudi Arabia and Libya with the primary aim of tapping them for a generous flow of funds for this nuclear project. That was an important objective by itself, but there was a larger purpose too in getting them on board from the beginning. Bhutto projected this enterprise as an Islamic venture. By putting together a bomb, Pakistan would be doing the entire Islamic world proud.

There were also rumours that during meetings with the Saudi and Libyan rulers promises were made by him of sharing the technology with them. In the case of Saudi Arabia, some reports suggested that a few bombs were going to be set apart for delivery to this kingdom on demand.

Yet another foreign policy ambition of Bhutto during this period was to achieve a leadership position for Pakistan in the Islamic group and in the developing countries' groups like the non-aligned. It was to his credit that Pakistan began to be counted as an influential country, and it used these fora to advance its interests, especially its agenda on Kashmir.

Even as he had reason for some satisfaction on the external front, domestically his star was beginning to fade. The rich were upset because he had whimsically nationalized their industries. Workers were unhappy because of inflation and declining job opportunities; new jobs were hard to come by because those who could have invested in setting up industry did not have the incentive any longer to do so because of the fear of further nationalization. To complicate matters further, Bhutto banned alcohol and declared the Ahmadiyya sect, a minority in Pakistan, un-Islamic. As if this was not enough, Bhutto rigged the elections in January 1977; he ordered a near defeat for PPP to be changed overnight into a victory for it.

This latest act of his was the trigger for people to come out in the streets and protest. Within the army messes, too, resentment was beginning to brew again, and this time anti-Bhutto posters began to appear on their walls. All signs pointed that Bhutto had failed; the autocrat's rule was coming to an end.

The rest was easy; the 111th Brigade, also known as the coup brigade, fanned out and secured the vital installations on the night of 4–5 July 1977. This coup by General Zia was unusual by most standards. Shortly after his troops had surrounded the home of Prime Minister Bhutto, the two men were on the phone, calmly discussing details of the changeover. And in the weeks and months that followed the coup, the short, barrel-chested general insisted that he was taking over temporarily, merely to stabilize the situation.

Zia took over as the CMLA with the promise to the nation that he would soon relinquish that charge. Gradually, Zia developed a reputation for forgetting his promises.

*

At first people mocked Zia ul-Haq. How could a man such as Zia actually make it to the top in an army that prided itself on the physique of its officers? They were even more surprised that he should then have dethroned an unsuspecting Bhutto who was otherwise so cunning. There were other contrasts as well. Bhutto was a feudal aristocrat—tall, colourful and fond of the good life. Zia was short, unimpressive in appearance with protruding teeth, deeply religious and uncomfortable in large social gatherings. He was an immigrant from India and his origins were humble; his father was a clerk in the Indian army in Jalandhar. Could this man be taken seriously in a country that had so far been ruled by the likes of Jinnah, Ayub Khan and Zulfikar Bhutto?

It took some time for Zia to grow out of Bhutto's shadow, and get over the fear of his presence. A legend has it that when Bhutto was the prime minister and Zia the army chief, the latter was smoking a cigarette when Bhutto walked into the room. Much to the amusement of Bhutto, Zia hastily hid the lit cigarette in his trouser pocket.

In fact, Bhutto never took him seriously. The Shah of Iran's sister, Princess Ashraf Pahlavi, talks of her visit to Pakistan in May 1977 when during a banquet given by Bhutto she expressed her concern about the role of mullahs and worried about its repercussions in the army. Bhutto replied cockily: 'As far as the army is concerned, you know that man (pointing to General Zia who was sitting at a distance), he heads the army. He is in my pocket.'

Two months later, on 4 July 1977, Zia was standing awkwardly during the National Day reception at the American embassy and nervously chain-smoking Dunhill cigarettes in a corner. Later that night he told his commanders to move against the government of Zulfikar Ali Bhutto. But he remained tense and worried till Corps Commander General Faiz Ali Chishti told him, 'We have got all of them.' Zia managed a faint smile then.

That tentativeness was the hallmark of his initial days in power, so much so that many of his announcements had a reversible quality. The running joke about him as the CMLA was that the designation stood for 'Cancel My Last Announcement'.

Right from the beginning, though, Zia had an unshakeable faith in God. It was Zia who introduced Islam in a big way into the Pakistani army; flowing beards were no longer frowned upon. The British practices of dancing and alcohol-laced parties in officers' messes belonged to a bygone era.

Zia was the first post-independence army graduate to become the president of Pakistan, and by serving for eleven years he was its longest-serving dictator. He is often criticized for being a harsh military dictator. He kept many of his opponents in horrible prison conditions—Benazir used to complain that she lost her hearing in one ear because of the rough treatment in prison. But it is often forgotten that her father Zulfikar Bhutto was equally brutal in dealing with his opponents.

Like Bhutto, Zia too, did not launch a war against India. But he did much worse. He launched a clandestine war of a thousand cuts that continues to make India bleed. It was under Zia that Pakistan tested its first nuclear bomb in China. Psychologically, Zia set Pakistan apart from India by introducing the salwar-kameez as the national dress for men. It was also under Zia that textbooks were rewritten with an

Islamist bias. Pakistani historian K.K. Aziz described the revisions as teaching of prescribed myths. Students were taught to believe that Pakistan was the fortress of Islam, the advent of Islam reformed Hindu society, and that Hindus are indebted to Muslim culture and civilization.

If Jinnah was the creator of Pakistan and Bhutto its destroyer, or at least the catalyst that led to the bifurcation of Pakistan into two, then Zia's role was equally original. He made his country a nuclear state, introduced fundamentalism in its army and implanted terrorism as a 'state policy' of Pakistan.

As with all his predecessors, India was an obsession with him. But unlike them, he introduced yet another dimension to Pakistan's strategic policy. Afghanistan became a major preoccupation for him and set in motion events that have kept the Afghan cauldron boiling ever since. It could be argued that he wasn't alone in stirring up things in Afghanistan and that Afghans themselves were inviting trouble by their internal dissensions. It may be true, but Pakistan's was the critical touch—it instilled terror in an already troubled Afghanistan.

19

Pakistan–Afghanistan Relations

The Pakistan–Afghanistan relationship has been mostly acrimonious. As a matter of fact, tensions between the two regions have pre-dated Pakistan's coming into being as an independent state. Among the many reasons for it, a principal one is the treaty of November 1893 which the British had imposed. It resulted in an artificial division of Pashtun lands through the Durand Line. Earlier, all the areas inhabited by Pashtuns belonged to Afghanistan, but the effect of this 1893 agreement was to split the Pashtun tribes and divide their land. A people who recognized no boundaries were suddenly expected to respect borders.

The dispute over the Durand Line has become the subtext for nearly every other disagreement between the two neighbours. Despite this, it has never been explicitly discussed in negotiations. There are at least 38 million Pashtuns living in the two countries. In Afghanistan, the Pashtuns are an estimated 42 per cent of the population, which at around 11.8 million makes them the largest single ethnic group in the country. In Pakistan, Pashtuns are approximately 15 per cent of the population, which, at around 26.2 million, makes them the second largest ethnic group in the country. Family ties, marriages and tribal affiliations still bind them in various cross-linkages. Yet, they continue to be divided by a British imperial treaty that was forced on Afghanistan under duress.

It is a pity that neither then nor later was the doubtful nature of its legality put to a serious test. Partly, this indifference was on account of the episodic global interest in remote Afghanistan till the early 1970s. By then, Pakistan had read out its interpretation of the agreement repeatedly to the casual Western academic. Since that overlapped broadly with the imperial British version, the occasional curious enquiry was easily satisfied. There was rarely ever a realization that the agreement may not actually have been a boundary settlement and essentially might have been a British colonial device to contain and restrain marauding tribes.

In fact, the background to this treaty is indicative of its transient nature. The British rulers who had annexed Punjab in 1849 were irked by regular raids by the hill Pashtuns on the settled lowland areas of Punjab during the greater part of the nineteenth century. Their attempts to bribe the Pashtun tribes into cooperation did not produce results. Besides this, there were considerations of the Great Game, the rivalry of Britain with Russia to reign supreme in Central Asia, because of which the British had to decide where British India's north-western frontier ought to lie.

Some in London were emphatic that the frontier should stretch up to the line joining Kandahar, Ghazni and Kabul. Others argued that the physical frontier on this sector lay along the Indus. It was with this background that Mortimer Durand was deputed to Kabul to obtain territorial concessions in the Pashtun belt. Durand was to carry with him a rough sketch of the area with a line drawn on it that would turn out to be a compromise between the two extreme positions. At the time of receiving Durand in Kabul, the Afghan Amir was highly susceptible to pressures due to financial problems and internal dissensions.

In November 1893, the Afghan Amir, Abdur Rahman Khan and the foreign secretary of British India, Mortimer Durand entered into an agreement comprising seven short articles which created the Durand Line. This line was marked on a small-scale map of the Pashtun areas.

The Durand Agreement was written in the English language, with translated copies in Dari. But Amir Abdur Rahman Khan was asked to sign only the original English version of the agreement, a language which he could neither read nor write.

The Amir refused to sign the map that was attached to the agreement. However, the British claimed that because the Amir had signed the main agreement, the map too had his sanction. Along with this the British committed themselves to giving the Amir Rs 1.2 million (equal to about £120,000) annually besides some military equipment.

As A.M. Payne writes:

> The treaty designates large sections of what eventually became known as Balochistan, the Northwest Frontier Province (NWFP),

> and seven sections of the Federally Administered Tribal Areas as the possession of the British Empire. These seven 'semi-autonomous agencies' (Bajaur, Khyber, Kurram, Mohmand, Orakzai, South Waziristan, and North Waziristan) have a long history of occupation of tribes at least nominally under Afghan rule.[1]

According to A.S. Ghaus, the agreement essentially makes 'demands, according to which territories and people who since time immemorial had been considered part of the Afghan homeland and nation were arbitrarily included in British India'.[2]

Interestingly, the NWFP had originally included the districts of Multan, Mianwali, Bahawalpur and Dera Ghazi Khan as well, as these areas had formed a part of Afghanistan from 1747 until the 1820s, when Maharaja Ranjit Singh of the Sikh Empire took possession of them.

There is no doubt that the treaty of 1893 was forced upon a weak Amir. The treaty and the unsigned small-scale map can hardly pass muster today as a legitimate basis to amputate a country. Moreover, it has been argued that according to the terms of the agreement the Durand Line was valid for only a hundred years (that is, up to 1993).

Let's take the example of Hong Kong, which had a parallel case history in some respects. Hong Kong's territory was acquired by three separate treaties: the Treaty of Nanking in 1842, the Treaty of Beijing in 1860, and the Convention for the Extension of Hong Kong Territory in 1898, which gave the UK control of Hong Kong Island, Kowloon and the New Territories respectively. Although Hong Kong Island and Kowloon had been ceded to the UK in perpetuity, the control on the New Territories was a ninety-nine-year lease.

China regarded these as unequal treaties that needed to be revised by communist China as the successor state. Under pressure from it, the UK agreed to first contacts on the issue in the late 1970s. Matters came to a head during British prime minister, Margaret Thatcher's visit to China in September 1982 when Chinese leader Deng Xiaoping told her bluntly that China could easily take Hong Kong by force, stating that 'I could walk in and take the whole lot this afternoon.'[3]

It didn't take long for Britain to accept the inevitable. The transfer of sovereignty over Hong Kong from Britain to China took place on

---

[1]A.M. Payne, *The Durand Line: History and Implications of British Imperial Policy in Afghanistan.*

[2]A.S. Ghaus, *The Fall of Afghanistan.*

[3]Kwasi Kwarteng, *Ghosts of Empire.*

1 July 1997, when the ninety-nine-year British lease over the New Territories expired. Along with this Britain also handed back the Island and Kowloon over which it had acquired rights in perpetuity.

The important point to note is that a principle had been established—that a morally wrong treaty cannot be cited as a justification for sovereignty. In this case it was all the more important because two of the treaties were in perpetuity. Axiomatically, therefore, the same principle should apply in similar situations elsewhere. The Hong Kong example sets a clear precedent for Afghanistan to demand the restoration of its sovereignty over territories that were taken away from it in 1893.

Resentful Pashtuns have consistently agitated against the treaty and every Afghan government since 1947 has protested against the matter. Afghanistan claims that Pashtunistan includes the NWFP (or Khyber Pakhtunkhwa, KP, as it is known now) and that its geographical boundary extends up to the right bank of the Indus.

A recurrent objection by Afghanistan was that during the partition, the Pashtun regions should not have had to choose only between joining India or Pakistan, but should have been offered the additional options in the referendum conducted by the British of becoming an independent state or joining Afghanistan. Afghan leaders also argue that the various agreements between British India and Afghanistan, including the Durand Line, lapsed when the British left India and were not transferable to the new state of Pakistan. And even if Pakistan was deemed a legal successor state, the Afghans argue, the Durand Line remained illegitimate because the Amir had been coerced by the British into accepting the agreement.

After Pakistan's statehood, Afghanistan voted against its admission to the UN arguing that Afghanistan's treaties with British India were no longer valid because a new country was being created where none had existed at the time of signing the treaties.

Border clashes with Pakistan in 1949–50 and an embargo by Pakistan on oil supplies caused serious hardship to Afghanistan. This provided an opening for the Soviet Union which shared a long border in its south with Afghanistan. It stepped in first with an alternative route for the oil supply and then with aid. Between 1953 and 1973, Soviet aid to Afghanistan at US$1500 million was thrice that of America at US$450 million.

In the 1950s and 1960s, Afghanistan used to regularly protest against the Durand Line, much to the consternation of Pakistan. Thereafter it was distracted by its internal convulsions, but the passage of time has not dimmed the Pashtun desire for a greater homeland.

Afghan demands concerning a greater Pashtun region trouble Pakistan. The possibility that a strong and united Afghanistan might force the issue, or at least cite the Hong Kong precedent to muster support in its favour, presents Pakistan with a potential source of worry. Therefore a weak, divided and unstable Afghanistan suits Pakistan. A Taliban-type regime may or may not be weak, but being friendly with it will present Pakistan with the additional benefit of strategic depth. Its interference in Afghan affairs may well have its roots in this twin logic.

Pakistan saw its chance when King Daud began a crackdown on the Marxist elements in Afghanistan. Besides the Marxists, those fleeing Daud's repression included Islamists like Burhanuddin Rabbani and Gulbadin Hekmatyar. This was an ideal opportunity for Pakistan to step up its activities and an Afghan cell was set up in Pakistan's foreign ministry in 1974. After Bhutto's ouster, Zia ul-Haq began to guide the activities of the Afghan cell.

Coincidentally, the pace of events began to pick up in Afghanistan. It is a little-known fact that as early as 3 July 1979 President Carter signed the order giving assistance to the opponents of the Afghan regime. Whether it trapped the Soviets into rushing into Afghanistan for what was eventually a Vietnam-style debacle is a subject of speculation, but that is exactly what the then US National Security Advisor Zbigniew Brzezinski claimed.

On 24 December 1979, Soviet forces crossed the Amu Darya and marched into Afghanistan to save the Babrak Karmal regime. Soon thereafter, Pakistan began being wooed by the Western powers.

It was the same Pakistan which, for much of the 1970s, had been under the sanctions of the US because of its nuclear programme. But changed circumstances led to a rethink by US about those nuclear trespasses. The events in Afghanistan, and the Soviet invasion of it, necessitated this revision of US priorities. It now needed Pakistan's collaboration in organizing a guerrilla force against the Soviet occupation of Afghanistan.

After a long hiatus the US president picked up the phone to speak to Zia and to offer him financial aid besides promises of other cooperation. Under the changed circumstances and as the US need was greater, Zia had famously dismissed the offer of US$400 million aid as peanuts.

Soon, financial and defence aid started pouring into Pakistan in such huge quantities that even the American embassy computers had difficulty keeping track of the full numbers. In this non-stop shower of largesse, there were benefits galore for Pakistani armed forces—they were being modernized at a dizzying pace, their battlefield techniques benefited from exercises with some of the best-trained troops in the world, and they picked up the latest in military strategy and anti-insurgency operations.

Pakistani society, too, changed irreversibly. Estimates vary, but some put the number of Afghan refugees in Pakistan to be as many as three million. They were accommodated initially in the refugee camps in the NWFP, but in course of time some went back to Afghanistan, many settled in and around Peshawar while others spread out in different Pakistani cities. Naturally, this intermingling had an impact on Pakistani society.

A more obvious one was closer business links with the drug cultivators in Afghanistan. As a result the drug culture in Pakistan proliferated; estimates put the number of addicts there in many millions. Pakistan is a major trading post for Afghan drugs and over the years it has itself become a producer of drugs, earning for the Taliban and sundry other groups hundreds of millions of dollars. But far more fundamentally, the basic character of the country has changed. Hundreds of thousands of madrasas churn out cadres year after year for the Taliban. And poverty in the countryside forces families to sell their sons for suicide missions for a few thousand rupees. There is, therefore, hardly ever any shortage of suicide bombers with the Taliban.

There is a blow-back of all this for Pakistan too. As Hillary Clinton put it, 'if you keep snakes in your backyard they are bound to bite you'.[4]

But back in the 1980s, Zia was being courted by the US and both took pride in rearing the snakes of terror together. Throughout that decade the Western powers applauded him for what he was doing against the Soviet Union in Afghanistan, occasionally in Soviet territory too. Zia had perfected the technique of bleeding the Soviets in Afghanistan without provoking them into a direct confrontation. 'Water must not boil over' was his approach.

Encouraged by his success in Afghanistan, Zia decided to extend terror activities in India too. Zia adopted a slight variation of this policy in India; deniability was to be the mantra of terror operations there. Pakistan was to carry out clandestine operations to weaken India while simultaneously appearing to seek a durable peace. To

---

[4]Altika Rehman, 'Work harder to squeeze Haqqanis…' *The Express Tribune*.

complicate matters further for India, Zia started patronizing other neighbours too; every South Asian country which had some grouse against India found a very sympathetic Pakistani shoulder to cry on. The ISI set up operations in Nepal, Bangladesh, Sri Lanka and Myanmar to monitor and to provide invaluable help in insurgency operations in India. Like poison, the ISI had spread its tentacles everywhere, inside India as well as all around it.

With all his plans in place, Zia was able to launch a highly effective campaign of terror in India. Terror strikes became a matter of routine, bombs went off regularly in cities and killings by the dozen were not uncommon. Kashmiri Pandits were terrorized into migrating en masse out of Kashmir, and people started to shift out of Punjab as well. Both Punjab and Kashmir were balanced on a razor's edge in that decade. Yet another bomb blast and one more terror strike brought India that much closer to desperation. Some pessimists were quick to predict the break-up of India.

The ISI was a very busy agency then. Besides a successful India operation, it was organizing regular blows to Soviet forces in Afghanistan. Like Pakistan's foreign ministry, it too had set up an Afghan Bureau. It had three branches to deal with operations, logistics and psychological warfare, obviously a sophisticated operation on the lines of the latest in management techniques. In the five-year period between 1982 and 1987, the Afghan Bureau of the ISI trained 80,000 Afghans for terror operations in Afghanistan. Additionally, it sent Pashtu-speaking Pakistani soldiers to guide the mujahidin in battle conditions. But all this did not prevent the siphoning off of millions of dollars meant for aid to Afghan refugees in Pakistan, or the monies that were to be delivered to the mujahidin groups. In those years and thereafter, ISI officers developed an extra swagger and considerable personal riches.

At a macro level, Zia succeeded handsomely in his foreign policy goals. Afghanistan was within his strategic grasp and India was gasping for breath. All this may have pleased Zia immensely, but he failed to anticipate the consequences of it for Pakistan. The deadly destabilization was not only poorly anticipated but also ineptly managed by the establishment, which was solely interested in short-term goals and self-preservation.

In April 1988, the Geneva Accord leading to the Soviet withdrawal from Afghanistan was signed. Pakistan was now close to acquiring its strategic depth and the goal of installing a Taliban regime in Kabul seemed within reach. With that the issue of the Durand Line too would be sealed once for all; at least so Zia had hoped.

But soon after the Soviet withdrawal from Afghanistan, Pakistan and the US were engaged in a game of mutual deception. Pakistan wanted to keep the CIA in the dark about its support to Gulbadin Hekmatyar. The CIA on its part was bypassing the ISI to conduct a direct dialogue with its favourites among the mujahidin. To complicate the picture further, an enormous ammunition dump at Ojhri Camp, near Rawalpindi, was blown up in April 1988, resulting in the death of 1300 people. Though an enquiry was instituted, it did not address the speculation that one of the two superpowers may have been responsible for this sabotage.

In what can only be termed as an amazing coincidence, another mishap happened within four months of the blast at Ojhri; this time the plane carrying Zia and the US ambassador besides some generals blew up soon after taking off. This was the bloody end of Zia. Like the predecessor he had hanged, he too, died an unnatural death.

As in life so in death, people have underestimated Zia. For one thing he did not fit into the normal image of a dictator. As a man he was charming. As a politician he was clever. He overthrew a prime minister who was elected, albeit in a highly rigged poll. When studied in action, he was found to be quite ruthless. Like Bhutto, he was a great showman and adept at image-making. Foreigners became his greatest admirers. But politically he lived precariously; Pakistanis were not greatly enamoured of him.

Yet Zia's deadly legacy is sure to live long years after him. He changed the Great Game most fundamentally and in the process the Soviet Union got reduced to Russia. Encouraged by its success in Afghanistan, the US was convinced that in the newly emerging unipolar world, its word was going to be law and that the American standard for state behaviour had to be the new measure of morality in the world. Like the US, but in a radically different manner, Pakistan too wanted to impose its writ in the region. The resultant forces of terror and fundamentalism that Zia unleashed continue to haunt the region, and increasingly, Pakistan as well.

Future generations may point out that had it not been for the turmoil of the 1970s in Afghanistan, the region may have been far more peaceful. The US would not have been involved militarily in the region. And without the confidence of plentiful American arms and finances, Pakistan may not have had the gumption and the resources to launch its campaign of terror in India.

Future generations would also do well to remember that four years after the Durand Agreement was signed in the hope that it would keep the Afghan tribes away from British India, young Winston Churchill arrived to fight yet another war against the Afghans. His experience in that enterprise of 1897 was frustrating enough to make him write, 'Financially it is ruinous. Morally it is wicked. Militarily it is an open question, and politically it is a blunder.'[5]

As with Churchill, many others have found an Afghan adventure pointless and ruinous. But Pakistan feels otherwise. Every leader after Zia has pursued the goal set by him, that domination of Afghanistan is vital to Pakistan's integrity. Meanwhile, the Afghans continue to seethe. A century of strife and wars later, they still rail at the iniquitous Durand Line Agreement.

---

[5]Con Coughlin, *Churchill's First War*.

20

Talking About Our Neighbour

In Russian fairy tales, the hero often finds himself at a crossroads; standing there he reads less-than-encouraging signposts. If you go left, reads one, you lose your horse. If you turn right, reads the next, you lose your head. If you go straight, says the third, you find nothing. That is the typical conundrum.

I was reminded of it as I stood facing a volley of questions from a hundred of Delhi's bright young professionals and undergraduates. The questions came in thick and fast, and went on much beyond the allotted time despite appeals by the organizers. Almost without exception, the questions were well framed and pointed.

I had expected anger, even raised voices from a group so young. Instead, there was the confidence of conviction and clear, well-articulated questions. The other thing that amazed me was the uniformity of emotion. They were all equally puzzled at India's helplessness in fashioning an effective response to Pakistan.

A young lady asked, 'Do we have a policy on Pakistan?' Others asked, 'Why can't we stop them from killing our soldiers?' 'Why indeed are we scared of Pakistan?' 'Did we get anything by giving them all the documentation on 26/11?' queried yet another. 'Is dialogue the only way out, don't we have any other option?' 'Who should India negotiate with in the Pakistani establishment—should we talk to the ISI and the terrorists?' 'If Kashmir is ours, including the part occupied by Pakistan, why are we talking to them on Kashmir?'

There was a sense of puzzlement that after six decades of dealing with Pakistan, we had not got the measure of the country except once in 1971. Otherwise, and for the most part, it seems to be leading India by the nose. And we look content at being led.

The young were frustrated that rather than taking the fight into Pakistan to stop the menace of terrorism once for all, we seem content to remain in a defensive pose waiting to stave off the next blow.

Nehru came in for a lot of criticism for his mishandling of the Kashmir issue, but that was abstract anger because it happened a long time ago for this group with an average age of twenty-two or thereabouts. The details of what actually happened sixty-six years ago were hazy to them.

Their ire was obvious for what was happening now, in their generation. They railed against the Manmohan Singh government which, like Nehru, had been unable to confront the real and present danger. To them, the mishandling by Nehru must have been no different from what they were witnessing now.

The questions kept coming in a never-ending torrent. Is Pakistan really that much more powerful than India? Why do we let their terrorists roam free and kill at will? One young man went to the extreme of assuming that all Pakistanis are venomous when it comes to dealing with India.

As I stood there answering their questions, the thought came to me that if 'nationalism' is the dominant ideology, then in the minds of this representative selection of the best and the brightest of Delhi, the government has failed to prove its mettle. It was the cowardly inaction in the face of terror that this group's anguish was about. Even as the evening was coming to an end, and as the organizers resorted repeatedly to dimming the lights, questions hung about in the air trailing the distance between their seats and the podium like imaginary missiles; the arbitrariness of the government in deciding that we should sit back in fatalistic acceptance every time there is a terror strike bothered this group.

I did not want to embitter them further by stoking their anger. My effort was to tell them of the distinction between the state and society, that there are sections within Pakistan who genuinely wish to walk the peaceful path with India. But the youth gathered in the auditorium were impatient. They had no time for polite assurance. They spoke of the beheadings of Indian soldiers and the brutal killing in Lahore's Kot Lakpat jail of Indian prisoners like Chamel Singh and Sarabjit Singh.

I reminded them that before 1947 we were one, they shot back that since 1947 Pakistan has been busy manipulating and manufacturing history. Their textbooks falsify; there the Urdu version of 'Z' has a picture of a turbaned Sikh with the caption 'zalim', meaning brutal.

When I said it is logical that we should persist with dialogue, they shot back, 'Does logic help with Pakistan? No, it doesn't because Pakistan is an irrational state. Everyone in the world says so.'

I tried another approach and said, 'Let's not look at the half-empty glass—there is light at the end of the tunnel. One day terror will end,' I added brightly.

They gave me a pitying look and said the tunnel seems to get longer and longer. In any case, Pakistan's aggression is not an ad hoc impulse; it is a carefully calibrated strategy to keep Afghanistan weak and India off balance.

'But Pakistan has a civil society,' I persisted.

'Ha!' the entire lot of them guffawed as if I was a complete ignoramus. 'Pakistan's problem is that it has too much state and not enough society.'

'That's generalizing matters,' I countered, grabbing the chance. 'The issue is more complicated. From the very beginning, the masses there have been content to be led because there is no middle class to protest and articulate society's concerns.'

'Wrong!' they shouted back. 'Middle class or no middle class, the Pakistani nation has been the personal property of its military and political rulers. The army has its defence housing societies all over Pakistan to buy land at throwaway prices for its officers who can then sell it at a phenomenal profit, and politicians pocket the cream from government contracts. In case you don't know, the feudal lords own the people of Pakistan.'

'It's not like that,' I insisted with all the gravitas that salt-and-pepper hair can bring. 'There has been a lot of change in Pakistan in recent years. The judiciary is assertive and the media is independent. There is real democracy now in Pakistan.'

'Really?' they mocked again. 'There is, in fact, very little difference between Pakistan's civilian regimes and its military ones. Democracy in Pakistan is constantly threatened by the sheer scale of its religious and economic difficulties. When terrorists are quiet, the army threatens the political party in power. Democracy is a big drama in Pakistan. Remember what happened to Salman Taseer, who was assassinated by his own security guard? And who knows where democracy has taken the son of former Prime Minister Gillani?'

There is no doubt that they had got the better of me. They were well informed, articulate and sure of their facts. And they didn't hesitate in saying what they felt should be told.

I had been tentative and defensive, in imitation of official India. Still, I wanted to try one last time.

I told them that I didn't want to poison their young minds with the prejudices about partition that people older than them carried. That's why I was giving them a rational and non-venomous view of Pakistan. It was my hope that they and their counterparts in Pakistan would succeed where the previous generation had failed.

Even as I said this piece I knew I was sounding a bit false, that to their young uncluttered minds I was clutching at non-existent straws. Yet, with the desperation of a drowning man I made the effort and brought in the great man. This, I thought, could not fail. 'Our founders were saintly,' I said with all the authority I could command. 'The creation of modern India is an act of moral imagination; the idealistic conviction spread across the land by Mahatma Gandhi that we could win our freedom by peaceful persuasion. If he could get us freedom from the mightiest empire on earth by persuasion, why can't we persuade Pakistan?'

They didn't respond immediately, but there was no nervous shuffling of feet in the hall. Nor did they look at each other hoping that someone else in the audience, rather than they would speak. No, it was not the pause of the meek. They were still supremely confident. Instead, they gave me a look that a person gives when he sees a very diseased limb. To them, I seemed beyond hope.

A determined-looking young man got up from the very back of the hall and said, 'Sir, I'm sorry to differ, but Pakistan behaves like Josef Goebbels. Remember, sir, Goebbels used to say, "Oh, how wonderful it is to hate." Pakistanis are like that. They hate us every waking moment of their day and they plot our destruction in their dreams.'

A young lady followed immediately. 'In 1933 while Gandhiji was spinning peace, Albert Einstein wrote to Sigmund Freud, "every attempt to eliminate war had ended in a lamentable breakdown…man has within him a lust for hatred and destruction."'

I had barely time to let out a dispirited sigh, when a serious-looking man got up to wave his fist in the air and say, 'To me, Pakistan's singular success has been the perfection of the terror machine. It breeds, trains and sponsors terrorists as in a hatchery and despatches them in distinct batches: one for the US, the other to be sent across to Afghanistan but the most lethal are reserved for India."

Frankly speaking, I felt a burden had lifted off my chest when the session ended. Thank God, the ordeal is over, I said to myself. But the encounter kept haunting me for long thereafter.

Why were the young disillusioned with the official stance? Why did they say that Nehru had saddled India with an avoidable millstone? And why did they insist that the Indian case is not understood in the global councils? There was a huge disconnect between their thinking and the government's policy.

It wasn't just this group of the young who were frustrated with the government's response to Pakistani aggression. I had encountered the same angst throughout the country, in heaving metropolises like Kolkata and in smaller cities like Dehradun and Indore. They were vehement that except for an episode or two, India has prided itself for being a non-threatening power. To them this was rooted more in India's weaknesses rather than a moralistic compulsion.

The thought that kept worrying me was this—that the next generation may not have the infinite patience that Indians have exhibited during the last six decades. Given the anarchic unpredictability of its neighbourhood, and as it grows in power, India will be tempted to enforce its will.

A 26/11-type attack five or ten years from now could lead to a massive retaliation by these young men and women who might be in positions of power by then.

21
Terror Trail

Lahore's infamous Kot Lakpat jail contorts to a human face temporarily when a foreign VIP visits. In one famous effort to please, the jailor asked the visiting VIP if he would like the jail to organize a special demonstration of flogging for him.

Since the 1980s the Pakistani state has taken to organizing special shows—a bombing in Delhi, a deadly blast at the German Bakery in Pune, or better still, take on Mumbai and show the world how only ten men can hold an entire city to ransom for three days.

Then, there is a permanent fireworks display in Afghanistan. At first, in the 1980s, Pakistan was the joint producer of this show with the US and the target of their attacks was the Soviet army in Afghanistan. It is a fact widely acknowledged that together they had put up a magnificent show. But even then, they were fickle in their loyalties, there were rumours that both flirted a little on the side.

Two decades later, Americans replaced the Soviets as the occupying force in Afghanistan. Technically speaking, Pakistan continued to partner the US in this millennium as well. But in reality, it maintained an adulterous relationship with the Taliban; Pakistan was the surreptitious mentor and protector in this new show run by the Taliban. Therefore, when crackers explode in American faces, Pakistan calls it collateral damage or mistaken friendly fire. Often, Pakistanis deny all knowledge of it. Riled Americans say that treacherous Pakistanis are playing a double game. But soon after letting off steam, they woo the Pakistani army again.

Pakistan would like the world to believe its denials, but no one trusts it any more. Every bomb strike, anywhere in the world, is linked somehow to Pakistan, or so the world has come to believe. As a result, it has come to be regarded as a neighbourhood drunk who makes a spectacle of himself and is dangerous to those around him.

In theory, at least, it could be said that India has got off lightly; there has been no war between the two neighbours since 1971. It could also be argued that Kargil was only a daring and deep incursion with bloodshed on both sides. It had all the makings of a war, but since India took the decision to keep the action confined to the Kargil sector and not cross the international border, let us for our present purposes not call it a war. Or to put it more correctly, while statistically it too should be considered a war, militarily let's call it a local affair. If that is agreed to, then it follows that the last war between India and Pakistan was fought in 1971.

Ordinarily, that should be a reason for satisfaction because it means that for over four decades India and Pakistan haven't exchanged bombs and bullets. Alas, such a conclusion would be an exercise in deception. We may not have fought a conventional war, but we have been engaged in bloody conflict almost constantly from the 1980s up to now.

Terror has stalked India continually, causing destruction. Its losses have been enormous but have never been clinically evaluated in statistical terms of financial and human loss as the US is apt to do after every natural disaster or a terror strike. Worse still, each terror attack has only an episodic value for India; the angst lasts for the duration of the attack.

It is difficult to pinpoint a precise cut-off date for when Pakistan started sponsoring terrorism as a state enterprise. Strictly speaking, it started in 1947 when Pakistan came into being and began to push Mehsud and Afridi tribals into India. It was the same in 1965 too. But the big difference between those efforts and the one that began in the 1980s is that the latter is a continuous enterprise; it carries on regardless of whether there is a state of war or the hope of peace between India and Pakistan. The second big difference between the earlier efforts and this phase is that both the security forces and civilians are the target now. Moreover, the economic base of India is also under attack. All this can happen only under the guidance of an organization like the ISI and with the resources of a state.

America must bear some responsibility for the spread of terror in the world. It was the massive infusion of arms and money into Pakistan by America in the years starting from 1979 that led to Pakistan becoming a vast repository of weapons for jihadis against the Soviet occupation of Afghanistan. Once arms are distributed generously, there is no knowing who might use them and for what purpose. Moreover, Pakistan became a sophisticated training ground for terrorists who gathered there regularly from across the world. Here, too, the US Special Forces were of great help; they joined enthusiastically in this enterprise of preparing jihadis, as in a hatchery. There was a fresh batch of eager trainees all the time, and the overjoyed Americans taught them all they knew of sabotage and the killing techniques. Had they paused to think of the consequences, of the snowball effect of this dangerous knowledge, the American trainers may have wondered if all of it was necessary.

But in the 1980s, they were driven by the mission to crush the Soviets; therefore, no one bothered to think of the other consequences. Those were heady days for Pakistan, jihadis and for the US. It was then that Zia decided on a side adventure by the ISI in Punjab first and later in Kashmir. Saudi Arabia, too, contributed with money. But basically it was American arms and the American training of jihadis that made the big difference. And its Afghan engagement with the US gave Pakistan the confidence that America would ignore its terror trespasses in India as long as it needed Pakistan to fight the Soviet Union in Afghanistan.

This is exactly what happened. As we know, at one point, the traffic of arms flowing into Pakistan from the US government was so massive that even large computers installed in the US diplomatic missions in Pakistan had difficulty coping with it. Given that enormity, it was difficult to control how many weapons came in and which ones were used where. Moreover, the training camps that America and Pakistan jointly organized for the battle in Afghanistan could always accommodate a dozen or so extra trainees who could then be consigned to India for operations there.

Once the momentum builds up for such an operation, it becomes an unstoppable machine, a self-perpetuating monster. The jihad factory that the US had helped set up in the 1980s for operations in Afghanistan resulted directly or indirectly in the biggest terror attack the world has seen so far. And it was on American soil.

Two months prior to 9/11, Russian President Vladimir Putin and US President George Bush met during a G-8 meeting in Genoa in July 2001. Condoleezza Rice records in her memoir: 'He [Putin] excoriated the Musharraf regime for its support of extremists and for the connections of the Pakistani army and intelligence services to the Taliban and Al Qaeda...'[1] Putin added prophetically that it was only a matter of time before it resulted in a major catastrophe. At that time

[1]Condoleezza Rice, *No Higher Honor.*

Bush and Rice thought that Putin was exaggerating. It was only after 9/11 that they must have realized that he was right.

Many American strategists grudgingly acknowledge now that the threat to America isn't so much from the war zone of Afghanistan, but from further south. Pakistan, with its nuclear arsenal of over 100 bombs, and some 100,000 Taliban of various hues, is the real threat in the immediate, medium and long term. Its instability adds further to the gravity of that threat.

Mike McConnell, Director of National Intelligence in the Bush administration, had focused on this threat in his first briefing of the President-Elect Barack Obama. He said bluntly:

> Pakistan is a dishonest partner of USA in Afghan war... In exchange for $2 billion a year from US, Pakistan's powerful military and its spy agency (ISI) helped USA, while giving clandestinely weapons and money to the Afghan Taliban.[2]

What McConnell was conveying to the incoming president was grim news, that US-supplied weapons were being used to kill American soldiers. McConnell also told him that Bush had directed that Pakistan should not be given advance intimation of drone attacks because the ISI was known to pass on that information to the intended victims.

Obama's reaction to that briefing was:

> It corroborated some of my deepest concerns about the fact that the Taliban had strengthened, were controlling many parts of the territory, and that we did not have a strategy in Pakistan for the FATA and the Northwest region.[3]

Obama spoke too soon. Had he waited, and gained a little more experience of dealing with Pakistan, he would have added that he couldn't fix the problem called Pakistan. Whether one president failed or both did equally badly in dealing with Pakistan is not the question. The issue is: why are the Americans and others shy of tackling the reality that stares them in the face and acknowledging that unless they eliminate the roots of terror in Pakistan they will just be trimming the branches of this menace in locations like Afghanistan?

Bush had recognized this need when he spoke to his fellow Americans on the evening of 9/11: 'We will make no distinction between those who planned these acts and those who harbour them.'[4]

---

[2]Bruce Riedel, *Deadly Embrace.*

[3]Ibid.

[4]Ibid.

Despite this presidential declaration, the fact is that Pakistan harbours the largest number of Al Qaeda and Taliban operatives anywhere in the world. Osama bin Laden and Hakimullah Mehsud were killed in Pakistan; till their final day they had been living within gazing distance of Pakistani army establishments. Mullah Omar, Ayman Al Zuwairi and Jalaluddin Haqqani, the leadership of the militant organization Quetta Shura, and countless others live in Pakistan and continue to plan and direct their attacks against Americans and American interests in Pakistan, Afghanistan and elsewhere. Yet, the presidential doctrine does not seem to affect them.

As a former CIA operative and presidential aide on intelligence, Bruce Riedel, said once, 'Pakistan is the most dangerous country in the world today, where every nightmare of the 21st century converges—terrorism, government instability, corruption and nuclear weapons.'[5] He also said that the ISI had a direct hand in creating, supporting and bankrolling Islamic extremists.

Right in the beginning of his first term, Obama turned to Riedel for a quick strategic review of what America needed to do in Pakistan and Afghanistan. Riedel had his recommendations ready within the promised sixty days.[6] Its essence was that the American focus (of operations) must shift from Afghanistan to Pakistan. His reasoning was that Pakistan has a convoluted relationship with terrorists in which it was the patron, the victim and the safe haven—all at the same time. Extremists based in Pakistan were undermining the Afghan government and in a vicious cycle, Afghanistan's insecurity was feeding Pakistan's instability.

Riedel's solution to this complex web was 'to disrupt, dismantle and eventually defeat Al Qaeda and its extremist allies, their support structures and their safe havens in Pakistan and to prevent their return to Pakistan or Afghanistan.'[7]

It was the right prescription, but one that was stumped by a problem called Pakistan. There was not a single stick that the US could use to prod Pakistan into good behaviour. The new president was told that there was no question of invading a country of 170 million people and armed with dozens of nuclear bombs. If Pakistan were offered a civil/nuclear deal of the type that was given to India, it wouldn't even say thank you, because it would only feel that a wrong

---

[5]Ibid.

[6]Ibid.

[7]Ibid.

had been corrected. And there was no question of trusting anyone in Pakistan.

Some of the dramatis personae in public life then, such as Army Chief General Ashfaq Parvez Kayani, were considered liars by the US: in turn, General Kayani found President Zardari incompetent and the then opposition leader Nawaz Sharif untrustworthy!

Given such a bleak scenario, there was very little elbow room with Pakistan, except maybe to hope for the best and to keep giving more money and arms equipment to keep it appeased. The presidential review in Washington had changed nothing. There was no lever that the US could use effectively enough against Pakistan. Therefore, the presidential declaration warning those harbouring terrorists was non-implementable, except to the extent that Pakistan chose to cooperate. Here, it is best to recall the analogy of the jailor from Kot Lakpat; like him, Pakistan puts up a show occasionally to please the foreigner. But it does so selectively, on its own terms, at a time and on a scale that it chooses.

Still, three of the recommendations made by Riedel to Obama stand out: while not minimizing the need for integrated counter-insurgency operations in Afghanistan, the president needs to stay focused on the real, central threat that is Pakistan. Second, the Al Qaeda is relentless—until Americans destroy them, they will continue to kill Americans. Third, while drone strikes are killing the bad guys, it is like going after a beehive one bee at a time. Drones would not destroy the beehive.

They could have added a fourth recommendation—stop all aid. If the US cuts off all financial aid and leans on multilateral agencies to do likewise, and if it stops supplying arms to Pakistan, that may have some effect.

Obama spent a huge amount of time in finalizing a strategy for the Afghanistan–Pakistan region. In the end he set certain benchmarks when he announced a surge of 30,000 troops in Afghanistan. This strategy for Afghanistan and Pakistan was announced on 29 November 2009. Its five-page memorandum was notable for its stated aim: the US goal in Afghanistan is to deny a safe haven to Al Qaeda and to deny the Taliban the ability to overthrow the Afghan government.

In so far as Pakistan was concerned, the document set the following markers:

- Are there indicators that we [the US] have begun to shift Pakistan's strategic calculus and eventually end their active and passive support for extremists?

- Has Pakistan approved our [the US's] specific request for assistance against Al Qaeda and other extremists, including the Afghan Taliban and the Haqqani network?

Beyond these objectives there is a larger test that the US should subject itself to. It should ask the question whether six decades of engagement with Pakistan has lived up to the premises and promises that it was built on.

22

The US–Pakistan Connection

The US–Pakistan engagement started in the 1950s. The US could have been in a relationship with India instead because India was bigger, a functioning democracy and temperamentally a natural partner. But that was not to be, and one reason for it was the tepid response of the Indian leadership.

US secretary of state, Dean Acheson gives one such instance in his biography, *Present at the Creation: My Years at the State Department.* Nehru did not support the US position during the Korean War. Instead, he advocated a permanent seat in the UN Security Council for China on the plea that its presence there would have averted the war! This attitude was one of the reasons why Dean Acheson described him as, 'one of the most difficult men I have ever had to deal [with].'

A few years later, in 1953, Vice-President Nixon undertook a sixty-eight-day tour of Asia, including India where he met Nehru. He wrote in his memoirs that Nehru was the least friendly leader he had met in Asia. Regarding Pakistan he recommended, 'Pakistan is a country I would like to do everything for. The people have fewer complexes than the Indians.'[1]

These assessments, among other factors, must have contributed to the American tilt in favour of Pakistan. It was presumed by the American strategists that Pakistan along with Iran and Turkey would be the West's southern flank to check the spread of communism and the Soviet influence. A second assumption was that the Pakistani connection would be invaluable in building bridges with the Arab world. Along the way, many other reasons were thought of to keep the Pakistan–US connection in a steady state. Sometimes the secret approach to China, on another occasion the desire to drive the Soviet Union out of Afghanistan provided the bonding glue. Each such need

[1]Richard Nixon, *The Memoirs of Richard Nixon.*

became an opportunity for Pakistan to assert its pivotal role for American interests.

But was its role really vital for the US? There was a historical momentum that was going to push some events anyway in the direction that they eventually took, and that would have happened with or without Pakistani help. The Soviet Empire was overstretched in the immediate post-Second World War period. It was an unwieldy geographical entity; difficult for the best of administrations to govern and hard for any politician to keep the multiple ethnic pots from boiling over. Economically, it was an unviable state that was somehow kept going by statistical jugglery. Yet, this vast conglomerate was expected to subsidize its satellites in Eastern Europe and from time to time reassure them that it was strong enough to take on the Western imperialists.

The East Europe of the East–West era and the Amu Darya river to the south should have been the geographical limit of the Soviet reach, yet it gave in to ambition and ventured into Afghanistan in 1979.

That was the turning point for Pakistan. It is true that Bhutto had set it on a nuclear course in 1972 and the Chinese had started arming Pakistan. But its armed forces were demoralized and underequipped. Moreover, with the American sanctions in place the critical spare parts for the US-supplied equipment were in short supply. Had the Soviet invasion of Afghanistan not taken place, the Pakistani army might have continued to languish as a defeated army—dictators at home but of no great menace abroad—but 1979 provided it the booster shot.

From that point on, Pakistan played a central role in organizing an insurgency against the Soviet forces in Afghanistan. But the question that must be asked is whether Pakistan's role was critical. Would the Afghan resistance and the headaches of occupation not have tired the Soviets in due course? After all, sustaining an army of 100,000 in a foreign state and maintaining the supply line of food and equipment over a prolonged period is a costly affair. Moreover, the morale of an army suffers when it is uncertain about why it is there; what is the objective that it is fighting for?

It took nearly a decade of combined efforts by the US, Pakistan and the mujahidin to drive out the Soviets. It is quite possible that the Afghans may have, by themselves, driven out the Soviets in that long a time. Or, the Soviets may have tired of staying on as unwelcome guests.

Perhaps, it wasn't really necessary for the US to intervene in the

Afghan quagmire. Had it stayed away, it would not have become so critically dependent on Pakistan either then or post-9/11. Nor would it have lulled itself into believing that the roots of terrorism lay elsewhere, not in Pakistan. By the time the US came to this realization it was too late; it had exhausted its military energies in pruning the branches of terror in Afghanistan. Meanwhile, it had armed Pakistan with the latest and the best that its defence industry had to offer.

The other assumption that Pakistan's is a vital connection to the Islamic world is, once again, a premise of doubtful validity. It assumes that the Islamic bloc is a monolith, and that all Islamic countries are somehow beholden to Pakistan. Facts paint a different picture, however; Pakistan and Pakistanis are not always the first on the guest list of an Islamic state. Its excessive Islamic zeal unnerves them. When the first Pakistani ambassador to Egypt reeled off various Islamic unity-related proposals to him, King Farouk remarked, 'Islam seems to have come to this world on August 14, 1947.'[2]

The Islamic world is divided by ethnic, cultural, geographic and economic differences. It might unite against an external challenge, but religion does not always determine national interests. The national priorities of Saudi Arabia are vastly different from those of Egypt and diametrically opposite those of Iran or Syria. Neighbours like Iraq and Kuwait have fought two bloody wars, and tiny Qatar growls constantly at bigger Saudi Arabia.

It is true that Saudi Arabia exercises an extraordinary influence on Pakistan, mediating in its internal political squabbles as well. In turn Pakistan has been of use; it has trained Taliban cadres at Saudi behest, and despatched its Sunni soldiers to put down the Shia revolt in Bahrain and to aid the rebels in Syria. Large contingents of Pakistani soldiers are stationed in Saudi Arabia to help protect the kingdom and to keep the restive Shia population in the eastern part of the state in check. Gulf states, principally Saudi Arabia and Kuwait, have given it grants of billions of dollars and often oil at concessional rates. All along Saudi Arabia has acted as the bigger brother in their relationship, deciding the direction and the extent of it. But the obverse is hardly true. Pakistan may be a convenient drop box for charity by the oil-rich Gulf sheikhs, but by and large, the more liberal among the Arab states are wary of too close a Pakistani embrace. It is not the state that they rush to for counsel of wisdom on their internal affairs.

Pakistan is essentially a rabble-rouser in Islamic councils; it gets

---

[2]Sultan Khan, *The Memories and Reflections of a Pakistani Diplomat*.

routine endorsement for its views on India-centric issues like Kashmir. But it does not determine the intra-Islamic power equations nor can it influence the policies of major players like Turkey, Indonesia, Iran or Saudi Arabia on their relations with the outside world, especially the US. Therefore the American assumption that Pakistan could be a vital key to the Islamic world never really stood up to the test.

If in a belated realization of this, the US were to cut all its civil and military aid, would Pakistan retain its swagger? Would that affect its capacity to sponsor terror? This should be so axiomatically; sadly, however, the real world does not run to logical equations.

23

The Great Game

A hundred years ago, India was a prize catch of the 'Great Game'. In John Buchan's *Greenmantle,* the hero Richard Hannay is told by the fictional head of British intelligence, Sir Walter Bullivant, 'There is a dry wind blowing through the East, and the parched grasses wait the spark. And the wind is blowing towards the Indian frontier… I have reports from agents everywhere.'

That was fiction. John Buchan wrote his novel in 1916, in the middle of the Great War. But sometimes truth is stranger than fiction and within three years of Buchan writing his book, the Bolsheviks were aiming the Marxist torch towards the East. Lenin declared in1920, 'England is our greatest enemy. It is in India (the richest of all imperial possessions) that we must strike them the hardest.'[1]

The Bolsheviks could not reach the blue waters of the Indian Ocean; they had to be content with consolidating Central Asian states back into the Soviet fold. Their foray further south beyond the 'stans' (state or country) would have to wait another sixty years. They ruled Afghanistan for a few years in the 1980s but in the process, the Soviet Union exhausted itself.

Ironically, it was this foray south of the Central Asian 'stans' into Afghanistan that resulted in the loss of territories it had consolidated in the 1920s. Neither the Soviet Union in the 1980s, nor America after 9/11 thought of marching further south into Pakistan. Even venturing into Afghanistan has for long been a curse-ridden enterprise; rarely in recorded history has an invading army emerged from Afghanistan with its glory intact. Afghanistan consumes them all. The entire British army, except one soldier, was slaughtered there. So many Indian soldiers perished on the cold heights of a mountain there that it was

---

[1]Giles Milton, *Russian Roulette: A Deadly Game—How British Spies Thwarted Lenin's Global Plot.*

named Hindu Kush, the killer of Hindus. The elements there, and the Afghans themselves, have consistently posed formidable odds for invading forces. The Soviet Union was splintered into fifteen pieces and the US has vastly downsized its global ambitions after its Afghan travails. Though Afghanistan has stymied the military reach of the two superpowers, Pakistan would be a much greater challenge.

Regardless of what happens to the US and its presence in Afghanistan, chances are that the Pakistan-supported Taliban would pull out all stops to prevail over Afghan security forces. The Taliban may not succeed immediately but they would carry the battle as deep into the Afghan heartland as possible. They will then keep nibbling at the territory outside Kabul till they are finally in control of all Afghanistan south of Kabul. It may take them longer to conquer the Tajik and Uzbek part of the country.

Would that state of instability then percolate down to Pakistan or the Pashtun part of it at least? Either way, India has reason to be anxious about the times ahead.

If the US is apprehensive about crossing the Rubicon and taking the fight to Pakistan because it has 100 nuclear bombs, India has many more reasons to be worried. It is the next-door neighbour, and Pakistan's nuclear bombs, terror incursions, drug trade, fake currency operations, an India-allergic clergy and army are all directed in the easterly direction.

On top of this there is the certainty that, sooner rather than later, some of the Taliban cadres may shift to India. This is a real threat and dangerous in its implications. But it is just one part of the problem for India. Thousands, perhaps substantially more as Rabbani had promised, of terrorists crossing into India would stir up a nightmare beyond the wildest imaginings of the security experts.

Second, the Taliban, who are engaged in fighting the Afghan government forces, are bound to attack the foreigners in Afghanistan; Indian diplomats and the personnel working in Indian aid projects in Afghanistan would be high up on their hit list.

Since the Taliban have no fixed address, who will the Indian government take its complaints to in case of a terrorist attack on its nationals? Pakistan would deny any link with or responsibility for the terror strike. The Taliban, if at all they are approachable, would make impossible demands as they had done during the Kandahar episode. Whether India has devised an effective counter-strategy remains to be seen. Thus far the evidence is not encouraging and India's record of protecting its people and interests can hardly be termed reassuring enough.

In one form or another, the Great Game will go on. But will it be as exciting as before, or will the participation of the Taliban turn it into a blood sport rather than the exciting adventure that it once was? On the other hand, the ascension of the Taliban in Afghanistan might lead to its suspension. That is exactly what happened in the years following the defeat of the Soviet forces, and till 9/11. The Great Game had virtually ground to a halt because of America's disinterest, Soviet disengagement and other players' fear of the Taliban.

This acknowledgement of their supremacy had the effect of fuelling the Taliban's ambitions for more. Consequently, besides extending their hold over North Afghanistan, expansion in Central Asia through its terror network became the next major focus of the Taliban. That region's vast energy and mineral resources were the objectives and the majority Islamic population in those 'stans', a likely asset.

By turning northwards towards Central Asia, the Taliban had reversed the direction of the traditional Great Game. Earlier, reaching the warm waters of the Indian Ocean was the objective and rich India the ultimate prize. Now, the Taliban were seeking oil and gas of the Central Asian republics, and their population as converts to their cause. In the months preceding 9/11, the Central Asian republics were apprehensive whether they would be able to hold out for long. Tajikistan was fighting a bloody civil war against the Taliban-inspired forces and Uzbekistan was repeatedly being attacked by the Hizb ul Tehrir and the IMU (Islamic Movement of Uzbekistan) cadres.

The stern Taliban with their uniformly unwashed, identically clad and bearded look sparked fear and loathing. When they ruled Afghanistan, theirs was the law of the untamed jungle where only one word counted and that was theirs.

Then 9/11 happened.

To the extent of checking the Taliban, the US intervention in Afghanistan was welcome. But the Americans let the victory slip out of their grasp by supping with Pakistan. While the US was trying to figure out what went wrong with its policies in Afghanistan, another variation of the Great Game may have begun to unfold. It could be macabre, with multiple competitors and it could turn very vicious.

India would have reason to be very wary and very apprehensive.

24

Breakfast in Delhi, Lunch in Lahore

At the start of his long ten-year term in office as the prime minister of India, Manmohan Singh expressed a wish to have breakfast in Delhi, lunch in Lahore and dinner in Kabul. Besides the civil nuclear deal with its uncertain benefits, the principal foreign policy priority of Singh's ten-year term was the fulfilment of that culinary adventure. Sadly for him it could not materialize.

Given the gathering storm in Kabul, even the most adventurous do not opt to stay for dinner in Kabul. The US leaders, on a rare visit now, prefer the safety of their army compound north of Kabul if a scheduling issue forces them to spend a night in Afghanistan. Others have simply struck Kabul off their list of the must-visit capitals.

Manmohan Singh's preferred lunch destination, Lahore, isn't a killing field yet, but LeT chief Hafiz Saeed roams there freely, hurling challenges at the US and India. His vitriol inspires thousands, and his actions have led the US to declare a US$10 million bounty on him. Whether he would be an ideal lunch companion for a visiting Indian prime minister is open to doubt.

Experience indicates that India is overly tolerant of the despicable. Where else in the world would a foreign minister escort three dreaded terrorists to the safety of a Taliban sanctuary? Yet, despite knowing the consequences, India did precisely that in Kandahar. The country has paid the price ever since, suffering further acts of terror by Pakistan.

Besides being tolerant, India can masochistically ascribe to itself crimes that it never committed. Which other country would readily agree to be bracketed with Pakistan on terror? Yet India did that voluntarily in Sharm el Sheikh in Egypt when Manmohan Singh agreed to equate the happenings in Baluchistan with the terrorist attacks in India. This self-goal defied logic because in one stroke India had bracketed itself with Pakistan as a sponsor of terror. Obviously, this delighted Pakistan, giving it a handle to bad-mouth India internationally. Yet, in a statement in November 2013, the chief minister of Baluchistan clarified that there was not a shred of evidence to indicate that India was involved in any act of terror in Baluchistan.

This is not all; India has tripped repeatedly in other ways too. Were the multiple nuclear tests of 1998 really necessary? India had exploded a device in 1974, and though it did not belong formally to the elite club of nuclear haves, everyone knew that it had turned nuclear. Pakistan was suspected of possessing the capability, but no one wanted to let it come out of that purdah and get anywhere near the nuclear power status formally.

The fact of the matter was that though India was an interloper, it was a declared nuclear interloper. Pakistan was already the bad boy of the international community on multiple counts. If it crossed the nuclear red line as well, it risked being ostracized.

That was bad enough, but it could have been much worse had Pakistan tested a nuclear device all by itself. Economic sanctions were sure to have followed a nuclear test. This fear and the precarious state of its economy was the reason why it did not test a bomb. Surreptitiously, however, China had already facilitated a test on its territory to give Pakistan the confidence that its bomb worked.

Still, for all practical purposes, the world kept up the pretence that Pakistan did not have the bomb. This charade may not have been an effective check, but as long as it lasted, it kept Pakistan on the leash; it could not threaten others with the nuclear option because it pretended not to have one.

In the early 1980s, the situation began to ease for Pakistan because the US now needed it as an ally against the Soviets in Afghanistan. As an immediate reward for that cooperation, the US agreed to sell F-16 fighter jets to Pakistan. This was done despite the fact that these jets would become the most important air platform in Pakistan's air force. Not just that, the US also knew that F-16s were going to be the most likely delivery vehicles of a nuclear weapon.

But when the Soviets retreated from Afghanistan and the US interest in the region declined, there was yet another twist in the tale. Soon, the nuclear-proliferation-related sanctions (under the Pressler Amendment) came into force in 1990. The US government cancelled the sales of the F-16s which had already been paid for by Pakistan to the tune of US$486 million, and the fighter jets were kept parked in a disused airfield in the US.

The Pressler Amendment had banned most economic and military assistance to Pakistan unless the president certified on an annual basis that 'Pakistan does not possess a nuclear explosive device and that the proposed United States assistance program will reduce significantly the risk that Pakistan will possess a nuclear explosive device.' No president had issued this certification since October 1989 when President Bush determined that Pakistan had developed such a weapon.

But India's five nuclear tests on 11 and 13 May 1998 changed the picture radically. Ironically, India was the catalyst that set Pakistan free from fear. It was no longer the only bad boy in American eyes.

Soon after India's five tests, there was considerable pressure on Nawaz Sharif from Bill Clinton and Tony Blair not to test. Clinton made five telephone calls to dissuade him, and offered US$5 billion to Pakistan if it did not test. But there was counterpressure on Nawaz from within the country; people wanted the Nawaz government to respond to India. Benazir Bhutto had once quipped at a public rally, 'Nawaz is trying to put handcuffs on me. But I'm going to put bangles on him.'[1]

Moreover, this was the ideal opportunity for Pakistan to come out of the closet and declare to the world that it, too, was a nuclear power. India's tests gave Pakistan just the opening it was looking for.

Pakistan carried out five nuclear tests on 28 May 1998 and in an address to the nation Prime Minister Nawaz Sharif said, 'Today, we have settled scores with India.' Soon thereafter, on 30 May 1998, Pakistan was to do one better than India and explode a sixth bomb.

Eleven bombs going off, one after the other, within the space of a fortnight was scary stuff. Others from the nuclear club, the ones who were the original members, had tested one or two at a time, but this was unprecedented. To the horrified world this hyperactivity was a confirmation that the next war between the two nations could really go wild. Naturally, global condemnation followed. But the resentment did not last long. Pakistan was soon to emerge out of the doghouse, to become a most important non-NATO ally of the US. More importantly, its declared nuclear capability made it a power that could not easily be trifled with.

India had already tested a bomb in 1974; to that extent it need not have tested again to assert its nuclear power status. Critics of this decision maintain that India had shot itself in the foot by making

[1]Saba Imtiaz, 'Wikileaks on 1998 nuclear tests', *The Express Tribune*.

Pakistan cross the nuclear threshold publicly. The net result of nuclear bombs going off by the dozen was the alarming evidence that India's and Pakistan's nuclear weapons status would complicate, but not necessarily deter, future conflicts.

As far as India was concerned, one unintended result was the sobering thought that the other side had a declared nuclear capacity too. Earlier, if ignorance about Pakistan's bomb was a matter of some bliss, now the certainty of it had become dangerous knowledge. India would henceforth be constrained by it.

Kargil demonstrated that and Operation Parakram was proof of it.

25

Pakistani Politicians and the Army

It is suggested sometimes that Pakistani politicians do not have a say on vital strategic issues concerning India. It is also advocated that the army and the ISI drive the hardline agenda against India. The argument goes on to add that left on their own, politicians would be inclined to extend an olive branch to India—and that it is the army that is the spoiler. Nothing could be further from the truth; after all, it was Zulfikar Bhutto who drove the hardline agenda against India.

Moreover, an army cannot run an entire country all by itself. Even the most powerful dictator would need civilian aides to execute domestic and foreign policies. When politicians are in power in Pakistan, there are sufficient ways and means for them to be the main drivers of policy unless they begin to tread on the turf considered sacred by the army. The fact is that as far as the policy towards India is concerned the politicians are essentially in sync with the army; they practise policies that do not conflict with the grand plan of the army.

Some Pakistani politicians, when they are out of power, aver that given another chance they would change Indo-Pak relations for the better. They add grandly that peace alone can promote prosperity in the two countries. This is only natural because the worldview of politicians tends towards a benign sweep when they are out of power. But once in power they sing a different tune. The foreign ministry, the intelligence agencies and the pressures of politics combine to influence the leaders in the government, and to remould their views. It is not just in Pakistan that power brings a new dimension to responsibility. It happens in India too—but the difference is that at the core of Pakistan's neurotic view of India is a sense of insecurity about why India is a presence at all.

When he first came into power in 1990, Nawaz Sharif was told that the army exercised control over policies relating to Afghanistan, the Kashmir issue and the nuclear policy—all this was the army's turf. To reinforce that point Army Chief Mirza Aslam Beg met him, but his visit was also to convey the message that the army is always available to guide the civilian authority in deciding policy on difficult subjects!

On the Kashmir issue, however, there was no difference at all between Sharif and General Beg, or for that matter with President Ghulam Ishaq Khan. As scholar Shuja Nawaz writes in *Crossed Swords*:

> They saw the fight for Kashmir to be a jihad that was incumbent on Pakistanis and supported whatever trouble they could foment in Kashmir for India, even if it meant using the Islamic radicals from the North West Frontier region or the newly freed up fighters that waged the successful jihad against the Soviets in Afghanistan.

Sometimes, politicians stand their ground and the army concedes.

Benazir was liberal by temperament and her western education had made her more receptive in her relationship with the outside world. It is true that she was swayed by low-level intelligence gossip and it is also true that her husband's misdemeanours were largely the cause of her fall from office twice. But it is also a fact that on occasion she stood her ground against the army. This may have prevented the Kargil invasion at least once during her spell in office.

As she recounted to Shuja Nawaz in an interview:

> A Kargil-type operation was being discussed at a war game in Joint Staff Headquarters. Major General Pervez Musharraf, DGMO, was heading one side of this game. So then I put him through a series of questions, which I hadn't put to [General] Beg when on an earlier occasion a suggestion had been made to open the Kashmir front because that time… I didn't have the same confidence. But this time I had a little bit more confidence. So I said, 'Then what will happen, once you take Srinagar?' So he said, 'Then we will put the flag of Pakistan on the Assembly of Srinagar.' And I said, 'What will happen after you put the flag?' He said, 'Then you will go to United Nations and tell them we have taken Srinagar.' I said, 'Then what will happen when we tell them we have taken Srinagar?' He said, 'Then you will tell them change the geography of the map.' So I said, 'And then what will happen?' So then he stumbled, he said, '…What do you want me to say? What's happened, we've won.' So I said, 'No, General, if I say that they will tell "withdraw from Srinagar". Don't only withdraw from Srinagar, but withdraw from Azad Kashmir too. Because under the United Nations resolution

> first the plebiscite—we have to withdraw even from Azad Kashmir where the plebiscite has to be held.'[1]

Since then apologists for Musharraf have tried to explain it away by saying that it was only a war game, a theoretical classroom exercise that had nothing to do with reality. But that explanation doesn't stand the scrutiny of subsequent events. After all, Kargil happened when Musharraf was the army chief.

Some versions of the account from Musharraf's point of view have also emerged, putting him in less damaging light. But Musharraf has been known to economize on truth. At any rate Benazir's account would be a rare instance where a Pakistani leader has taken on an army general to caution him against a misadventure. Otherwise, the record says that from Jinnah right up to the present leadership, politicians rush forward to wish the army godspeed in any aggressive plan against India.

Yet another remarkable feature of this encounter was the reference by Benazir Bhutto to the UN resolution. It is even more remarkable that she acknowledged the fact that by the UN resolution, Pakistan had to withdraw from POK before a plebiscite could be held.

Indian formulations rarely point it out with this clarity. The fact is that Nehru had taken the reference to the UN under British pressure, and in an unnecessary stroke of idealism. He lamented, 'Why must two brothers quarrel?...if a vote had to be taken to ascertain the wishes of people then so be it. Let's have a plebiscite.' He held this view because of his confidence that the people of Jammu and Kashmir would vote overwhelmingly to remain with India. But in taking the matter idealistically to the UN, he had also implored the organization to ask Pakistan to first vacate its aggression regarding Kashmir. That was the basic prerequisite.

It was this background that Benazir was talking of when she quoted the UN Security Council resolution which seeks the vacation by Pakistan of POK before a plebiscite could be held. That resolution also mentions that the Indian administrative and security machinery would be stationed in the entire state of Jammu and Kashmir, including in the portion to be vacated by Pakistan.

Isn't it strange that India rarely recalls that prerequisite? Anyway, Benazir was soon replaced by Nawaz Sharif. Ironically, like Benazir's father in the case of Zia ul-Haq, Sharif, too, chose in his second term

---

[1]Shuja Nawaz, *Crossed Swords: Pakistan, its Army and the Wars Within.*

as prime minister to catapult Musharraf over many other deserving generals in the hope that as a Muhajir (groups that migrated to Pakistan from United Provinces and Bihar) he was less likely to be a coup-maker. As was the case with Zulfikar Bhutto, Nawaz too had misjudged the situation. And like Zulfikar, he was given the third degree by his chosen appointee. But unlike in the case of Benazir's father, the appeals of foreign powers worked for Sharif and he was spared the gallows. Later, he returned to become the prime minister for a record third term.

Before that, Sharif and Musharraf collaborated in an audacious adventure, the one that Benazir had shot down.

26

Kargil and the Attack on Parliament

When movie star Dev Anand and the prime minister of India, Atal Bihari Vajpayee crossed over from the Wagah border into Pakistan in February 1999, there was an expectant crowd waiting in welcome. From the way they rushed forward towards the prime ministerial bus, and mobbed the colourfully clad Dev Anand, it seemed at least for a moment that they had come to see the mega matinee star of the subcontinent.

Regardless of who they had come to see and greet, there is little doubt that the atmosphere was electric. Indians were glued to their television sets and the country was ecstatic. Euphoric TV anchors termed this unconventional bus ride across the border as historic, epochal and a game-changer. Indo-Pak relations would never be the same again, claimed banner headlines in newspapers the next morning. One called it: 'A moment that could given time, patience, statesmanship and a little bit of luck go down in history as an event comparable to Richard Nixon's flight to China and Anwar Sadat's embrace of Menachem Begin.' Even the otherwise sceptical strategic experts gushed that it was history in the making.

It certainly was history in the making, but of a dangerous variety. Why is it that we in India fail to recognize the signs when trouble is beginning to brew? It is not every day that an Indian prime minister visits Pakistan, yet Army Chief Musharraf decided not to turn up at any function marking Vajpayee's visit. Close to the bus, Nawaz Sharif was looking distinctly uncomfortable as he bent forward to embrace Vajpayee.

Sharif had reason to look sheepish because Pakistani soldiers were already occupying the heights in Kargil. The Pakistani army's Operation Badr had been put in place earlier that month to take over the posts that the Indian army routinely vacated in the winter months. By March–April, the Pakistani soldiers had consolidated their hold by building concrete bunkers in areas that were as far as 9–10 kilometres inside Indian territory. Altogether, Pakistani soldiers were in occupation of 140 Indian bunkers. In a later admission, Musharraf also claimed that he had spent a night deep inside Indian territory in one of the bunkers occupied by Pakistan.

There is no reason to doubt that claim. But what is astounding is the fact that neither in 1999, nor for nearly thirteen years thereafter, did India have any inkling about the fact that the army chief of Pakistan had spent a night 9–10 kilometres deep inside Indian territory.

It is all the more worrying because this is not the first time India has been caught unawares. In the 1950s, China had built a road in the Aksai Chin region without India knowing about it for at least two years. In Musharraf's case, it is an even greater cause for concern because it happened on an active and theoretically heavily patrolled border.

Musharraf wouldn't have just walked over one night into a bunker situated at a height of 12,000 feet or even more because some of the bunkers were located in mountains as high as 18,000 feet. The Pakistani army would have taken all possible precautions to ensure that their chief wasn't discovered in the Indian territory. They would have undertaken at least a few reconnaissance trips at the colonel and brigadier level to ensure that there was no chance of discovery by the Indians. Moreover, Musharraf may have spent more than one night inside Indian territory because he might have halted en route for high-altitude acclimatization.

Yet, despite all the hectic activity that must have gone on for many days, the Indian security authorities remained unaware of the lurking danger. In fact it was only in May 1999 that the Indian army raised an alarm when it was tipped off by two shepherds about the Pakistani presence.

There is also the riddle of what and how much Nawaz Sharif knew of the operation and at what stage. Shuja Nawaz writes in his book *Crossed Swords*:

> It was at the 17 May [1999] briefing [at ISI Headquarters for PM Nawaz Sharif] that General Ziauddin of the ISI recalls a discussion of the Kashmir operations in general and Kargil in particular… The briefing map indicated the location of the 108 bunkers that Pakistan had occupied or constructed… At the end of the briefing, there was a suggestion…for a 'dua' or prayer for the success of the venture.
>
> …Zia [General] recalls Nawaz Sharif saying, 'This is a military operation. All I can say is that…there should be no withdrawal, no

> surrender of any post because that will greatly embarrass us.' He [Sharif] asked if we could hold on. Both [Generals Aziz Khan and Mahmud Ahmed] said they could. In assessing the Indian reaction, they talked about the possibility of attacks across the international boundary, but also thought that Indians would be unable to counter-attack in force...surprisingly for him [Sharif] he actually asked questions... [General] Zia also states that Mahmud used to take maps to the PM house to brief him as posts fell... According to [General] Zia, the Prime Minister had the authority to order a halt to the operation at any point if he had serious doubts. But he did not.

There is enough here to confirm that Nawaz Sharif knew about the Kargil operation, the knowledge of which he has denied consistently. Moreover, the fact that as prime minister he could have called a halt to the operation, but did not, is also significant. It is also an important indicator that the civilian authority in Pakistan (the prime minister in this case) is not as helpless in controlling the army, as it is sometimes made out to be.

The discussions of 17 May at the ISI headquarters also convey a message as far as their assessment of Indian capabilities is concerned. The fact that the ISI could work on the construction/repair of bunkers deep in Indian territory, and that neither the noise of the equipment and tools nor the activity of men attracted the attention of Indians is a comment by itself.

Pakistanis weren't flawless either. Their confident assessment that 'Indians would be unable to counter-attack in full force' proved to be way off the mark. Yet, the Kargil operation was brilliant tactically and Musharraf almost pulled it off. This range of snow-covered mountain peaks is vital strategically because it overlooks the valley below and controls the access to the Siachin glacier. The Pakistani control of Kargil would have given its army a trump card over the Kashmir valley too.

Militarily, Musharraf had chosen well. But as usual he had not thought it through, and that proved to be disastrous for him and his army. It was also India's good fortune that having crossed the LOC, Pakistan's luck ran out. Its civil and military leadership developed cold feet and did not follow it through with aerial attacks. Had they done so, they would have found masses of exposed Indian artillery guns and army men in the open grounds below the high hills. A single successful sortie by Pakistani planes would have done immense damage.

Should India have been surprised by Kargil? As a matter of fact it should have anticipated it. The history of Pakistani adventurism pointed in this direction, that sooner or later Pakistan would want to do something that had brought it close to success earlier.

In 1947–48 it had managed to grab nearly one-third of the territory of Jammu and Kashmir and its forces had almost reached Srinagar airport. The Pakistanis were close to that airport again in 1965. Moreover, its infiltration and terror activities in Kashmir over the last thirty years have consistently raised unsettling questions about Pakistan's capacity for dangerous ventures. There are also reasons to doubt its ability to subordinate its loathing of India to the more rational demands imposed by the nuclearization of the subcontinent. Despite all these warning signs, India was not prepared for a Kargil-like adventure.

But nor was Pakistan prepared for India's swift and strong response thereafter. That, combined with transparent and full coverage of the Kargil war by the Indian media, brought the reality of it not only to the Indian people but to Pakistanis and the larger world as well. Moreover, some deft diplomacy brought in Clinton's intervention, and worldwide opprobrium on Pakistan.

Isolated diplomatically and on the verge of a military defeat, Nawaz Sharif rushed in panic to Washington. On 4 July 1999 Clinton took time off from the US National Day celebrations to get Sharif's word that he was ready to withdraw his troops and end the conflict. The joint statement issued that day by Clinton and Sharif is significant for the fact that it upheld the sanctity of the LoC and reiterated twice in that short statement the centrality of the Simla agreement.

Did the solemn promises made by the prime minister of Pakistan, with the concurrence of his army chief, have a lasting effect? It seems unlikely; it may at best have had a temporary effect.

The Nawaz–Clinton joint statement is seldom recalled by Pakistan, and it is unlikely that the three-month-long conflict (mid-May to the third week of July 1999) will be the last of its type. Did the international condemnation sober the Pakistani army sufficiently to make it swear off adventure in future?

As Shuja Nawaz writes:

> There was a broader Kashmir plan at work that had been presented and discussed by the army chief with the Prime Minister and his key aides in early 1999, although interestingly, even after all the subsequent public spats about who said what to whom and when, not one of the participants will talk about that aspect of discussions... One aspect of this plan may have been the use of reinforcements

> from Afghanistan. Mullah Mohd. Rabbani, the Afghan President... was asked by Pakistan to provide 20–30000 volunteers for the Kashmiri jihad. He startled the Pakistanis by offering 500,000.

That was then. The next time, and there is certain to be a next time somewhere along the LOC, the Pakistani attack is likely to be preceded by large-scale infiltration into Kashmir. Perhaps, at long last even the Chinese may chip in. That two-front war is the cause of many nightmares in the Indian military mind.

*

Operation Parakram was to have been a swift military strike on Pakistan for its nefarious sponsorship of an attack on the Indian Parliament, and its leadership, on 13 December 2001. Five terrorists belonging to the LeT drove a car that afternoon into Parliament House in central Delhi. The vice-president of India, the home minister and a large number of MPs were in Parliament, though the session itself had broken for lunch recess. The terrorists came very close to getting inside the main chamber and causing huge mayhem. But in the exchange of fire with security personnel all five terrorists were killed.

India reacted to this attack on its sovereignty with deadly seriousness. Pakistani officials were quick to reject out of hand New Delhi's accusations that the attacking militants were Pakistani nationals or aided by Pakistan's military and intelligence services. Islamabad charged New Delhi with trumping up an incident to malign Pakistan and pressed for a joint investigation to establish the identity of the terrorists. This suggestion was dismissed by India.

As India mobilized forces, Pakistan responded in kind. By January 2002, India had mobilized around 500,000 troops and three armoured divisions on the Pakistani border and along the LOC in Kashmir. Pakistan responded similarly, deploying around 300,000 troops in that region.

It was a strange mobilization. All the previous wars between India and Pakistan had an element of surprise. For the first time, it threatened to be an announced one. But when the army chief sought the objectives of Operation Parakram from Prime Minister Vajpayee, he closed his eyes, and after some time opened them and said, '*Woh baad me battayenge* (will tell you later).'[1]

---

[1]A.G. Noorani, 'Vajpayee's Foreign Policy', *Frontline*.

The Indian army chief, General S. Padmanabhan announced to the media on 11 January 2002 that the mobilization for war was complete and the armed forces were waiting for the political nod. On 12 January 2002, Pakistani President Pervez Musharraf gave a speech intended to reduce tensions with India. He declared that Pakistan would combat extremism on its own soil, but he also added that Pakistan had a right to Kashmir. Still, this was good enough for the Indian leadership. In response, the Indian prime minister told his generals that there would be no attack 'for now'. But the troops remained lined up on the border, exposing their military build-up to the Pakistani view.

The situation remained in this state of limbo for another four months. Then, tensions escalated again. On 14 May 2002 three terrorists crossed over from Pakistan and attacked the family quarters of an Indian army garrison at Kaluchak near Jammu. Before they could be hunted and shot down, they managed to kill thirty-one people. Among those killed were three army personnel, eighteen army family members and ten civilians. There were forty-seven wounded, including twelve army personnel, twenty army family members and fifteen civilians. The dead included ten children.

Following this provocation, all military leave was cancelled. On 22 May, Prime Minister Vajpayee visited the front lines in Jammu, near where the attacks had occurred. There he delivered a chilling message to the troops that the time had come for a decisive battle (*aar paar ki ladai*). He added confidently, 'We will have a sure victory in this battle.' Then, oddly, Vajpayee left on 24 May for a five-day rest in the mountain resort of Manali.

For senior White House officials and the State Department's '7th floor', the 13 December terrorist attack on India's Parliament marked the start of an 'additional crisis'. Under ordinary circumstances, the attack would have been the dominant concern of the administration. But 9/11 had occurred a mere three months earlier, and it was the principal preoccupation of the US. For America that was the 'main fight' and Pakistan had a central role in the help that the US thought it needed in its Afghan mission.

Moreover, this was the time when the US was zeroing in on Osama in Tora-Bora, and it felt that here, too, Pakistan could play a critical role in its support. Thus, for many Washington policymakers, the 13 December attack and the subsequent Indian and Pakistani military deployments were serious but unwelcome diversions from the war on terror. The diplomatic challenge facing Washington was to play for time and eventually to 'tell the generals [Indian and Pakistani] that their best service was...to pull back'.

The longer the Indian army was deployed in the field, the more unwise the deployment seemed, harming morale and training. In fact, as one senior US official recalled, 'after a while, the generals were ready to go home' if they were not going to be given orders to fight.

The options considered in the US strategy sessions on India–Pakistan tended to be fairly narrow. The principal reason was the unpredictability of the Pakistani generals and the continuing Western belief that, for one assumed reason or the other, the West needed Pakistan. Driven by that sense of dependence, the only viable proposal they could zero in was for joint monitoring by the US and the UK of militant camps operating in Pakistan. But even this failed to catch on as US officials worried that disbanded camps would simply be reconstituted elsewhere. This realization was further evidence, if one was needed, of the severe limits of Western influence on Pakistani generals.

The best strategy under the circumstances became the game of attrition, to tire the Indians into boredom. The feeling was that if they continue to stare into the distant horizon, instead of into their gun-sights, they were bound to blink. So, the US and others began to 'choreograph' a stream of senior official visits to the region from Washington, London, the European Union, Tokyo and Beijing, in order to keep the two sides 'talking and thinking' about peace.

The strategy worked—not a shot was fired. Frustrated, and having run out of options, India decided on 16 October 2002 to pull back troops from the western frontier after keeping them in fighting formation for ten months.

Fortunately for the Indian leadership of the time, it escaped the critical examination, and the censure that was otherwise its due. The principal reason why it got away with doing nothing was the esteem that Vajpayee was held in. It was not the policy of the government, but the personality of the prime minister that saved the leadership from the sharp questions that should have been asked. Why did the government commit the country to an exercise that was doomed from the beginning; the Indian strike corps took far too much time to mobilize to a battle-ready position, and the stalemate at Kargil was a recent memory. Could India have cracked the Pakistani resistance this time over an entire border?

By the time Operation Parakram was called off, it had long become counterproductive. Musharraf's personal stature had risen in Pakistan for posing a dare to India's military mobilization. And in that ten-month standoff, the US had become more than a mere facilitator between India and Pakistan.

Commenting on it, defence analyst Praveen Swami writes:

> It marks an end to arguably the most ill-conceived manoeuvre in Indian military history. Intended to signal India's willingness to go to war, if Pakistan continued to aid cross-border terrorism, Operation Parakram ended as an ignominious retreat after having failed to secure even its minimum objectives. But the worst may be yet to come. Pakistan has called India's cards, and discovered that its much-hyped hand contains no aces.[2]

Others were equally scathing. According to another defence expert, Brigadier Gurmeet Kanwal:

> ...the most important lesson emerging from the standoff was the inordinately long time that strike corps needed to mobilise for war. By the time these elite formations were ready to deliver a massive punch, the international community had prevailed upon India to give General Musharraf an opportunity to prove his sincerity in curbing cross-border terrorism. These strike corps are designed to penetrate deep into Pakistan and run the risk of crossing Pakistan's nuclear threshold early during an offensive.[3]

Former air chief A.Y. Tipnis said, 'Inaction is damaging our credibility; people have begun to believe India incapable of taking any action.'[4]

Strategic affairs specialist Brahma Chellaney, lamented:

> The harsh truth is that the government played a game of bluff not just with Pakistan but also with its own military... When a nation enjoys credibility, it can usually achieve its objectives with a mere threat to use force. However, when there are serious credibility problems, even modest objectives are difficult to accomplish. Vajpayee ended up practising coercive non-diplomacy.[5]

Former navy chief, Sushil Kumar, too, was blunt in his judgement: 'There was no aim or military objective for the Operation Parakram... I don't mind admitting that Operation Parakram was the most punishing mistake for the Indian Armed Forces.'[6]

In statistical terms the ten-month long standoff cost India about US$2 billion and the lives of over 1500 soldiers to mine explosions,

---

[2]Praveen Swami, 'Beating the retreat', *Frontline*.

[3]Gurmeet Kanwal, 'Lost opportunities', Centre for Land Warfare Studies, (CLAWS).

[4]B.N. Bhatia, 'Army as an instrument of national power', *Tribune*.

[5]Gurmeet Kanwal, 'Lost opportunities', Centre for Land Warfare Studies, (CLAWS).

[6]News report, Rediff.

ammunition mishandling and the sheer heat of the desert in summer. In contrast, the loss of lives during the Kargil conflict was only around 550. There were some less publicized losses as well. At the very start of Operation Parakram, two major ammunition dumps were blown up in a suspected act of sabotage. Were they the work of Pakistani agents? How much was the damage? Were preventive steps taken to ensure that there was no next time? These questions may have been asked. But if any answers were found they remain outside the public domain, and even that of Parliament for which the entire Operation Parakram had been launched.

The US succeeded in its mission of and tapering Indian anger. The delay took away the surprise element and the long-lasting line-up of the Indian army and the equipment on the border was an unnecessary exposure to Pakistan of India's military and tactical plans. Along the way there were whimsical decisions galore.

One instance must be cited. Prior to the start of the 1971 hostilities, India had banned overflights between the western and eastern wings of the then Pakistan. The objective was to severely cramp Pakistan's ability to send across troops and military equipment to the then East Pakistan. This was a sound policy move and it had the desired effect. Pakistan was forced to take the time-consuming sea route and the longer air detour via Sri Lanka. It stretched and severely curtailed its logistical abilities, which was the intention of India's decision to ban overflights.

Thirty years later, in a slavish replication of that move, India decided to ban overflights during Operation Parakram between what had now become Bangladesh and Pakistan. This was a bizarre move, with no tangible benefit for India. There was hardly any air traffic between Bangladesh and Pakistan, and none of any strategic nature that could affect Pakistan in any material way.

In a quick countermove Pakistan banned all overfights over its air space by aircraft flying from and to India. This began to hurt India immediately by adding to flying time. All aircraft flying to and from India in the westerly direction had to negotiate a path away from Pakistani airspace; besides the inconvenience of it, there was also the issue of additional fuel cost.

It was decisions such as this which made people wonder whether India had gained anything at all from the so-called Operation Parakram. It is also often said that the only imaginary shot that may have been fired during the ten-month period by half a million Indian troops was the one that went through India's foot.

Because of 9/11, the US had merely made sympathetic noises in the beginning. It was only when 800,000 men stood poised at the border, hand on trigger, that the earlier mild concern of the US turned into alarm. Had these tensions escalated into a war, it could have become the first nuclear war of the millennium. That was precisely the reason why the US was so keen to manage the Indian rage.

Is it possible that in a similar face-to-face confrontation between the two armies one day, the US reaction might come too late, or that its cajoling might not work?

The fundamental issue, however, is one of self-esteem. The international community conducts the business of diplomacy in a transactional form; every time a favour is sought, the other side expects a bigger one in return. Moreover, it is also a remarkable turn in values for a country which had once prided itself on self-reliance and now has the pretensions of a big power. In that league, big boys don't rush to others for help.

Let's pose the question in a different manner: what if Pakistan was the injured party? Let's assume its National Assembly had been attacked by a group of Indians, and let us also assume that a further attack by another batch from India had taken place on one of its military cantonments, resulting in the death of soldiers and their family members. Would the Pakistani generals have played the game of 'patience' with their troops, letting them fall to the ground out of sheer boredom? Or would they have fired first to avenge their and their nation's honour? It is more than likely that they would have fired first to take full advantage of the element of surprise. Then, and only then, would the Pakistani generals have responded to the international calls for patience.

The other question is the efficacy of the culinary quest. Do lunches in Lahore work? Manmohan Singh may have missed his meal in Lahore, but Vajpayee was feasted there in 1999. The Kargil war, the Kandahar hijacking, the attack on Parliament and Operation Parakram followed that feast in Lahore in quick succession. Were all these a mere coincidence? Or is it a sign that the quest should be for substance rather than form in so prickly a relationship? There, the memories of betrayals and multiple prejudices set us apart.

27

Article 370

The issue that often agitates the Indian people is this: why doesn't India assert itself? Why is it always on the defensive? Is the Indian leadership out of synchronization with the mood of the nation? Let's qualify that question and ask whether Indian leaders, after Indira Gandhi, have for some reason decided that peace must be pursued, whatever the cost. There seems to be reasonable ground for reaching this conclusion, considering the fact that the provocations from the Pakistani side have been many and continuous.

Sometimes, it seems that we are keen to clutch at the imaginary straws that they dangle; that terror is the work of non-state actors and that official Pakistan has nothing to do with it. We fall for that line because we find it convenient to be deceived.

I still recall vividly the summer afternoon of 14 July 1993 in Karachi. It was the French National Day and the reception was being held in the chancery premises. I had just walked into the splendid garden, when an eminent former judge of the Pakistani Supreme Court shook my hand and said quickly, but sotto voce, 'The blasts in Bombay were done with the approval of Prime Minister Nawaz Sharif.'

'How do you know?' I asked, stunned.

'A sitting judge of the Supreme Court, who should know, told me.'

I had no reason to doubt a man of his eminence. He had a sterling reputation in Pakistan and it was out of the question that such a man might make a comment on the basis of half-baked information. His anguish was genuine, and he seemed visibly concerned that the terror attacks had taken place, resulting in so many deaths. As a judge, he seemed to have been morally outraged that they should have been sanctioned at the highest level.

It isn't as if the Indian establishment is not aware of such complicity at the highest levels in Pakistan. But successive Indian leaders have stopped reacting to provocation, resulting in criticism that they follow a policy of appeasement.

India does not even register the proforma protest any more on some vital issues, as was the norm once. For example, it doesn't register a protest any longer like it used to against the cessation of 5180 square kilometres of territory in POK by Pakistan to China. The despatch of such diplomatic protest notes was a regular practice in the 1960s and 1970s.

Or, for that matter why is the Indian government diffident on the issue of Kashmir. Kashmir did not come into being in 1947, yet by letting the Pakistani narrative link the two intrinsically we have allowed this impression to befog all logic.

Etymologically, 'Kashmir' is derived from 'ka' (water) and 'shimeera' (desiccate). Twelfth-century author Kalhana mentions in his definitive book on Kashmir's history, *Rajatarangini,* that as the two words suggest the Kashmir valley was once a lake. The local legend gives further credence to this claim by adding that the lake was drained by the great Rishi Kashyap (hence another etymological connection to the name Kashmir). It was in this drained land that Kashyap settled high-caste Brahmins. These and other accounts testify to the ancient link of many millennia between Kashmir and the rest of the country.

Yet, some insist on making the claim that Article 370 is the only link between Kashmir and the rest of the country, and that with the abolition of that article the link between the 'state' and the 'union' would be ruptured. That such an assertion should be aired indicates how easy it is to get away with the outrageous when people do not pay attention to the facts of the case.

Let us therefore start chronologically. Article 370 came into being as a part of the Constitution adopted by India on 26 November 1949. As a matter of record it should be added that Dr B.R. Ambedkar, the principal architect of the Indian Constitution and the law minister then, had refused to be associated with the drafting of this article. It was then that Nehru entrusted the job to Gopalaswami Ayyangar who in close consultation with Sheikh Abdullah drafted this article.

Among many reasons for its introduction, some point to Sheikh Abdullah's determination to rid Jammu and Kashmir of the maharaja's rule. Others refer to Nehru's idealistic belief that India had nothing to fear from a plebiscite. To keep the Indian side of the agreement, this article gave a special status, but temporarily, to the state.

Since then, the passage of time has obscured the real intent. Over time, politics, passion and Pakistan's interference have led to a stage where any discussion on the issue is fraught with volatile consequences.

This was not always so.

The Constitution makers were clear that it was a 'temporary article', and it was stated as so right in the beginning of this provision. They were also unambiguous in giving full powers to Parliament via Articles 1 to 4 of the Constitution—to admit/establish new states and to alter their names/areas and boundaries. Jammu and Kashmir is one of the states included in the list of twenty-nine states mentioned in Article 1.

The Constitution makers were also clear that scope should be given to the Constituent Assembly of Jammu and Kashmir to consider aspects of Article 370. That's why item 3 of this article mentioned:

> Notwithstanding anything in the foregoing provisions of the article, the President may, by public notification, declare that this article shall cease to be operative or shall be operative only with such exceptions and modifications and from such date as he may notify: Provided that the recommendation of the Constituent Assembly of the State referred to in clause (2) shall be necessary before the President issues such a notification.

Sadly, this provision has since been misinterpreted to mean that the president's powers are limited, and that every time there has to be an amendment it should be approved by the Constituent Assembly of Jammu and Kashmir. Is this logical? Could the framers of the Indian Constitution have included a provision that involved a virtual succession of Constituent Assemblies in Jammu and Kashmir?

That was neither the intention of the Indian Constitution makers nor indeed the interpretation by the Jammu and Kashmir Constituent Assembly. Their intent was logical and transparent. Since a Constituent Assembly of Jammu and Kashmir was to be convened after the framing of the Constitution of India (which included Article 370), let it convey its views on any issue covered by it. More importantly, it should also convey the will and the verdict of the people of Jammu and Kashmir as Nehru had wished. This is precisely what the Jammu and Kashmir Constituent Assembly did following its deliberations from 5 November 1951 to 17 November 1956. The Preamble to the Constitution adopted by it declares:

> We the people of the State of J&K, having solemnly resolved, in pursuance of the accession of the State to India which took place on

> the twenty sixth day of October 1947, to further define the existing relationship of the State with the Union of India as an integral part thereof...

As if to reinforce the point further, it mentions in Part ii, para 3 of the Constitution: 'The State of J&K is and shall be an integral part of the Union of India.' If this is not a categorical expression of the will of the people and their decision to merge with the Union, what else is it?

Moreover, the same Constitution gave the powers to the Union to appoint the governor and the high court judges and the power to conduct elections and to finalize the electoral rolls. All this was far beyond the scope of Article 370.

Since then, Article 370 has been amended and modified repeatedly. For instance, ninety-four of the ninety-seven entries in the Union List[1] and twenty-six of the forty-seven entries in the Concurrent List have been extended to Jammu and Kashmir over the years. Moreover, 260 of the 395 articles of the Indian Constitution have been extended to Jammu and Kashmir; besides there are presidential orders which have eroded the original substance of the article.

Home Minister Gulzarilal Nanda told the Lok Sabha on 27 November 1963:

> Article 370 of the Constitution occurs in Part XXI of the Constitution which deals with temporary and transitional provisions. Since this Article was incorporated in the Constitution, many changes have been made which bring the State of Jammu and Kashmir in line with the rest of India. The State is fully integrated to the Union of India. Government are of opinion that they should not take any initiative now for the complete repeal of article 370. This will no doubt be brought about by further changes in consultation with the Government and the Legislative Assembly of Jammu and Kashmir State. This process has continued in the last few years and may be allowed to continue in the same way.[2]

Prime Minister Nehru also confirmed this position to the Indian Parliament in that session.

Once again, in 1969, the law minister introduced in the Lok Sabha a bill entitled the Central Labour Laws (Extension to Jammu and Kashmir) Bill, 1969 to extend the application of a large number of labour enactments of the Government of India to Jammu and Kashmir. While introducing the bill, the law minister said:

---

[1]Dileep Padgaonkar, 'Open the Pandora's box at your own peril', *Outlook*.

[2]Behram Contractor (Busybee), *Uday India*, and the Lok Sabha Debates Archives.

> ...it is the attempt of the Government to see that the special position of Jammu and Kashmir State as mentioned in article 370 of the Constitution is eroded little by little and in course of time it will be entirely corroded, resulting in Jammu and Kashmir having the same status as other States.[3]

To give another example, on 30 July 1986, the president made an order under Article 370, extending to Kashmir Article 249 of the Constitution in order to empower Parliament to legislate even on a matter in the State List on the strength of a Rajya Sabha resolution. 'Concurrence' to this was given by Governor Jagmohan.

Article 370 is discriminatory against the spirit of democracy in as much as it bars citizens from other parts of India from settling in Jammu and Kashmir. It also runs counter to the strategy followed by Pakistan in the part of Kashmir it had occupied (POK).

Unlike India, Pakistan acted quickly after annexing POK to change the demographic complexion of that region. A large number of Punjabis were settled there by Pakistan to ensure that the result of any plebiscite there went its way. In an almost parallel operation post-1947–48, the indigenous population of POK was encouraged to migrate out of Pakistan. Besides swinging the demographic balance in the direction it wanted, the physical presence of so many Mirpuri Kashmiris (from the Mirpur district of Kashmir) on British soil was a constant reminder of the Pakistani plaint against India. As a result, 70 per cent of the Pakistanis living in the UK are from POK.

Other countries follow a similar practice of swiftly changing the population mix. Thus, after the First World War, when South Tyrol was awarded to Italy, Benito Mussolini lost no time in changing the demographic complexion of the region by settling the toughies from Sicily and Naples in South Tyrol till they outnumbered the local population by 51 per cent to 49 per cent. China carried out a similar exercise in Tibet and Xinjiang. The US simply wiped out the indigenous Native Indian population, and colonial Spanish changed the progeny in Latin America. Israel has walled out the Palestinians. Ethnic cleansing, as a tool, was used most ruthlessly to change the demographic mix of Pakistan in the months preceding the partition. Pakistan also has the unique distinction of being a rare country in the world where the demographic profile of its minorities has been in a steady decline ever since the partition. All this is an assertion of the same basic theme—by changing the population mix and presenting a fait accompli it is possible to win more than half of the argument.

---

[3]Lok Sabha Debates Archives.

In sharp contrast, half a million Kashmiri Pandits have been driven out of the Kashmir valley. For years, they have been living in miserable conditions in makeshift refugee camps. Their condition, and that injustice, hardly causes human rights activists to lose sleep. India has compounded the problem by denying its population the right of settlement in Jammu and Kashmir, thereby weakening its case. The fact of this denial makes the foreigner wonder why this is so.

Sometimes, it seems that India follows its laissez-faire policy a bit too far. Thus, it allows visiting Pakistani leaders to meet the leaders of the militant Hurriyat organization. Mostly, they do so even before they begin the official meetings in New Delhi. Besides the questionable propriety of it, there is also the issue that every such meeting of Pakistani leaders with the Kashmiri separatists constitutes interference in the internal affairs of India. Moreover, the fact that such meetings take place on Indian soil with Indian acquiescence is a further point in Pakistan's argument that it has a role in the issue.

On the other hand, the question can legitimately be asked about whether the Pakistani government would permit any visiting Indian minister to meet Baluchi separatists or Muhajir leaders in Islamabad. As a matter of fact it has never happened in the last six decades. And if some Pakistani separatist were to dare make such an attempt, the chances are he would either end up dead the next day or languish in prison for years thereafter.

That apart, the effect of each such meeting between Pakistani leaders and Kashmiri separatists in Delhi is this: if the Indian government does not object to such meetings right under their nose, what is to stop ISI operatives from meeting them and planning out destructive operations in other venues? As it is, Pakistan's declared moral, political and financial support to the Kashmiri separatists is an encouraging shot in the arm to the campaign of violence in Jammu and Kashmir.

Suppose, for a moment, that the entire state of Jammu and Kashmir was gifted one day to Pakistan, would it then follow that a satiated Pakistan will stop sponsoring terror and not covet any more of the Indian territory? The answer to this must be a firm no. Rather, it will only encourage Pakistan to greater aggression; if it has succeeded once, why not try and get some more? Besides, what is the basis of Pakistan's claim to Kashmir besides a very tenuous religious one? That, anyway, is a deeply flawed argument; the fact is that there are more Muslims today in India than in Pakistan. Moreover, some day the question can be asked about the very legitimacy of Pakistan since it was carved out whimsically by the prejudiced British.

Still, Pakistan has followed a systematic plan in pursuit of its objective to obtain Kashmir. The plan covers interference, terror, financing and propaganda too. Domestically, to excite passions, it terms Kashmir as Pakistan's *shah rag* (the jugular vein). Bilaterally with India, it tables the issue as the unfinished agenda of the partition. The sheer intensity of its propaganda blocks out the occasional appeal for reason by India. Its international campaign has taken multiple forms. To the world it projects Kashmir as its right denied and as the core issue that bedevils the relationship between the two neighbours.

28

'Cutting India Down to Size'

One of the more prominent propaganda efforts was run by Syed Ghulam Nabi Fai. He founded the Kashmiri American Council (KAC), with ISI funding in 1990. It wasn't a mere coincidence that Pakistan-supported insurgency in Jammu and Kashmir should have started around the same time. According to the FBI, the Kashmiri American Council would arrange seminars, conferences and lectures on Kashmir and the funding for these activities came from the ISI.

Ultimately, Fai was arrested by the FBI on 19 July 2011 for concealing the transfer of US$3.5 million from Pakistan's ISI to fund his illegal lobbying efforts and to influence the US government on the Kashmir conflict. In March 2012, Fai was sentenced to two years of imprisonment by a US court for 'conspiracy to defraud the US' by concealing the transfer of funding from Pakistan's ISI for his illegal lobbying efforts on Kashmir.

Besides influencing parliamentarians in the West and utilizing every Islamic forum to denigrate India, Pakistan exploits NGOs and bodies like Amnesty International for its purposes.

India went through a harrowing time in the 1980s and early 1990s when year after year it was hauled up at the United Nations Human Rights Council (UNHRC) meetings in Geneva over the alleged human rights abuses in Punjab and Jammu and Kashmir. Often, the basis of this was the reports of human rights abuses brought out by NGOs. Amnesty International was in the forefront of this campaign against India.

Amnesty's was a formidable name then; it was the acknowledged high priest of human rights worldwide. But invariably the focus of its reports was on the developing countries and the Eastern Bloc. Within the developing world, however, there were some notable exceptions; for instance, Amnesty rarely ever found fault with the state of affairs in the Arab nations. Pakistan, too, got off lightly despite frequent news reports of the human rights abuses against the Baluchis, the Muhajirs and the minorities.

All this largely escaped Amnesty's critical eye. India, however, was a convenient target for periodic whipping. Amnesty's reports damning India used to appear before every human rights meeting as if on cue. Pakistan would get into the act quickly to give the matter widest possible publicity. Its diplomatic missions circulated the reports worldwide. Pro-Pakistan or Pakistan-sponsored groups would then hold demonstrations against India in the UK and other European countries. Usually, Amnesty International issued its India-focused reports in September, in the weeks preceding the human rights council's meeting.

I recall one notable incident. One sunny morning in September 1994 in London, when I was scanning the mail on my desk in the Indian High Commission, a brochure caught my eye. Its cover had a picture with the caption: 'Kashmiri woman in mourning'. The story inside was titled sensationally, 'Kashmir: Where India has turned Heaven into Hell'. It was an Amnesty International publication which proclaimed proudly that this special investigative issue on human rights abuses in Kashmir was based on the testimony of the Kashmiri widow shown in the picture. The report was strident enough to make a convincing case for India-bashing in Geneva.

Yet something about the picture bothered me. The widow shown in it looked far too dark of complexion to be from Kashmir. I double-checked with my colleagues, and then with some Indian journalists. Their verdict too was the same: this woman, they all said, is not from Kashmir. Quite clearly, it was a forgery and I would have liked to confront Amnesty immediately, but as it was an international holy cow then, I wanted a solid proof of its lie.

The next step, therefore, was to look for the photographer, identified as 'Kash'.[1] We found out that he was a freelancer who worked on a commission basis with Amnesty. Being a practical man who visited India often, he admitted readily to my colleagues that he had taken that photograph in Kerala. He had used a local model to bow like a mourner at an old grave. He said he had not hidden that fact from Amnesty International when he showed them the portfolio of his photographs from this latest trip to India. But for reasons of its visual appeal they chose the photograph he had taken in Kerala for their brochure on Kashmir. After this admission, Indian journalists based

---

[1]Vijay Dutt, *Times by the Thames: An Indian Cruise*.

in London interviewed him and got his confession that the photo was a forgery and that the accompanying report inside the brochure by Amnesty International was largely a fabrication.

This was sufficient for me to challenge Amnesty International. Initially, Amnesty reacted venomously. Their luminaries and I engaged in almost daily debates in the electronic media in the UK. At first, they were vehement in their denial, but given the enormity of proof against them their confidence began to slip.

A major blow for Amnesty came through a young British–African journalist who was working for the *Telegraph*. The article that he wrote was in the finest tradition of investigative journalism. A number of other articles followed in the British and Indian press. Each new day brought another blow for Amnesty till finally in a rare act, it issued a formal apology owning up to the forgery in the photograph.

But there were questions in my mind. Why was Amnesty International obsessed with India? Why were its reports timed to come out just before a major human rights conference?

Eventually, the picture that emerged was simple in conception but highly effective. It turned out that a large number of Amnesty's members in the UK, and in other parts of Europe, were people of Pakistani origin. The membership fee at about seven pounds was low enough to be affordable by almost everyone and for those who could not pay seven pounds, there was always the ever-resourceful ISI. Consequently, Pakistanis formed the single largest group of Amnesty's membership.

This piece of information came as a huge surprise to us as British Pakistanis are not known to be particularly vocal on human rights issues. Nor do they generally show interest in the worrisome human rights conditions of Pakistan. So, how was it that such a huge number of them should want to be members of Amnesty International? The only explanation for this was that it was a sponsored drive for a so-called national cause.

Every year on cue, these Pakistani members would flood the Amnesty headquarters in the UK with faxes and letters asking it to investigate human rights abuses in some part or the other of Kashmir. Under pressure from so many members, Amnesty responded with yet another report on India.

It is strange though that the Amnesty hierarchy didn't see through this game. And for that matter, how could Fai escape scrutiny of the US and European intelligence agencies for so long?

*

If this is the effort they put in internationally, what do the Pakistani leaders think of India in their private moments? Since Pakistan has been ruled by military dictators for half its life, is there a difference between the approach of a democratically elected leader and a dictator regarding relations with India? In short, does it matter who is in power in Pakistan as far as India is concerned?

Let's take a recent example. In September 2013, Pakistani Prime Minister Nawaz Sharif rather colourfully compared Manmohan Singh to a 'village woman' for taking his complaint to Obama about ceasefire violations by the Pakistani forces.

While Indian leaders do not use similarly colourful language in describing their Pakistani counterparts, it will be fair to balance the picture and acknowledge that Indian leaders do not hold their Pakistani counterparts in high esteem.

But we digress. Let's put the focus back on the query that we started with: what are the policy inputs that affect Pakistani decision-making and its strategy? Is hurt betrayal the dominant theme of its interlocution with the outside world? Its military and political leadership use it constantly to tell the US how it has betrayed them. This despite the fact that Pakistan may be the only country in the world which has got the better of the US in a transactional relationship, receiving one of the largest global shares of the US's arms and financial aid without conceding much in return. In so far as India is concerned, it seems that opposition to India is the sole basis of its existence. Often it seems that it defines itself not in its own terms, but in opposition to India. Its sulk, its negativism, and its charge that the world is against it, is often the reason why it is said that Pakistan is insufficiently imagined. Pakistan's policy so far has been negative and destructive in equal parts. It has yet to find an ideology to hold it together, and an idea to burnish it.

Can India help Pakistan create a political culture that works, works free of army interference, and does not view others in antagonistic terms? It would be a difficult enterprise in the best of circumstances, but a lot more so now. There are far too many conflicts taking place in slow motion in Pakistan—a class war between the elite and the poor, the violence between Sunnis and Shias, the revolt in Baluchistan against the national government and the ethnic wars in Karachi between the Muhajir, Sindhi, Pathan and the Taliban groups there. And throughout Pakistan, suicide bombers and masked abductors have crippled its urban life and shattered its national economy.

Still, there is no harm in trying, or at least trying to understand what this undertaking might involve. In any such exercise it is vital to get a sense of the pulse of the people, because masses can influence the behaviour of rulers. And the opinion-moulder of masses on a day-to-day basis is the media.

The mass media and the social media might irritate the establishment, but they reflect merely what they see. And what they see is the mood of the nation. Yet they remain underrated in their ability to inform and influence. There is no denying the fact that the media in Pakistan is immensely active and exceedingly influential. It agitates issues as well as people, giving instant solutions.

In the Indo-Pak context there are some additional factors at work all the time—emotions, the folklore of alleged excesses by the other side and the short acrimonious history since partition. All of these are in play at one time or the other. Ironically, the distrust is mutual. Indians feel the Pakistani Foreign Office and its military establishment delight in devising new pinpricks, and laying virtual landmines on any road to peace. Pakistanis suspect that devious Indians are busy sabotaging every move towards peace. Little wonder then that India should rank consistently as the most hated country for the Pakistani people or that Pakistan is cast villainously in the Indian imagination.

There are multiple inputs that inform and advise the Pakistani leadership, ranging from strategic considerations to advice from diplomats and intelligence agencies. The other source of information is the interaction with foreign governments; the exchanges at the official, ministerial and prime ministerial levels are important in informing and influencing each other, in some cases even for forming strategic alliances where policy interests may coincide enough to formulate a joint plan. All of this is the normal and the accepted way of conducting state business. But the big difference in Pakistan's case is that in addition to all this, the advice of its army and the ISI is paramount. It is rarely ignored on policy matters relating to India and the US. When, exceptionally, a leader tries to follow a soft line, the army steps in with a quick rap on the knuckles.

It happened to Benazir Bhutto early on in her first term that began on 2 December 1988. She was barely thirty-five years old then and, with her Western education, a democratically inclined modern lady. She had wanted to explore new ground in relations with India. It was, therefore, hoped that Rajiv Gandhi and she, as two young leaders with a modern outlook, would be able give bilateral relations a new push. There was clearly excitement in the air when they met in

Islamabad in 1989 during a SAARC summit, but Benazir was also conscious of the fact that the ISI were listening in to every word spoken between them. Despite her liberal approach and the positive chemistry between them, the establishment in Islamabad ensured that the script dictated by it was followed by her to the letter.

So if she was liberal and modern in her outlook, she was also a woman of grand aspirations and complex manoeuvrings. In that calculation, the army and a political opponent like Nawaz took priority, and relations with India became subordinate to domestic considerations. So towards the end of her short two year first term (1988–90) she was shrieking 'jihad, jihad' (over Kashmir) at every public rally as if she was herself willing to lead the march of people across the LOC.

This is what her opponent Nawaz Sharif tried to do on two occasions which led to firing by Indian security forces on the crowd. Rich Nawaz Sharif was only thirty-six years of age when he first stepped into power as the chief minister of Punjab. He was also young, at forty-one years, when he became the prime minister in 1990. Though short and stocky, he has never been short of gumption and that's why he has been described as Sher-e-Punjab, the lion of Punjab. Nawaz was picked by Zia ul-Haq as a politician of choice and his political party, Pakistan Muslim League (N), was to be a counter to Bhutto's PPP. But with all the luck on his side, and having survived death threats by Musharraf and exile to Saudi Arabia, Nawaz has at best been a mediocre administrator and less than successful as prime minister.

He, too, tried to normalize relations with India because he felt it would facilitate his economic agenda. He had sent feelers to Prime Minister Chandra Shekhar on these lines. But the ISI stood firm about pushing terrorists into Kashmir and Sharif did not take long to fall in line and even considered conducting a nuclear test in his first term. Some critics maintain that the soft, pro-good-relations-with-India façade of Nawaz Sharif is just that, a good Venetian mask to hide the real intent. Like his mentor Zia ul-Haq, he too is playacting. Otherwise if you look at his record, it is pretty grim; the Bombay blasts of 1993 took place in his first term, the Kargil war happened during his second term.

If these two young leaders failed, there is hardly a chance that a military dictator would seriously try walking down the path of peace with India.

In 1981, Zia asked General Akhtar Abdur Rehman, director general,

ISI (1979–87) and chairman of the Joint Chiefs of Staff Committee (1987–88) for his views on India. General Akhtar said, 'Indians would never understand the language of decency...their objective is still the creation of Akhand Bharat (greater India).'[2]

General Akhtar also put in place a plan which resulted in the ISI spreading its wings deep inside India. Several top secret files were taken from Prime Minister Indira Gandhi's office and insurgency in Kashmir was speeded up. Meanwhile, Zia continued to drip sugar and honey in his dealings with the Indians he met in Islamabad. Invariably, he would personally escort the visitor out to his car, and insist on opening the car door for him. Shrewd Zia knew that the overwhelmed visitor would mistake the gesture for the genuine stuff. To that extent, Indian visitors to Pakistan have consistently confused the Pakistani hospitality for policy.

Sometimes it is also said in Zia's favour that there was no war during his time. That is true, but he unleashed terror which was far more deadly and bled India economically, while being a low-cost, high-deniability operation for Pakistan. Outwardly, Zia was on a peace offensive while actually encouraging the ISI to speed up its plans for destabilizing India. Terror activities in Punjab assumed frightening proportions then, and Kashmir began to boil.

'Cutting India down to size' isn't merely a figure of speech. It has consistently been the Pakistani military's ethos. Colonel Javed Hassan (later lieutenant general) claimed to have researched 2000 years of Indian history and came to the conclusion in a study done for the Pakistan army, *India: A Study in Profile*: 'India has a poor track record at projection of power beyond its frontier and what is worse a hopeless performance in protecting its own freedom and sovereignty.' Pakistani army officers are also told that India has a centrifugal rather than a centripetal tradition and that India has a historical inability to exist as a single unified state.

In the early 1990s, the US became seriously concerned over Pakistan's support to terrorism. But the ISI advised the Pakistani officials dealing with Americans to flatly deny any involvement and if pressed, to ask for supporting evidence. The documentation would give the ISI clues to the methods that the US was using to collect evidence, and with that the ISI would be able to cover its tracks better.

When the Pakistani denials persisted as did its terror activities, the US delivered an ultimatum: first in the form of a letter by the US

---

[2]Hussain Haqqani, *Pakistan between Mosque and Military.*

secretary of state, and this was followed quickly in May 1992 by US Ambassador Nicholas Platt's protest to Prime Minister Nawaz Sharif. In an unusual step he also handed over to the prime minister the speaking note that his embassy officials had prepared for him. The blunt message in it was:

> ISI and elements of the army are supporting Kashmiri and Sikh militants who carry out acts of terrorism... This support takes the form of providing weapons training, and assistance in infiltration... If the situation persists, the Secretary of State may find himself required by law to place Pakistan on the USG state sponsors of terrorism list...[3]

A few days after Ambassador Platt's message, Sharif took a meeting where Army Chief Asif Nawaz and ISI Chief General Javed Nasir were present. Nasir argued that the jihad in Kashmir was at a critical stage, and that they had been covering their tracks well and would cover them even better in future... He added that the US threats were empty and it would not declare Pakistan a terrorist state. He recommended a better diplomatic and public relations effort in the US.

Nawaz Sharif agreed with that approach and sanctioned an additional US$2 million for lobbying efforts with the US media and the Congress.

During Benazir's second term (1993–96), Pakistan went a step further and stopped apologizing for the terror activities in Kashmir. In 1995, Kashmir became an international worry when Harkat-ul-Ansar took six Western tourists hostage. The US declared Harkat-ul-Ansar a terrorist organization and to placate the Americans, Benazir ordered the arrest of the Harkat's leaders. But the ISI turned around and told Benazir with a straight face that it had no idea about the group, or the whereabouts of its leaders! A few days later the leaders surfaced on the streets of Pakistan.

On another occasion following American protests about foreign participation in terror activities in Kashmir, she told the army and ISI chiefs that this contradicted Pakistan's claim that the insurgency in Kashmir was indigenous. The ISI's chief, General Javed Ashraf Qazi, told her that as Indians had killed all Kashmiris over the age of sixteen, foreigners had to fill in the gap. Benazir swallowed that lie, and faithfully repeated it to her foreign interlocutors thereafter.

---

[3]Chidanand Rajghatta, 'Pak on track to being named terrorist state', *The Times of India*.

These are illustrative of the influences that work on the leadership, and how they shape their policy. But why go that far into Benazir's second term or the Kargil misadventure during Nawaz Sharif's second term? The fact is that the principal strands of foreign and strategic policy are common to all regimes, and they are determined by the army with an accommodating wink by the Foreign Office. Hence the common strand of promoting terrorism in India during every leader's term.

These then are the influences that work on civilian leadership. But are the military leaders equally guided by the army and the ISI? There, the equation is different as long as the dictator is also the army chief—he determines the policy. Let's turn to Musharraf for a bit.

Despite Kargil and many other episodes of varying intensity he is projected by some as a leader who could have delivered on a peace package. It is also said that during his time peace held and by way of evidence it is claimed that no terror attack took place after 2004 when he gave a promise to that effect. Sadly, this argument is based on a selective interpretation of facts. It ignores the train blasts in Mumbai of 2006 when over 200 people were killed. It also ignores the fact that the preparations for 26/11 were begun during Musharraf's regime, and that the go-ahead for the operation was given by Kayani as the ISI chief under Musharraf.

In fact, speaking to newspaper editors on 4 February 2004 President Musharraf laid out his policy: 'Pakistan has two vital national interests; being a nuclear state and the Kashmir issue.'[4] Both these were aimed at India.

Musharraf should have added that a new factor was increasingly beginning to determine national interests—the forces of fundamentalism and terrorism. A jihadi finger on the trigger would have completed the picture he was painting for editors. The LeT and Tehrik-i-Taliban influence the civil and military leadership in as significant a way as the other, more conventional types.

Therein lies the danger for others as also for Pakistan. The jihadi worldview is all-consuming; they would like a war between India and Pakistan because they are basically nihilists.

That's not all; no true jihadi likes the Pakistani state as it exists. They would rather that the whole structure crumbled so that they could build it again. If that happens all restraint would have gone.

---

[4]Gorden Correra, *Shopping for Bombs: Nuclear Proliferation, Global Insecurity and the Rise and Fall of the AQ Khan Network.*

Like Nixon, they could then play happily their own extreme version of the 'Game Theory'.

This is a worrying picture, one that Musharraf had hesitated to sketch. It will be futile to pretend that there is no such thing as the influence of the jihadi. It is there, and dangerously so.

But the question that should be asked is this: will a jihadi leader of Pakistan be any more negative than a dictator? Pakistan's first military dictator Ayub Khan's diary reveals the following entry for January 1968:

> Two things have unbalanced India completely; the 1962 clash with China and the 1965 war with Pakistan... So, whilst wanting a Kashmir solution, we should show no undue anxiety. Let India bleed till she can no longer bear the burden of big power chauvinism. She may then come to her senses...

Jihadis declare openly that their aim is to make India bleed. Is it too much of a coincidence that Ayub Khan had thought likewise? Considering the overwhelming unanimity of views among the civil, military and the jihadi elements regarding India, would it not be a vain enterprise for India to imagine that it could influence, moderate or reform Pakistan?

29

The Nuclear Threat

Actor George Clooney recalls in an interview in the December 2012 issue of *Esquire* magazine:

> I talked with the President [Obama] at one of those fundraisers some months back, and I asked him, 'What keeps you up at night?'
>
> And he said, 'Everything. Everything that gets to my desk is a critical mass. If it gets to my desk, then no one else could have handled it.'
>
> So I said, 'So what's the one that keeps you up at night?'
>
> He goes, 'There are quite a few.'
>
> So I go, 'What's *the one*? Period.'
>
> And he says, '*Pakistan*.'

Do Indian leaders lose any sleep because of Pakistan? There is nothing in the public domain to suggest that they do. However, one thing is certain, and it is this that Indian leaders lose no opportunity in convincing the world at large that they have no ill will towards Pakistan, and that a prosperous and stable Pakistan is in India's interest. They also go on to say that they would do all they can to help promote stability in Pakistan.

How exactly will they help, and what form India's help would assume, is never clarified. Nor is the fact taken into consideration that help by India would be seen as the kiss of death for anyone in Pakistan who receives or agrees to receive such assistance, be it a political party or an individual.

On the other hand, if the desire is to shore up Pakistan economically by cash transfers, it will be well worth recalling the US experience. Its billions have disappeared without trace, and without any stabilizing effect, in a bottomless pit called Pakistan.

Therefore critics of a realistic persuasion have often asked, 'Is Pakistan an Indian responsibility? Or is it a dangerous distraction?'

Political scientist and economist Francis Fukuyama wrote in his book *State Building*, 'Weak and failing states have become the single most important problem for international order.' Fukuyama may or may not have had Pakistan in view as the perfect model for his conclusion, but the vast body of international writing on Pakistan has consistently maintained that Pakistan is weak as a society and failing as a state.

There is no indication so far that Pakistan would, at any identifiable future date, be able to put in place a system that delivers efficiently and reasonably transparently. Nor is there any sign that the massive effort required to industrialize the country is about to begin in the immediate future. Without the necessary wherewithal of job creation, the large numbers of unemployed youth will take the only option available to them. And that is the path of terror. There is no antidote that India can provide to prevent that from happening.

In fact India's equanimity in the face of a very grim situation surprises observers.

The US worries endlessly about a nuclear bomb that Iran is nowhere close to possessing. It fought two wars with Iraq on the suspicion that there were weapons of mass destruction in its basement. The US's treatment of Libya bordered on impetuous brutality despite the fact that it had already forced Muammar Gaddafi to dismantle the nuclear process that was still in a nascent stage. And the US keeps worrying about the trigger-happy Pakistani generals and their arsenal of hundred-plus nuclear bombs. But the US sits thousands of kilometres away, well out of the reach of Pakistan's nuclear delivery systems.

So, is Obama right to have sleepless nights over Pakistan? Given all the information at his disposal, he may have many reasons to be worried. A principal one could be the unpredictability of the Pakistani generals. No one is denying the fact that they are solid, professional army men. But if they can commit atrocities of the type they did in Bangladesh, and continue to do in Baluchistan, and if they gloat over 9/11 and 26/11, who and what can stop an angry general from ordering a nuclear strike? The record shows that they are prone to using violent means. Look, for instance, at the number of wars they have dragged Pakistan into. If you count the two Afghan wars and the continuing terror enterprise, then Pakistan has fought a major war in every decade of its existence; sometimes even two wars simultaneously. Or look at the number of coups it has had over the years. No other major country is held to ransom as whimsically as Pakistan is by its volatile generals.

Therefore, if they are happy providers for the likes of Mullah

Omar, and long-time protectors of terror icons like Osama bin Laden, what is the guarantee that one day some angry general may not give in to the temptation of knocking more than a few heads and decide to hand over one or more of the bombs to a Mullah Omar or a Haqqani? It might sound far-fetched, and it could also be said in their favour that Pakistani generals are highly motivated.

Alas, that high motivation is the problem—their desire to shape the world around them in their mould leads them to adventures that no other professional army dares engage in. Every such action is a constant reminder that if faith in Pakistan is full of rules, its policies defy all rules. Despite the many wars and multiple coups, there is no evidence to suggest that there is any fundamental shift in their approach. Therefore, whatever can be said about the Pakistani generals at any given point of time, the opposite is equally true.

When a general decides to reach for the nuclear trigger he will not aim it towards the distant US, but at a convenient target nearby. Yet India sits comfortably. It has also given Pakistan the additional assurance of a no first strike. That's good and that's decent neighbourly behaviour. It is also one more way of making Pakistan feel safe and stable. But what if some extremist were to get hold of a nuclear weapon in Pakistan? Or, what if a general were to get very angry? Or as mentioned in that State Department note for Nixon in 1971, 'Over the longer run if Pakistan is internally unstable and deeply divided…'

As former Pakistan ambassador to the US Hussain Haqqani writes in his book *Pakistan between Mosque and Military*:

> …of all the countries in the world where terror breeds, Pakistan is the only state that actively sponsors it as a long term instrument of State policy, and as a matter of strategic choice. It is also the only such state that is nuclear armed and uses the threat of that weapon as a deterrent to support its terror activities. Alas, it is also the only state in the world that cavalierly chooses to rotate a part of its nuclear arsenal in trucks through city roads. It claims to do so to keep the arsenal safe by constantly dispersing them.
>
> The worry that grips the strategic community the world over is this: what if a truck breaks down or has an accident in rush hour Lahore or violent Karachi. Or what if some Al Qaida or Taliban cadre were to successfully track such a moving arsenal and hold it up successfully. This is not inconceivable: the terrorist groups have successfully attacked army and navy bases in the past.

There, then, is a very real doomsday scenario, not so much for the rest of the world as for the easy-to-reach and a decidedly desirable target called India. Yet, the Indian leadership rests peacefully at night.

I remember a friend in Karachi recalling for me a conversation he had the previous evening on a flight from Islamabad. He was seated next to the foreign minister of Pakistan who happened to know him well. In the course of a long conversation he asked the minister what his greatest wish was during his ministerial tenure.

The minister stretched both his hands in front of him, opened his palms facing skywards and said, 'If God were to grant me a wish I would ask him to place a nuclear bomb each on my palms.' Then, with a satisfied smile, he turned his palms downwards and added, 'One I would drop on Bombay, the other on Delhi.'

*

In late October 1969, Richard Nixon ordered a squadron of eighteen B-52 bombers, loaded with nuclear weapons, to race towards the Soviet Union's border. For three days they flew along the edge of Soviet airspace, taunting Moscow. This was a calculated move by the White House to convince the Soviet Union that Nixon and Kissinger were just a little mad, that unless the Soviet Union blinked they were capable of the most whimsical decision.

The purpose of this dangerous show was that Nixon wanted the Soviet Union to put pressure on North Vietnam to end the Vietnam War. In this extreme variation of the Game Theory, he concurred with Kissinger's view that nuclear blackmail might work on the Soviet Union. He was right theoretically, at least, because in many confrontations the prevailing side is the one most willing to take the fatal step. But in this case, the Soviets refused to be cowed down and on 30 October, the B-52 bombers were called back. Still, the world had come close to a nuclear confrontation.

Nixon and Kissinger were leaders of the greatest power in the world. Some consider them to be great statesmen. Yet they were willing to think the unthinkable and unleash Armageddon.

Consider then a situation where an angry Pakistani general controls the nuclear trigger, or a bearded Taliban leader sits in the seat of power in Islamabad. Let's also assume that aircraft bearing nuclear bombs have been ordered to keep flying close to the Indian border. Would the Pakistani leader order the bombers back? Or would India just wait it out till the man in Islamabad tires of playing a deadly version of the Game Theory?

The US and the Soviet Union were geographically thousands of miles apart; that large distance would have given them the crucial few minutes to pause and reconsider even if the first nuclear exchange had already taken place. But India and Pakistan are so close geographically that they will not have even that minimal comfort of time. Once the other side's bombers are in the air and near the border, the reaction time would at best be that of a knee jerk. The reaction would have to be immediate otherwise huge devastation will follow; there would be no time to ponder over doctrines like 'no first strike'.

In the 1969 crisis between the US and the Soviet Union, both countries had disciplined armed forces which were conscious of the possible danger. Still, the experienced Soviet ambassador in Washington Anatoly Dobrynin was shocked by the irrational outburst of Nixon when he was summoned to the White House to receive Nixon's ultimatum that Moscow should fall in line—or else.

Would a bearded leader controlling the nuclear trigger in Islamabad care to summon the Indian high commissioner to deliver an ultimatum? Instead, he might just give the go-ahead if he has decided to launch his version of the B-52 bombers. But catapulting B-52-type bombers is not the only choice a Pakistani dictator would have.

As Pakistani journalist Ahmed Rashid writes:

> Pakistan has one of the fastest growing tactical nuclear weapons programmes in the world today, with the capacity to put miniaturised nuclear bombs on short-range rockets, artillery and tank shells. [Moreover] Pakistan refuses to adopt a 'no first use' of nuclear weapons in its strategic focus and therefore every crisis the two countries have been involved in since they became nuclear weapon states has forced Islamabad to adopt a threatening and risky posture in order to avoid total war with India, which it would surely lose.[1]

Tactical nuclear weapons give the Pakistani dictator a far wider choice than merely the B-52 bomber that Nixon despatched. This option makes it psychologically easier for a dictator to use them, rather than having to decide about an all-out nuclear war.

What is the likely profile of the person who may have his finger on the nuclear trigger? Let's consider their catchment area first. Unlike other Taliban groups like Tehrik-i-Taliban Pakistan (TTP), which largely recruit the Pashtuns, though lately from Punjab as well, the LeT is basically a Punjabi group. It recruits from the same families and neighbourhoods as the army; hence an army operation against the LeT would be an oxymoron. A large number of LeT training camps are next to army bases and retired Special Services Group

---

[1]Ahmed Rashid, 'Beware Pakistan's small nuclear weapons', *Financial Times*.

officers train the LeT cadres. So whether it is the army or someone from the TTP or LeT, the background is likely to be more or less similar. This can be consequential; it is said that in most successful revolutions, soldiers have refused to fire on demonstrators because of family and neighbourhood loyalties. In Pakistan, the association is even more intricate because there are clan and religious linkages besides the common bond of conviction.

The other issue is whether it will be a city-bred middle-class leader or someone from a business or feudal background as has been the case up to now. There too, it might be a case of diminishing possibilities. It is increasingly more likely that he might emerge from a semi-rural or even a rural background. And regardless of whether he is from the army or belongs to a Taliban-like outfit, his education may have been influenced by what is being taught in madrasas.

More than sixty years after partition, Pakistan ranks at the 113th place among 120 countries in literacy, with a combined men's and women's literacy rate of 55 per cent. But even among this 55 per cent, there are a considerable number who have received a rudimentary education either in ill-equipped government schools or in madrasas. In 1947 there were only 189 madrasas in Pakistan, but in 2002 the country had 10,000–13,000 unregistered madrasas with an estimated 1.7 to 1.9 million students. A 2008 estimate puts the number of madrasas at 'over 40,000' and the number of students at close to 5 million. This large number studies little beyond the Quran.

Lately, occasional calls have been given by some politicians that Pakistan must put greater emphasis on education. But no one has suggested that the madrasa system should be replaced by one offering liberal education.

This idea of building Pakistan around religious nationalism has backfired badly. In practical terms, religious nationalism has given rise to extremism. Since Pakistan is not only a Sunni state but has a 20 per cent Shia minority too, it has meant extremism from both sides. And then there is the extremism of the Pathans, Muhajirs, Sindhis and the Baluch, which is perhaps not religious but a reaction to the extremism of the others. As a result, Pakistan is in a virtual state of civil war between various sects and militias attached to these sects who do not tolerate each other.

The other defining feature of Pakistan, almost from the beginning, is the certainty with which aid keeps pouring in. Despite more than US$20 billion in US aid since 2001, despite regular financial injections by the International Monetary Fund, generous grants by the Gulf

Arabs and their concessional oil supplies, Chinese economic benevolence, billions in annual remittances from its overseas citizens and billions that filter into the country because of drug trafficking, Pakistan ranks thirteenth on *Foreign Policy* magazine's Failed State Index, edged out only by such wonders as Somalia, Haiti and Zimbabwe from descending into a still more humiliating status.

Once again the reason is not far to seek. The army is the biggest employer in Pakistan; the business side of its activities make it worth close to US$21 billion. In so far as the private sector is concerned, the lack of security has kept foreign investors out. That, plus phenomenal corruption, discourages Pakistani businessmen from going in for expansion and making fresh investments. The public sector, such as it is, is inefficient, even the railway system inherited from the colonial times barely totters along. Except for the occasional Chinese-aided investment in an infrastructure project, there is hardly any fresh foreign investment in industry. As a result new job opportunities are hard to come by even as the number of employable youth rises inexorably year after year. Therefore, the youth look to the army, army-owned industries and the fundamentalist outfits for employment. Whatever the label of the employer, the result is the same—more of the religiously indoctrinated youth are added to the Pakistani rolls.

Since the catchment area for the army and the Taliban is either the same family or the neighbourhood, in a subtle and covert way it breeds an alliance between the clerics and the officers. It is true that faith made Pakistan, but the problems thrown up in the country's way are not of the kind that a Hafiz Saeed can resolve.

As a series of its failed governments show, Pakistan seems ungovernable. There is order in Lahore and Islamabad, but Karachi teeters on the edge of chaos. In the regions beyond, the authority of the state is challenged by banditry and tribal warlords and religious pretenders. There is long-standing unrest in Baluchistan, a huge impoverished province with more than 40 per cent of the country's land mass, but only 6 per cent of its population. Among Baluchis, the authoritarian state is an instrument of the Punjabis and the Pathans. Like the East Pakistanis once, the Baluch too feel that their resources serve only to enrich the Punjabi businessman. The situation is getting no better in Sindh or the Khyber Pakhtunkhwa, or in some of the interior parts of Punjab.

To exploit it all for temporary gains is the vast apparatus of intelligence agencies. The ISI, in particular, dominates the rest. Under

Zia, the size of the ISI increased vastly; its staff jumped from 2000 in 1978 to 40,000 in1988. With a billion-dollar budget it was omnipotent—tapping every telephone call, keeping informants right down to the village level in Pakistan. Politicians and media people were on its payroll and those who dared oppose it disappeared. Outside Pakistan, the ISI maintains a vast network among Pakistani taxi drivers in the Gulf states, London and New York. By the late 1980s, the ISI was a hugely feared organization in Pakistan and one of the most potent intelligence services in the world. Through it, Zia gave Pakistan a very explosive combination of jihad and extremism.

Illustrating the tight bond between the ISI and the jihadi groups, Bruce Riedel gives the example of the terror attacks against NATO troops in Afghanistan:

> A secret NATO study leaked in 2012 based on the interrogations of 4,000 captured Taliban, al Qaeda, and other fighters concluded that ISI support was critical to the survival and revival of the Taliban after 2001. It provides sanctuary, training camps, expertise, and help with fund raising...the ISI is thoroughly aware of Taliban activities and the whereabouts of all senior Taliban personnel.

Riedel goes on to add, 'Kayani ran the ISI's covert operation assisting the Taliban directly until his promotion to COAS in 2007... As DG/ISI, Kayani would also have been in charge of the early planning for the attack on Mumbai...'

There are some important points worth noting here. First, that Pakistan was in complete denial all along that its army or the ISI were aiding the Taliban in Afghanistan. Second, the Taliban would not have achieved the success they had without the ISI's active involvement. Third, Pakistan was using NATO/US funds and military equipment to engage, defeat and kill NATO soldiers.

As far as 26/11 is concerned, Riedel's statement quoted above makes it amply clear that the operation could not have been planned without Kayani's knowledge. What is worse is the fact that despite Musharraf's promise in 2004 to stop state-sponsored terror activities against India, the planning for 26/11 had started soon thereafter in 2005. In fact, Riedel adds, 'The attack was intended to change dramatically the future of South Asia, perhaps even by provoking a war between the two nuclear powers rising in the subcontinent.'

Taliban, terror and the ISI are so closely interlinked in today's Pakistan as to be indistinguishable for all practical purposes. Will the Taliban eventually dominate them all? That could be a real possibility because power is dispersing in Pakistan. Both dictatorships and democracy have failed—and the Taliban think it is their turn now.

I.A. Rehman, head of Pakistan's Human Rights Commission, apprehends that this might be the case, 'Taliban have people across Punjab and those terrorists are not fighting for small stakes. They are fighting to capture Pakistan...'[2]

We are back then to the question we started with. Will a bearded mullah grab one of those trucks carrying nuclear bombs from a chaotic Pakistani road and order the Pakistani version of a B-52 to take off with a full bomb load and head east? Or, will a whimsical general one day line up his armour along a stretch of the Indo-Pak border and lob some tactical nuclear shells across to the Indian side?

[2]Karin Brulliard, 'Pakistan conflicted over targeting rising extremists in its heartland', *Washington Post*.

30

Like Moths to a Flame

Osama bin Laden described the organization of the Islamic jihad against the Soviets in Afghanistan as a multinational enterprise: 'Volunteers from all over the Arab and Muslim countries...were trained by the Pakistanis, the weapons supplied by the Americans, the money by the Saudis.'[1]

As the Afghan war began to wind down in 1987, Abdallah Azzam, a close friend of bin Laden, set up an organization called the Markaz-ud-Dawa-wal-Irshad (MDI) with the help of Hafiz Saeed. Its mission was to apply the experience of the Afghan war to Kashmir and the rest of India. The ISI set up training camps in Afghanistan's Konar province for the purpose, and a deadly military wing of MDI called Lashkar-e-Taiba was the result.

Punjab, in India, had been on the boil for much of the 1980s. Now Kashmir was beginning to burn. Like the mythical Prometheus, India found itself tied helplessly as terror gnawed away at it with deadly regularity. It is often said cynically that India was saved from destruction by its stoicism and forbearance, but mainly by the heroism of its forces. It survived the 1990s by a whisker, but the trial by a thousand cuts continued.

It is also said that the most daring terror plots in the world were planned for the turn of the millennium. These were to be simultaneous terror strikes in Jordan, Yemen, the US and India. All terror strikes failed except the one in India. Under the direct control of the ISI and Osama bin Laden, an Air India plane was hijacked on Christmas Eve of 1999 from Kathmandu and taken after halts in Amritsar, Lahore and Dubai to Kandahar.

Indian authorities could have stopped the plane from taking off at

---

[1]Bruce Riedel, *Deadly Embrace: Pakistan, America and the Future of the Global Jihad*.

Amritsar airport but indecision and confusion let the hijackers slip away. India then tried to seek the permission of the United Arab Emirates government to send its commandos to Dubai to storm the plane, but the United Arab Emirates government did not wish to get involved in a complicated affair where both Pakistan and Osama had an interest.

All the hijackers were Pakistanis and the operation was spectacularly successful from the ISI's point of view. Much to the surprise of the security experts, and in a move without parallel in the world, External Affairs Minister Jaswant Singh flew along with three terrorists, Maulana Masood Azhar, Omar Saeed and Mushtaq Zargar, to Kandahar to exchange them for the hijacked passengers. It showed India's helplessness in the face of a terrorist operation; a helplessness that was to repeat itself every so often in the new millennium as well. Each new crisis brought about fresh hand-wringing and a resolve to be firm the next time, but little else concretely.

All through, Pakistan continued to talk terror and peace in the same sentence. Despite Pakistani promises to the contrary, there was no let up in terror. It has to continue because many of the jihadi groups really believe that their great opportunity for *Ghazwa-e-Hind*—the great battle of India—will come when there is a big war. The Pakistani state has given strength to that narrative by teaching children in schools that Pakistan came into being not in 1947 but in AD 712!

At first the rulers of Pakistan thought that ideas such as this were necessary to give Pakistanis a reference point that was distinct from India.

For three decades, deep tectonic forces have been tearing Pakistan away from the Indian subcontinent and driving it towards the Arabian peninsula. This continental drift is not physical but cultural, driven by a belief that Pakistan must exchange its South Asian identity for an Arab-Muslim one. Grain by grain, the desert sand of Saudi Arabia is replacing the rich soil that had nurtured a magnificent Muslim culture in India for a thousand years. A stern, unyielding version of Wahhabi Islam is replacing the kinder, gentler Islam of the Sufis and saints. Aadab has been replaced by As-salaam-wallekum.

This shift manifested itself in many other forms. An invented history in the school curriculum was one way, the injection of Arabic words into the Urdu vocabulary was yet another example of this obsession to distance Pakistan from its roots. So too was Zulfikar Bhutto's unwritten diktat that women should wear salwar-kameez rather than the saree, which he identified with India.

Gradually, Pakistan became a laboratory of Islam and its citadel as well. Pakistani leaders, without exception, played upon religious sentiment as an instrument to strengthen Pakistan's identity. This Pakistani pursuit of faith became so deeply ingrained as a jihadi objective that now it is very difficult for any government to put jihadis out of business. Like the army, jihadis have made themselves a part of the national narrative. Over time they have become so pervasive that Pakistan cannot find peace without putting all jihadis out of business.

The story does not end there because India, too, will not find peace while jihadis are in business. Alas, the India relationship is even more complicated than a mere matter of dealing with the jihadis. It is not just them who are India's headache; India will not find peace till the Pakistani army undergoes a fundamental change of mindset.

Anatol Lieven writes in *Pakistan: A Hard Country* that speaking of an average Pakistani officer of today, General Naqvi told him: 'He has no doubt that the adversary is India… His [Pakistani officer's] image of Indians is of an anti-Pakistan, anti-Muslim, treacherous people. So he feels that he must always be ready to fight against India.'

The issue of India as an eternal enemy is not just confined to the army and the jihadis. It is also a readily available and convenient emotional handle for the political parties to exploit. When a Pakistani leader feels threatened politically, India-baiting becomes a useful diversion. The crux of the issue is whether six decades of India-baiting have gained Pakistan much. Rather, it may have imposed hidden costs on its economy, besides much else on society at large. If that is so, hasn't the time come for Pakistan's elite to embrace a new liberal paradigm that there is no eternal enemy of Pakistan and that there is no existential threat to Pakistan?

The idiom of violence has to change because jihad is not enough for a nation to move forward in the twenty-first century; nor is a culture of grievance its panacea. Pakistanis need to worry about doing something other than having young people burn the flag of some country or the other.

Defence analyst Pervez Hoodbhoy points out the difficulties involved:

> A recent survey of 2,000 Pakistanis in the 18–27 age group found that three quarters identify first as Muslims and only second as Pakistanis. Just 14 percent of respondents chose to define themselves as citizens of Pakistan first. This result should be no surprise.

> Pakistani schoolchildren learn to chant in unison: *Pakistan ka matlab kya? La ilah illa Allah!* (What is the meaning of Pakistan? There is no god but God!)[2]

Hoodbhoy also reflects on the relationship between the army and terrorists:

> The army's plan, hatched decades ago, was to leech India in a proxy war to be waged on Pakistan's behalf by Islamist militants... The strategy has seemed safe enough—Pakistan's nuclear weapons are supposed to deter India. And it has seemed to work, on at least two occasions: after the December 13, 2001 attack on the Indian parliament by jihadis of the Jaish-e Muhammad and after the 2008 Mumbai attacks by Lashkar-e Taiba, India protested vigorously but did not retaliate... A score of militant outfits based in Muridke, Bahawalpur, Mansehra and elsewhere are left free to plan attacks on India at times and places of their own choosing.[3]

The rise of hardline Islam in Pakistan also has many and deep roots. Perhaps the most relevant lies in wounded pride. Faced by a decline from a peak of greatness many centuries ago, Pakistanis lived in the ruins of the Mughal Empire in India defeated by the British colonial power in the mid-nineteenth century. Their version of history is nostalgic for a time when Muslims ruled over India. Some blame this fall on Muslims who strayed from the faith.

There is also the matter of money. The ascendancy of Wahhabism in Pakistan has been paid for by rich Arabs and their governments. In November 2008, Bryan Hunt, an officer at the US consulate in Lahore, sent a cable to the State Department conveying that 'financial support estimated at US$100 million annually was making its way to Deobandi and Ahl-i Hadith clerics in South Punjab from organizations in Saudi Arabia and the United Arab Emirates ostensibly with the direct support of those governments'. These funds fuel the fire that is consuming Pakistan.

Can the Indian republic be a natural ally of such a virulent jihadi state? Whatever Pakistan may say for public effect, the fact is that it cannot get off the tiger it has chosen to ride. The army and religious fundamentalism are not going to give space to civil society at any time in the foreseeable future. Given that circumstance, what are the

---

[2]Pervez Hoodbhoy, 'Faith and nation: reinventing Pakistan', *Ahmediyya Times*.

[3]Pervez Hoodbhoy and Zia Mian 'Pakistan, the army and the conflict within', *Middle East Report Online*.

options for India? If talking to the jihadi groups is not on the cards, is opening a line to the army a possibility? It is an option that has been talked of from time to time, one that some advocate may unlock the doors to peaceful coexistence.

But people forget that that there has been contact in the past with the Pakistani army chief—Yahya Khan met his Indian counterpart on two occasions in 1966 and 1967. But did that prevent a war between India and Pakistan in 1971? However, it can be said that India has not in the recent past dealt directly with the Pakistani army—except on the battleground, and when it had 93,000 Pakistani soldiers as POWs, and at the formal level of director generals of military operations (DGMOs). Let's, therefore, look at the experience of others.

The US, more than any other country, has had the longest and most intense relationship with the Pakistani army. Almost every senior officer of the Pakistani defence forces has trained at an American academy. The children of many officers have studied on scholarships in American universities; many of them have also found employment there.

Beyond these personal links there are strong institutional links which bring the two forces together, beginning with alliances like CENTO and SEATO to joint operations against the Soviet forces in Afghanistan, besides regular training exercises. Then, there are the massive arms transfers which take place on a regular basis. No other army, not even the Chinese or the Saudi Arabian, is as closely linked to the Pakistani army as the American is—and in multiple ways.

There have also been rough periods when a disappointed US slinks back to its corner. For those months and years it regards the Pakistani army petulantly. But something or the other draws them close together again, till the next spat. One of these phases followed the withdrawal of the Soviet army from Afghanistan, and the Pakistanis were quick to condemn the American indifference towards it as a betrayal of an ally. But that rift was temporary.

A fresh phase of intensified relations between the two armies started after 9/11. America was in a sullen mood and wanted to destroy the Al Qaeda quickly, but it knew that to accomplish the task, it would need the full cooperation of Pakistan.

'You are either with us or against us,' Secretary of State Colin Powell told Musharraf. Deputy Secretary of State Richard Armitage was more blunt with the director general of the ISI. 'The choice is clear,' Armitage told him, 'America or the terrorists. And if Pakistan chooses the terrorists, it should be prepared to be bombed back to the Stone Age.'[4]

Powell and Armitage received promises of cooperation. But what actually happened was an exercise in deception; Pakistan passed on American funds and arms to the Taliban to fight against the NATO forces in Afghanistan. In time, the American experience grew steadily bitter.

In almost every meeting between the Pakistani military and intelligence chiefs and their American counterparts, Pakistanis denied that they were in any way helping the Taliban against the NATO forces in Afghanistan. Once, American intelligence officials asked General Kayani to shut down the Quetta Shura, the ruling council of Taliban members associated with Mullah Muhammad Omar. The Quetta Shura, according to reports, was based close to a Pakistani army division headquarters in Quetta. But General Kayani, who was then the head of the ISI, looked puzzled, and acted like he'd never heard of the Quetta Shura!

In 2008, Mike McConnell, President Bush's director of national intelligence, confronted the ISI chief, General Ahmed Shuja Pasha, with evidence that the ISI was tipping off jihadists so that they could escape in advance of American attacks against them. McConnell also asserted that American intelligence had concluded that most Pakistani assets were still deployed against India. 'How dare you tell me how our forces are deployed?' Pasha said to McConnell.[5]

Still the American generals kept giving assurances repeatedly to the Congress and officials of the Bush and Obama administrations that they had developed close and personal relationships with Pakistani military leaders, which would lead to a more productive alliance.

No other American worked as hard as Admiral Michael Mullen, chairman of the Joint Chiefs of Staff, to cultivate General Kayani, whom he visited twenty-six times in Pakistan. The two generals played golf in America and met during long working dinners in Rawalpindi. Some American officials joked about a 'bromance' between them. But in real terms, Kayani conceded nothing; rather, he continued to weave webs of deception round his American interlocutor.

---

[4]Kranti Kumara and Keith Jones, 'US threatened to bomb Pakistan back to stone age', *World Socialist*.

[5]'The ally from hell', *The Nation*.

Eventually, Mullen's patience was exhausted. A few days before his retirement, Mullen broke with Kayani publicly. In his final appearance before the Senate Armed Services Committee on 22 September 2011 Mullen exploded with anger and said:

> We have almost no strategic convergences with Pakistan, at any level. ISI-supported operatives of the Haqqani network had conducted a recent attack on the American Embassy in Kabul. The Haqqani network acts as a veritable arm of Pakistan's Inter-Services Intelligence agency.[6]

The American distrust of Pakistan is also brought out by cold statistics.

Besides the vast amounts it spends on aid, to placate Pakistan, it incurs many more billions to chase terrorists and proliferators on its own. In 2013, US spy agencies sought US$16.6 billion to fight Al Qaeda and other terrorist groups and asked for US$6.86 billion to counter the spread of nuclear, biological and chemical weapons. These two items accounted for nearly half of the US intelligence community's budget demand for the year. And Pakistan is the principal reason why these two categories—counterterrorism and counterproliferation—exist. The bulk of this US$23.46 billion was spent in Pakistan.[7]

The American record of dealing with the Pakistani army and the ISI cannot be termed happy by any standard. This intense US experience of dealing with the Pakistani army should serve as a guide for India on what to expect. If people like Admiral Mullen felt betrayed, what chance does a straight-thinking Indian general have against a counterpart whose ethos is counterfeit and practice suspect?

A dialogue of generals is unlikely to lead to peace between India and Pakistan.

Will this constant state of tension then lead to another war, and a nuclear conflict? Even if a war doesn't break out, the chance of a nuclear device falling into the hands of a terrorist group is real.

Pakistan would be an obvious place for a jihadist organization to seek a nuclear weapon or fissile material because Pakistan's military and security services are infiltrated by jihadist sympathizers.

At least six facilities associated with Pakistan's nuclear programme have been targeted by militants in recent years. In November 2007, a suicide bomber attacked a bus carrying workers to the Sargodha air-

---

[6]*BBC News*, 22 September 2011.

[7]*The News*, 4 September 2013.

base, which is believed to house nuclear weapons; the following month, a school bus was attacked outside the Kamra airbase, which may also serve as a nuclear storage site; in August 2008, Pakistani Taliban suicide bombers attacked what experts believe to be the country's main nuclear weapons assembly depot in the Wah cantonment.

It is true that the Strategic Plans Division (SPD) is considered to be a highly professional organization. Its soldiers and civilian staff are screened for signs of political or religious immoderation and investigated for ties to extremists, and to radical mosques, and for changes in their lifestyle and income. The SPD takes other preventive measures too. It is believed to maintain 'dummy' storage sites that serve to divert attention from active ones.

To ensure the safety of nuclear weapons, the SPD moves them among the fifteen or more facilities that handle them. Nuclear weapons components are sometimes moved by helicopter and at times by road—instead of moving nuclear material in armoured, well-defended convoys, the SPD transports them in civilian-style vehicles, in the regular flow of traffic. This low-security method is used to transfer not merely the 'de-mated' component nuclear parts but 'mated' nuclear weapons as well.

What if a jihadi group were to strike lucky and find that a van loaded with nuclear weapons has broken down ahead of them? If they get hold of the weapon, which is the nearest place they are likely to rush to test whether it works?

It is not only jihadis—the threat is equally grave from the uniformed soldiers. On 13 May 2011, the director general of the ISI, Ahmad Shuja Pasha, told the Pakistani Parliament, 'The Pakistani army had not only picked targets in India for retaliation but had also rehearsed striking them.'[8] He did not specify a nuclear attack or attack by missile-launched miniature nuclear warheads, but did not exclude them. This ambiguity, and the loose control over miniature nuclear warheads in a war or warlike situation, is potentially dangerous.

The previous assurances by Pakistan to the world were based on the understanding that its warheads and delivery systems were stored separately, and could not be fired without a specific instruction by the National Command Authority. But tactical nuclear weapons pose an altogether different set of risks, especially in conflict situations when they are likely to be deployed in multiple locations near the border.

---

[8]*The Economist*, 19 May 2011.

The command and control protocol is likely to be looser, and the officer on the spot may decide in favour of firing his weapon rather than risk giving the opponent a strategic advantage. And unlike India, Pakistan has not committed itself to 'no first use' of nuclear weapons.

An officer commanding a unit with tactical nuclear warheads may also feel encouraged by the signals he gets from the civilian top. On 3 December 2013, Prime Minister Nawaz Sharif told the POK's Council, 'Kashmir is a flashpoint and can trigger a fourth war between the two nuclear powers at any time.'[9]

It could be argued that Nawaz Sharif did not really mean to state this in such definite terms, or that he was merely paying lip service to the sentiments of the people in POK, or that his statement was merely reflective of the wounds of the partition that have still not healed.

Let's grant all that, but isn't a prime minister playing with lives if his words provoke a wildfire. India and Pakistan have already fought four wars (including that in Kargil). Since the early 1980s, India has also been fighting a proxy war sponsored by Pakistan. Still, efforts were made periodically during these six decades to try and somehow heal the wounds. Sometimes they led to a sense of euphoria that this time it would be different, and that we might finally live in peace and prosper in cooperation.

But each time, this faint hope fades fast. The wounds of the past are scratched raw every so often by a bloody violation across the LOC or a terror strike.

*

Are the two countries destined to remain engaged in conflict? Sometimes, it seems so. The pre-partition generation blames it on the bitter harvest of that poison.

The partition haunts them as a reminder of violence, displacement and of the unresolved problems of ethnicity and territory. Pakistan has complicated matters further by wholesale militarization. As a result, people live in the most militarized, least economically integrated region of the world. As Nehru said once, the fear and hatred of India continues to be an obsession in Pakistan. Its 600,000-strong army consumes 17 per cent of the national budget while education is allocated only 1.2 per cent. Inevitably then, the education standards are declining in a growing population and so are job opportunities.

---

[9] *Dawn*, 4 December 2013.

In 1947, West Pakistan had a population of 39 million. Today 53.5 per cent of its 180 million people are below the age of nineteen. If the present rate of fertility holds, by 2050 Pakistan's numbers will reach 450 million.

Imagine then the condition of a country where almost 400 million people are poor or absolutely poor with little or inadequate education and the bulk of them are unemployed. While that state of affairs may delight a future Hafiz Saeed, it will be a nightmare for Pakistan's civil society and for the region. And the world may have to coin even more damaging sobriquets along the way. Already Pakistan has been called a failed state, a state of nothing, an ally from hell, the birthplace of global jihad, the epicentre of terror and the most dangerous country in the world.

Yet, from time to time India renews its faith in Pakistan's good intentions. Is it because India is a masochist state that does not recognize danger when it sees it? Or is India inspired by its gods to try one more time?

A case in point about claiming that the glass is at least half full is the issue of a ceasefire on the LOC. The offer was made by Pakistan and readily accepted by India at the instance of its army. Since then, it has been promoted by India as an example of what goodwill can achieve. At first, the self-congratulatory noises were loud and frequent. Now, murmurs of dissent are creeping in. It is being said that the Indian army has fenced itself in a defensive posture by opting for a Maginot mentality, and thereby stifling the offensive response spirit of its troops. The Indian army with little to do across the fence, which is well within its territory, now looks inwards.

When it fights, it is in response to a provocation by Pakistan at a time and place of the latter's choosing. Pakistan also chooses the manner of engagement; whether it should be through its regulars, a combination of regulars and terrorists or terrorists backed by the Pakistan army's covering fire. The Indian army is forced then to engage in an asymmetric war.

A prime example was 26/11 as are the terror attacks in Jammu and Kashmir and elsewhere in the country. So was the Kargil war where about 3000 Pakistani soldiers engaged over two divisions of the Indian army besides its air force. Or for that matter the infiltration in early 2014 in the Keron sector by thirty terrorists who engaged a brigade of the Indian army for over fifteen days. This asymmetry is demoralizing for the troops and costly in terms of Indian lives and equipment. The Indian army is fighting this war in uniform, and therefore, fights by the rules. The Pakistani side has none.

It is said that military diplomacy works when two states have problems between them. But will such an engagement work between India and Pakistan? Now, in the background of tactical nuclear weapons and asymmetric warfare, let's briefly rephrase the game. The point at issue is whether the Indian army would be able to speak the language that the Pakistani army engages in, by threats, terror and force multipliers. Well, the short answer is a big no. The entire ethos of the Indian army, its discipline and the system of subordination to the civilian authority would have to change before it begins to emulate the methods of the Pakistani army. And that is just not likely, nor desirable.

If the dialogue between the governments gets us nowhere and if the two armies cannot engage across the table, is it then possible that civil societies might step in? Well, it has been tried.

There were meetings between the peaceniks of the two sides, soulful meetings at the border where they looked tearfully at each other in the flicker of wind-blown candlelights. But like the candles they held in their hands, the effect was temporary and ephemeral.

Once, after an emotional meeting of one such group of elderly peaceniks in Lahore, I remarked to an eminent Pakistani member of the group that '*Lahore ki mitti*—the soil of Lahore—would surely make the difference...this time peace would truly prevail'.

She smiled and said that 'peace and friendship stood a chance once all of them had merged with that *Lahore ki mitti*'. What she meant was that woolly-headed sentimentalism was hardly likely to lead to peace. A new generation was more likely to bring in fresh ideas, free of sentimentality. That practical approach might work.

She had a point. Already, the younger generation has made a difference. They are assertive and have changed the national narrative, in India at least. Aspiration is the driving mantra. The Aam Aadmi Party in India, despite its self-proclaimed goals, has brought in an entirely new discourse in politics. Moreover, the media, especially the electronic media, has made national issues instantly accessible and intensely debatable. There is hope, therefore, that one day one of these new approaches might smoothen Indo-Pak wrinkles too.

Still, if all else fails, what can India do? It is a difficult call to make, given the absolute unpredictability of the other side. However, options open up once there is the will to exercise them. Such a will may be required sooner than one imagines.

All told, India has three choices—do nothing, retaliate to each provocation with equal and exactly similar tactics, or hit hard. Doing nothing is cowardly. That's exactly what India has done over the last three decades with the exception of Kargil, where it had no choice but to stop the aggression against its territory. Otherwise, doing nothing has been the standard response to every act of terror and each provocation by Pakistan. The most bizarre example of this was Operation Parakram when India lined up 500,000 soldiers on its borders for a full ten months to do nothing. The most gutless was the state of its freeze after 26/11. India had two options then: it could have followed the American example in Afghanistan and attacked Pakistan or it could have talked to leaders of the country. It preferred to turn to the US in order to secure its goals. The result was an India–Pakistan contest for American favours.

This state of 'doing nothing' is dangerous. Passivity carries the risk that the next time the provocation might be bigger still. If India continues to tolerate the trespasses against it, this will only encourage Pakistan to up the ante. It will keep crossing the red lines and happily watch India blink. This Indian caution has meant the sacrifice of 100,000 human lives to terror. By some estimates it has also meant a recurring annual expenditure of US$20 billion on anti-terrorism-related security measures by government agencies and the private sector. Still, India is counting on its luck to protect it against the next major terror strike. This policy has no parallel in the world.

Essentially then, it boils down to a basic difference in DNA, between 'Brand India' and the 'Advertising of Pakistan'. In marketing terms, branding and advertising are intrinsically linked, just as India and Pakistan were before their turbulent birth. Therefore, ideally speaking, advertising and branding should have complemented each other. But the theory did not work in practice. They were an odd couple, and from the beginning they chose to go their separate ways.

India has built up its national brand as a stable, mature democracy with a reasonable rate of growth. On the other hand, Pakistan advertises itself as an Islamic state to the Organization of Islamic Cooperation (OIC) members, and as a country with a strategic geographic location to the US and China as well.

Thus far, for one reason or the other, for good or bad, the world has paid more attention to the aggressive advertising of Pakistan rather than to the ponderous effort at building a brand by India. So, even in a space where they could complement each other and gain from that combination, they have chosen to go their separate ways. Brands and advertising need not be intrinsically linked, says this exception to the rule.

There are other, more fundamental differences. As violence grows, pessimism about the country's future has descended upon the intelligentsia and investor class, prompting professionals and people holding financial capital to flee the country. Moreover, religion divides Pakistan and Pakistanis and increasingly, the Pakistani military as well. The Pakistani military, and the country that it runs, is bleeding from a thousand cuts inflicted by the foot soldiers of religious militancy.

Following the raid that killed Osama bin Laden, the Pakistani public too started to turn on the army. Derision and profanity replaced awe and fear. In Islamabad's Aabpara market, just a short walk from the ISI headquarters, protesters ripped down a huge military-sponsored banner praising the army and its vaunted spy agency. Such scenes had not been witnessed since the 1971 war with India. Or look at the public support for Hakimullah Mehsud, the TTP leader, who was killed by an American drone. These instances are indicative of a tightening hold on people of the forces of fundamentalism.

The nightmare scenario for India is twofold: first, what if some huge turbulence were to overwhelm Pakistan, forcing sections of its citizens to flee the country. What should India do then? Should it open its doors and simply accommodate them as it did for the 10 million who fled from East Pakistan in 1971? The flip side of it would be communal violence in India on an unprecedented scale, which is so deeply divisive as to force a major migration into Pakistan. Both situations, distasteful as they are, are not beyond the realm of possibility. Prudent nations must prepare and plan for such contingencies.

But India will need a more effective antidote than contingency planning and prayer in the coming days. Both Mao and Chou En-lai had advised the Pakistani leaders in the 1960s and 1970s that it should develop thousands of armed resources in the enemy (Indian) territory to supplement its war effort in the next confrontation with India. The extent to which this has been done will become known only in the next war. But if the ease with which the Indian mujahidin is able to plant bombs is any indication, it does not augur well.

31

Chasing Hope

Like a buzz that refuses to go away, my interaction with the youth of Delhi kept haunting me. I would lie awake at night wondering if that bitterness was representative of the young of the entire city and indeed of the country. Was it terror and the incidents at the border in 2013 that had affected them, making them so bitter? Or was it that the narrative of partition still overwhelms the poetry of healing.

The other question that kept bothering me was this: Why is the resentment limited to Punjab? The bitterness should have been equally intense in Bengal. It was the Direct Action in Calcutta (now Kolkata) in 1946 that was the precursor to violence in the rest of the country. And it is Bengal, rather than Punjab, which has always prided itself on its literary genius. Yet, the most moving accounts of the partition were written by people from both sides of divided Punjab—Saadat Hasan Manto's 'Toba Tek Singh', Amrita Pritam's *Pinjar*, Bhisham Sahni's *Tamas* and Khushwant Singh's *Train to Pakistan*, to name just a few. Was Bengal insensitive to its suffering or was there another reason to its writer's block?

The statistics of migration might provide a clue. A total of 7.22 million crossed over from India to Pakistan. Of this number, 6.52 million migrated to West Pakistan and only 0.7 million to East Pakistan. Among those who went to West Pakistan, only 1.16 million were headed towards Sindh, 5.36 million settled in West Punjab.

Similarly, in the other direction, 7.25 million Hindus and Sikhs migrated into India. At the time of the partition, 70 per cent of Karachi's population consisted of Hindus and Sikhs. Soon thereafter they were reduced to an insignificant minority. It was a similar story in Lahore. By the 1941 census, 240,000 Hindus and Sikhs formed a third of Lahore's population; this figure increased to 300,000 in April 1947. There were 433,170 Muslims in the city then. Most of the shops of the famous Anarkali Bazar were owned by Hindus and Sikhs, as were those around Shah Alami Gate and Chuna Mandi. In all they owned two-thirds of Lahore's shops, paid 70 per cent of its taxes and contributed greatly to making Lahore the most important educational, commercial and administrative centre in Punjab. Yet by August 1947, the Hindus and Sikhs were a mere 10,000 in Lahore.

These statistics explain in part the wrench of moving away, but not the violence. Why was it so horrible in Punjab and why is it that the anger of those times continues to affect the discourse of today? Besides the much larger number and a far more intense degree of violence, did the DNA of the region have something to do with it? Punjab has invariably been on the route taken by the conquerors of Delhi all through history. That repeated brush with war and warriors must have rubbed off on local people, making them so much more prone to violence themselves.

All that might explain the atrocities of partition, but these cold facts do not provide a way forward. Isn't there some way of winding back the clock to begin history afresh in a new format, away from 15 August 1947? If it were possible, let us imagine that we could live in friendship, because thus far both people have suffered.

It takes a poet of considerable sensitivity to articulate these sentiments. Ustad Daman of Lahore was such a poet who read out his poem at the First Indo-Pak Mushaira (poetry festival) in Delhi in 1954. Nehru was moved to tears on hearing his poem, the substance of which was regret that the partition should have divided an unsuspecting people. The last two couplets should be enough to convey the feeling:

Jagan waleyan rajj ke luttya hae
Soye tusi vi ho, soye assi vi haan
Lali akhiyan di payi dassdi hae
Roye tusi vi ho, roye assi vi haan
(The awake looted mercilessly,
While you slept, and so did we
The red eyes announce clearly,
Many a tear have you wept, and so have we)...

Despite anger and despite differences, both sides still wonder why there was so much violence. Yet the way forward is not easy. A basic test for countries that aim to be friends and allies is that they should have common attributes like governing systems, culture, strong people-to-people relations and convergence of interests. It also helps if their record on human rights, freedom of speech and the treatment of minorities is similar. Most importantly, there should be trust.

Isn't that a tough list in the Indo-Pak context? We bicker at every step and on each of the measures listed above for friendship. But why give up? Let's give friendship another try and start with the issues that bring us together undeniably.

Culturally, both India and Pakistan were born from the same womb. Mohenjodaro and Taxila are rich testimonies to that as are the links of the Urdu, Sindhi and Punjabi languages. The two Punjabs borrow each other's wedding songs and the two countries share TV soaps. They laugh at common jokes. The language of social discourse is similar.

There are other green shoots. Once, trade was the unbridgeable divide between the two. The archetypal story recalls that in the 1980s, the Pakistan Steel Company suggested that its negligible exports could get a major boost if it were allowed to export its steel products to India. The idea was promptly shot down by the Pakistani Ministry of Foreign Affairs; it grunted dismissively that Indians would melt that steel to make tanks and other lethal weapons to kill Pakistani soldiers.

Since then, there has been progress. Indo-Pak trade was a trickle at US$250 million in 2003. Ten years later it climbed to US$2.6 billion. It is still modest when you compare it with Indo-Bangladesh trade at US$4.6 billion or that of India with Sri Lanka at US$4.54 billion. But official statistics do not convey the complete picture. Besides direct trade there is also the switch trade of nearly US$10 billion which takes place through third countries, principally via Dubai. Much more can be done though as the major items of trade suggest. India has a large refining capacity for petroleum products and it exports a considerable quantity of this. Pakistan is a net importer of these products from long distances. Instead of spending large sums on transportation for export or import of these products, if the two countries were to trade directly, both would benefit from the savings on transportation cost. This logic can be extended to electric power, cotton and pharmaceuticals, to name just a few. The potential is considerable provided there is political will and a genuine desire of people to ensure that it happens, and that bureaucrats do not quibble over details.

Yet, the benefits of peace and tranquillity are being subordinated to excitable nationalism. It is said that if the two nations are not constantly on edge, wary of the other's intention, then they need not maintain the large military establishments that they do today. One estimate suggests that a reduction of only 20 per cent in the defence budget of Pakistan can open 7000 new schools a year or establish 1300 hospitals. A similar reduction of 20 per cent in the defence budget of India can establish 45,000 schools or 8000 hospitals.

It will be pragmatic to start with simple first steps. The signs of change are there—shopping arcades in India display Pakistani-made textiles and designer clothes. Business persons exchange visits and exhibitions. Pakistan's visual space is filled with films from Bollywood, just as the Indian public had once clamoured for Pakistan's TV soaps.

But there is still a long way to go. The two capitals, barely one hour's flying time apart, are not connected by air. There are only twelve flights a week between Lahore and Delhi and Karachi and Mumbai. There is no bank branch in each other's country and obtaining a visa remains an ordeal. Besides the Wagah–Attari route there is only the one road through Kashmir that is open for trade.

As against this there were as many as eleven land routes that were open for trade before 1965 and six Indian banks were operating in Pakistan, while Habib Bank had a branch in Bombay. Trade too was sizeable then. If India's exports to Pakistan amounted to a mere 0.99 per cent of its global imports in 2010, they were an impressive 50 per cent in 1947. And if Pakistan's exports to India were only 0.09 per cent of India's global imports in 2010, they were a good 25 per cent in 1947.

It is not just in trade that we have grown apart. We hesitate to interact even in the social space. Google in the words 'Indo-Pak friendship' or words to that effect and you would hardly be enthused by the response from cyberspace. Isn't it a sad reality for a people who instinctively gravitate towards each other in a foreign setting, who speak the same language, who laugh at the same jokes, who cook food largely the same way and who sing the same songs? Their shared heritage asks them the same question—why did that bend in the road happen?

It is a question they also ask each other when they visit the other country; the warmth and the sameness of everything is emotionally trying. The spirit may be there, hidden somewhere under the surface, but the finger that sends the impulse of friendship is unwilling to tap the words 'friendship' in. The fear of the other is all-pervading and the experience of the past a deterrent.

But this is not the first time in the history of this part of the world that we have bickered. A famous legend about Kabir, a fifteenth-century mystic poet and saint, narrates how his Hindu and Muslim followers massed for combat after his death, each side demanding to take charge of the body. Before the first blow is struck, someone removes the shroud to discover that a heap of flowers has replaced the cadaver. The two religious groups divide the flowers, and each goes off to bury or burn its half according to prescribed rituals.

Isn't it possible also for the two countries to lift the shroud of doubt and divide the goodwill that lies underneath? Indeed, there is no other way but the path to amity.

Yet, as the two countries have done so often in the past, they might opt once again to walk separate paths; those that run parallel. From there, they watch the gap between their chosen paths dubiously, afraid that a slight misstep might mean a leap into the abyss.

*

On a flight to Karachi in 1993, I was seated next to a young Pakistani banker. He happened to be a Shia Muslim and spent considerable time lamenting the constant state of strife with the majority Sunni community in Pakistan. We were about to land at Karachi airport when he came up with a unique solution to end the Shia–Sunni differences—mass marriages between the two communities.

Whether it was a case of naïveté or youthful innocence is difficult to say, but I hope he is still alive because in the last twenty years, violence against the Shias has multiplied in Pakistan. First it was the Sunni extremist group Sipahi Sabha, later its offshoot Lashkar-e-Jhangvi that took up arms against them. In the first two months of 2013, over 200 Shias were killed in a continuing pattern of systematic strikes. Pakistani commentators feel that this is likely to happen in the future too because the army and major political parties are averse to taking any seriously debilitating action against the Lashkar-e-Jhangvi.

The security authorities may occasionally arrest a few of its cadres, but that is only a temporary measure, meant to last for the duration of international pressure and public protest against the killings. The bitter reality is that the political parties are reliant on the Lashkar sympathizers for their mass electoral support, and the army taps them for the manpower requirements of the Taliban and sundry other jihadis.

As a Pakistani commentator, M. Iliyas Khan, wrote for the BBC:

> All the major political parties depend on this vote bloc in many areas of central and southern Punjab to win parliamentary seats. Therefore, any kind of a crackdown on these groups would run contrary to their interests.

> [...] These groups have provided both political and military support to Pakistani objectives against India in the disputed region of Kashmir. As things stand, the Afghan endgame, in which the Pakistanis are fishing for a major role, is yet to play out to the finish, and the border with India in Kashmir is far from stable. And if they continue to prove their anti-Shia credentials day after day, they will not have lost their utility for the Sunni-Wahabi sheikhdoms of the Middle East as well, from where they receive the bulk of their funding.[1]

In such a complex web, idealism and the hope for peace is unlikely to get a fair hearing in Pakistan. Consequently, that Shia youth's wishful thinking is bound to be negated repeatedly by the reality of violence in everyday Pakistan.

As with that young man, India too, has been living in hope, that somehow it will be able to get the bilateral relations on a peaceful track.

In that pursuit, Nehru remained an incorrigible idealist till the very end. He was certainly conscious of the realities of Pakistan, but his public posture and his policies were rooted in the hope that aspiration might somehow triumph over experience. Unfortunately, that was not to be.

Idealism alone has not shaped Indian policies. Like moths to a flame, Indian leaders have repeatedly been drawn to moulding a new beginning with Pakistan. Almost without exception, they have held on to the fatalistic belief that somehow, despite previous experiences to the contrary, they would be able to paper over the rough patches. And that through their efforts, amity and fraternity would begin to prevail in India's relations with Pakistan. Yet their failures do not deter those who succeed them. Invariably, each new Indian leader wants to make a mark in the history of bilateral relations. He wants to start afresh out of a conviction that a transformation in relations for the better could become his lasting legacy.

There was a brief departure from this idyllic vision in the early 1970s. Indira Gandhi's hard-headed realism had driven India's Pakistan policy then. She won a magnificent victory against Pakistan in the 1971 war. It wasn't just a victory on the battle front; it was an entire campaign to capture international imagination. But her vain hope that magnanimity, when you hold all the cards, may induce a

---

[1]M. Iliyas Khan, 'Formidable power of Pakistan's anti-Shia militants', *BBC*, 12 January 2013, in < http://www.bbc.com/news/world-asia-20983153>.

long-term change of heart in the other side was trumped by Bhutto's bluff.

The Pakistani leadership has consistently used each such generous turn to its advantage. The Indus Waters Treaty, the financial loans that Pakistan forgot about, the withdrawal of Indian forces from the strategic areas they had taken in the 1965 and 1971 wars, the Indian refusal to concede to the Bangladeshi demand that some of the Pakistani POWs be handed over to it for war crimes trials are some instances. But the issue is larger and the difference in approach more fundamental.

It is true that India and Pakistan were siblings of the same stock, who were surgically torn apart at birth by the British. But we tend to forget that the partition did not take place in the dim mist of long ago. The wounds are recent, raw and real. In the meanwhile, fences that are sturdy and barbed have sprung up between the two states and their people. Occasional attempts are made vainly to leap over the fences or even to break them down. But inevitably, Indians sit back tiredly, defeated by the effort. In part, these vain efforts and the many setbacks can be ascribed to India's inadequate understanding of Pakistan, of its establishment, its society and the societal churn it goes through periodically.

When a rare Indian manages to go across to Pakistan, his or her knowledge of the Pakistani state and its internal dynamics is shaped by a sanitized interaction with the establishment in Islamabad. The ferment in society, the torment of that young Shia man, the realities of the killing fields in Karachi, the oppression in Baluchistan, the angst in the northern areas and the anger in Khyber—all these escape the visitor's eye.

Sadly therefore, for a people who claim a shared ancestry, Indians are strangers to the pulse of Pakistan. Given that inadequacy ,the first question that must be asked is whether at a national level, Indian people understand the reality of Pakistan well enough. Second, any prognosis about the future shape of our relations must take into account the effect of the partition and the events thereafter.

Pakistan's beginning was undeniably christened with a coating of anger. Its leaders wanted to roll back time and rewrite history, and to claim as its own what was actually ancient India. Ever since, history for Pakistan is in a revisionary mode. Each new leader wants to leave his interpretation and stamp on it.

When Zia ul-Haq was alive, Pakistani wisdom maintained that he was the greatest man in the world. After he died, history began again and books were rewritten. Now there is fresh history-making in Pakistan. Extremists have made faith into a fortress. Like Jinnah, they refuse to recognize that faith cannot be partitioned. Islam was transnational; Jinnah made it a tool of his ambition. Moreover, ever since the extremists became the arbiters of war and peace in Pakistan, questions are being asked if the Pakistani state is a broken project.

Reflecting on the present-day state of Pakistan, and more specifically its military, Pakistani commentator Pervez Hoodbhoy maintains:

> ...there are now two armies. The first is headed by Gen Kayani (army chief) and is a national army. The second, as of now, has no known leader and sees itself as God's army. The same division is to be found in the ISI (the Inter-Services Intelligence), maybe even within the Strategic Plans Division, which has custody of Pakistan's atomic arsenal.
>
> Army-One and ISI-One, and Army-Two and ISI-Two, have similar but distinct mindsets. The officers and soldiers in both, like all Pakistanis, were reared on the 'two-nation theory', the belief of Pakistan's founding father Muhammad Ali Jinnah that Hindus and Muslims can never live together as equals in peace. Both sets of soldiers are steeped in anti-Indian prejudice...and also share a deep-rooted contempt for civilians. They differ on religion, however.
>
> ...For Army-One and ISI-One, religion is largely a matter of culture and identity...
>
> Army-Two and ISI-Two, on the other hand, are jihadis, for whom Islam and the state are inseparable. They are strict in matters of ritual and communal conformity: They pray regularly, insist upon strict segregation of officers and their wives, and keep an eye out for colleagues who furtively drink alcohol. Their political philosophy draws inspiration from the works of Maulana Abul Ala Mawdudi...the founder of Pakistan's Jamaat-e-Islami party, who insisted that seventh-century Arab Islam provides a complete blueprint for society and politics. Capturing state power is a means toward creating the ideal society along the lines of Medina in the time of the Prophet Muhammad. The majority of the Army Two are of Wahhabi, Salafi and Deobandi persuasion.[2]

So, the internal dynamic of today's Pakistan is a divided army that may sooner or later be led by a chief who belongs to Army-Two. He may then find ready support outside the army from the vast cadres

---

[2]Pervez Hoodbhoy, 'Pakistan, the army and conflict within', *Middle East Report Online*.

who belong to outfits like the Lashkar-e-Jhangvi or one of Hafiz Saeed's many organizations. Alas, the liberals may be a lonely voice in that army. As it is liberals in Pakistan find that their space is getting narrower by the day. On the other hand, the political discourse, such as it is, is loaded in favour of the rigid and the fundamentalist. It is true that the media has fought a valiant battle, but it has involved considerable sacrifice on the part of the media, setting a fearful example for those who might wish to follow them.

There is also the external angle—the external powers that for one reason or the other have found it necessary to cultivate Pakistan. At one time or the other they have, individually or collectively, felt the need to mentor Pakistan and guide its leaders. Invariably Pakistan has played along, while continuing to do exactly what it feels serves its interests best.

It is an indisputable fact that geographically, culturally and historically Pakistan belongs to South Asia. Some commentators in Pakistan, however, wish it was otherwise, preferring to trace their lineage from the Gulf Arab states. It was this supposed link, and the presumed Pakistani influence on the Arab states, that had first led the US to form an alliance with Pakistan in the 1950s. Let's, however, leave the Gulf states out of our present consideration; let's focus instead on the two most important Pakistani allies, the US and China. These two, directly or indirectly, provide military and economic sustenance to Pakistan. Afghanistan too is important, not because it provides sustenance to Pakistan, but because it gives Pakistan the hope that one day it may have in Afghanistan the much-sought strategic depth against India.

Overall, Pakistan has often proved to be of use to the US as a facilitator when America sought its first contacts with China in 1971, or later in the 1980s as a base for launching guerrilla attacks against the Soviet forces in Afghanistan. But these and other uses of Pakistan inevitably led to an inordinate reliance on its army. As Hussain Haqqani writes in his book, *Between Mosque and Military*:

> Support for the Pakistani military by the United States makes it difficult for Pakistan's weak, secular, civil society to assert itself and wean Pakistan from the rhetoric of Islamist ideology, toward issues of real concern of Pakistan's citizens... The United States has sought short-term gains from its relationship with Pakistan, inadvertently accentuating that country's problems in the process...the ability to secure military and economic aid by fitting into the current paradigm of American policy has made Pakistan a rentier state, albeit one that lives off rents for its strategic location.

Going by the above analysis, the US–Pakistan relationship is a lethal combination of mutual backslapping and opportunistic back-stabbing. The recent examples of this are the squeeze Pakistan puts occasionally on the supply lines through its territory for the American troops in Afghanistan, and the deceptive dealings with regard to the Quetta Shura and the Taliban. Pakistan, on its part, complains about the raid that took out Osama.

Neither side trusts the other, yet neither side believes it can do without the other. Consequently the objectives are transient, the strategy shifting and the methods opaque. A case in point is the fact that for long Pakistan pretended not to have seen the American drones that regularly targeted and killed Pakistani citizens in its territory. Like that Pakistani wink, the US often glosses over Pakistani perfidy in so far as India is concerned.

China is an even stronger ally for Pakistan. Antipathy towards India provides them their common strategic glue. Pakistan is the principal foreign market for China's defence production; its nuclear programme was founded on liberal help and guidance by China and it has been the beneficiary of frequent economic concessions from China. Still, if there was a doubt about the extent of their bonding, then the publicly known recent actions like the presence of Chinese troops in the northern areas, the grant of control over Gwadar port to China and the highway that will link Gwadar to China through POK are some of the many evidences that theirs indeed is an all-weather friendship.

But China also has reason to be wary: why, for instance, are Chinese nationals targeted in Pakistan and why can't Pakistan prevent the training of Chinese Muslim extremists on its territory?

China may build highways, it may supply arms and military aircraft to Pakistan. It may even set up many more nuclear plants on its territory. But will it trust Pakistan sufficiently to invest massively in it? Evidence so far suggests that while China may echo the Pakistani declarations about their relationship being deeper than the oceans and higher than the mountains, it will not trust Pakistan with its lives and property. That's why the Chinese physical presence in Pakistan is as sparse as its investment. Simply put, Pakistan doesn't inspire absolute trust among the Chinese.

For that matter, few Americans dare make Pakistan their base for business. If neither the Chinese nor the Americans find their lives and investments safe in Pakistan, can their respective strategic relationship with Pakistan be crack-proof? Experience tells them to keep looking over their shoulder as they walk hand in hand with Pakistan.

Contrary to the US assumption that aid translates into leverage, Pakistan's military has always managed to take American aid without ever fully giving it the leverage that it desires. This has been the pattern from the very beginning. During the 1950s and 1960s, Ayub Khan oversold Pakistan's willingness to help the US in containing communist expansion. Pakistan provided significant intelligence gathering facilities for a while but never provided the 'centrally positioned landing site' the US sought.

Later, Zia ul-Haq's cooperation in bleeding the Soviets in Afghanistan came with Pakistan's plan to install a client regime in Afghanistan after the Soviet withdrawal. Despite its swagger, the US could never control Pakistan's ISI, or for that matter the mujahidin, even though it paid for the operation. Pakistan's role in the jihad against the Soviet Union also inspired Pakistani jihadis to expand the jihad into Kashmir, a side engagement by the ISI that the US wasn't entirely happy about.

That brings us back to the question of the bilateral relationship. But before considering, finally, the Indo-Pak aspect of it, let us for a moment turn sceptical and question poet John Donne's assertion: 'No man is an island entire of itself; every man is a piece of the continent, a part of the main...'

Obviously, it will be churlish to suggest anything radical like Pakistan cutting off all relations with the rest of the world and living all by itself. That is neither practical nor possible in today's interconnected world. In that sense, every nation has to be a part of the mainstream as the poet suggests. But is it necessary for that interconnection to turn into dependence? Sadly, this is what happened when Ayub Khan first started to bind Pakistan so firmly to the US's security apron. Was that necessary, and has that been good for Pakistan and its people? One could pose that same question for its dependence on China?

What if Pakistan had decided to live as a self-respecting island, sufficient by itself, though connected to the world? Perhaps then its army may not have got the encouragement that it did from the US. Pakistan's politics, its internal dynamics and its value system may have shaped differently; more benign for itself and reasonably accommodative towards others. Left on its own, the state of its relations with India may have been vastly different. But like John Donne's man, it chose to be a piece of the continent, a part of the American universe.

India watched resentfully and sulked.

But all that is irrevocable history. The question now is: what of the future relationship and the state that it is likely to be in, battered or otherwise, in the coming years? Sadly, the crystal ball does not show a promising future. Whichever way one looks at it, the negatives loom large.

Let us, for example, take the most common assumption in India—that when Pakistan stabilizes, peace will prevail. This premise, unfortunately, is based on a false hypothesis that stability would mean the weakening of the army's hold on the government. How can it be presumed that stability would ipso facto lead to an obedient Pakistani army that bows to civilian rule?

The sad fact is that the contrary might actually happen. Freed from internal preoccupations, its army and its ISI are more likely to use that stability as a sanction for devoting greater energies eastward. It is, therefore, more than likely that every injection of strength in Pakistan may have a directly proportional reaction in its attitude towards India; greater stability might simply lead to greater gumption. Yet—and there lies the paradox—a state of strife, or that of a war with its neighbour, can hardly lead to stability at home.

Let's also examine a second assumption—that an accommodative attitude on India's part will catalyse Pakistan into a reciprocally positive stance. Unfortunately, the experience of the last six decades has shown quite the opposite. Every concession becomes a further proof that India can be bullied into conceding more. Thus, our sacrifice over the Indus waters goes unappreciated; in fact, there are increasingly shrill Pakistani voices demanding even more water from a water-starved India.

Or to take another example, Pakistan brazenly forbids Indian traders the transit facilities for trade exchanges with Iran, Afghanistan and Central Asia. The right to transit is enshrined in international law and sanctioned by historical practice as well. Yet, Pakistan behaves cussedly. Why should India be denied the legitimate transit rights with these countries, with which it has ancient trade and civilizational links? There wouldn't be many other examples of this nature in the world today. Yet, India doesn't protest. Is this docile acceptance on India's part the impetus for even more aggressive behaviour by Pakistan?

The third assumption we can be said to have made is our tendency to depend upon the big powers to intercede on our behalf with Pakistan. Thus, after 26/11, we virtually outsourced our responsibility to the US. It is debatable if that policy has paid us dividends. On the other hand, it seems to have reduced us to a state of helplessness vis-à-vis Pakistan while putting us under the obligation of the US.

The fourth false premise that we labour under concerns the belief in some quarters that Pakistan risks breaking up and, therefore, needs our understanding, support and help. Nothing could be further from the truth. Pakistan is not likely to break up soon and in the event it does, nothing that we do would prevent it from happening.

India should, therefore, not despair for Pakistan nor rejoice over its present condition, because like Houdini, it is capable of escaping all over again from an impossible bind.

Unlike India, others are more clear-sighted and less optimistic about the scope for serenity in Indo-Pak relations. In a report, the International Crisis Group commented that:

> Pakistan's fragile democratic transition, pivotal to the success of the dialogue, is endangered by a powerful military that is deeply hostile toward India and supports anti-India-oriented extremist groups. Another Mumbai-style attack by Pakistan-based jihadists would make the dialogue untenable and could even spark a new war.[3]

Still, there are the eternal optimists in India who live in the hope that one day there might be a massive change of heart among the Pakistani generals; from hawks they may just turn into peace-loving doves. It's a pity that the last six decades haven't produced even one such general. Consequently, there is little evidence to suggest that there might be a change for the better in the future; a change that could promote a really meaningful dialogue.

A former Pakistani ambassador, Zafar Hilaly, had this to say about the fate of his efforts to promote a dialogue:

> I was at the OIC summit in Casablanca with Benazir Bhutto in 1995. We had just finished making the rounds of the Heads of State and, feeling pleased with her efforts, Benazir seemed in a receptive mood. I started off by saying that if amity with India was not possible, perhaps managing differences more adroitly was a wise alternative but that this required engaging India far more robustly than we were doing then.
>
> 'Great,' Benazir remarked, 'now put it down in black and white, take it to them (the fauj—the army) and if they let you out of the room in one piece, come and tell me their response.'[4]

---

[3]'Pakistan's relationship with India: Beyond Kashmir?', 3 May 2012, in < http://www.crisisgroup.org/en/publication-type/media-releases/2012/asia/pakistans-relations-with-india-beyond-kashmir.aspx>.

[4]Zafar Hilaly, 'So should we build walls?', *The News*.

None of the factors described above is likely to change in the next ten or fifteen years. Nor is Pakistan going to tone down its act as the victimized smaller neighbour. It will also continue to repeat its alleged claim over Kashmir in every forum and at every opportunity. In doing so, Pakistanis will continue to enjoy the advantage of their aggressive complaints, while India would keep suffering the disadvantage of its dislike of rows. Moreover, India's case on issues like Kashmir will remain fogged in a mist of doubt and insufficient articulation.

Some other developments are also likely to impact directly or indirectly on Indo-Pak relations. A diminished American presence in Afghanistan will make it difficult for the Pakistani army to extract monies from the US on the scale that it has been used to since 9/11. But this reduced presence of its forces in Afghanistan will be an admission of American military failure. On the other hand, the Pakistani army will interpret this as their second, albeit indirect, victory in quick succession—first over the Soviet forces and now over the US-led armies. Consequently, this will give it a psychological high of having defeated, via the Taliban, two of the mightiest armed forces in the world. That, and its further ambitions for strategic depth, could put the Pakistani army at risk of a confrontation with the Afghan army, and perhaps even with the remnants of the US troops.

Separately, China's naval presence in Gwadar port and the neighbouring waters is bound to ruffle Indian and even American feathers. Moreover, the reported presence of the People's Liberation Army in the northern areas and along the Karakoram highway is not going to give comfort to India. All this, particularly Pakistan's strategic depth through Afghanistan if it materializes, is unlikely to inspire confidence in the Indian strategic community.

Still, let us turn hopeful again and assume that none of the above is likely to be detrimental to the bilateral relationship. Let us go a step further and say that a peace pact between the leaders of Pakistan and India will be signed in the not-too-distant future. But what good would that peace pact be if terrorists roam free and strike at will in India?

Yet, if by a miracle all terrorists were to be reined in, and confined to isolated barracks permanently, would that mean an end to the contestational relationship? Farzana Shaikh is not so sure. She writes in her book, *Making Sense of Pakistan*:

> This enduring rivalry between India and Pakistan is grounded not only in the rival interpretations of Partition, but also in two opposing

> national projects tied to distinct visions of nationhood; one (Indian) predicated on the principles of secularism, the other (Pakistani) founded somewhat problematically on the idea of a Muslim nation.

She adds, '...Pakistan's struggle against India is deeply embedded in a painful awareness of its own lack of a national history.'

There is nothing that India can do to alter that reality, or make that bitterness less painful. The act of its creation stunted Pakistan's choices. It cannot accept its common roots of history, culture and traditions with India. To do that would mean denying the logic of partition. Therefore, Pakistan alone must come to terms with the history that actually began for it in 1947, and not on some other imagined date. Till that happens an artificial construct of history will keep constricting it. Under the circumstances it'll be impractical to suggest that the mindset of the Pakistani establishment will change in the near future.

The last word must be reserved for Pandit Nehru. Some of his actions have no doubt led to the distortions of today, but it will be unwise to deny his prescience on Indo-Pak relations. As he recorded in a note of 15 June 1949 to K.P.S. Menon, the foreign secretary:

> ...it has to be admitted that they [India and Pakistan] are unfriendly to each other. More especially Pakistan is unfriendly to India. That feeling of hostility is likely to continue for a considerable time and certainly till the Kashmir matter has not been settled. It may survive even that settlement in the event of that settlement being unfavourable to either party... The whole of Pakistan policy, as that of the Muslim League that preceded it, is based on threats and bullying. Appeasement only leads to more bullying. We must, therefore, resist this and make it clear that we are not going to submit.[5]

Alas, India has chosen to appease Pakistan and that reality is sobering. Unless there is a miraculous change of heart, Pakistan's confrontational posture is likely to harden even more. If the economic conditions in Pakistan worsen, if ethnic strife is exacerbated, or if the likes of the Lashkar gain further ascendancy, all these will convey rough tidings for the relationship. Then, as in the past, Pakistan will continue to preoccupy and paralyse Indian strategic thinking.

*

[5]Avtar Singh Bhasin, *India–Pakistan Relations, 1947–2007: A Documentary Study*.

That's it. I have finished the book. The prognosis is dark, but what can I do? If there has to be a future of strife and confrontation, then so be it. I was resigned to that negative fate till I fortuitously happened to see a video uploaded by a visiting Indian of a debate in a Pakistani school. The young girls were speaking for and against the motion of the nuclear tests by Pakistan in response to the Indian tests of 1998.

Both debaters presented their arguments well and with vigour; the one in favour of Pakistan's tests also said a mild word or two against India. When at the end of the debate, these children were asked about those negative sentiments by the visiting Indian, they replied that both sides in the debate had to present their arguments as best as they could. Their aim was to win the debate. It was as simple as that. Then the visitor asked them their opinion of why there was a negative view of India in Pakistan.

The children responded spontaneously, 'It is all because of politicians. But people don't want strife.'

The Indian visitor nodded and in response he said, 'It is the same in India.'

The youngest in the group cut him short, as if she didn't like the business of apportioning blame on one side or the other. She said with the amazing grace that only the innocence of youth can bring forth, '*Hum maafi chaahte hain,* we seek forgiveness.'

If only the two nations could take a cue from that child and decide to forgive and forget the past.

Bibliography

Calling this a select bibliography may have been more appropriate. An enterprise that seeks to understand two large countries cannot be limited to a recent reading of books. There are a vast number of newspaper reports, magazine articles, fiction and non-fiction books from India, Pakistan and other countries that have helped me in writing *Where Borders Bleed*. Since they are too numerous to be listed, and some too distant in time to recall accurately, I have opted for the pragmatic step of enumerating my recent reading. Except for some inadvertent slip, I have acknowledged them wherever I have made use of their views.

Aijazuddin, F.S. (ed.), 2003, *The White House & Pakistan: Secret Declassified Documents, 1969–1974*, Karachi: Oxford Publishing House.

Aggarwal, J.C. and S.P. Agrawal, 1995, *Modern History of Jammu and Kashmir: Ancient Times to Shimla Agreement*, New Delhi: Concept Publishing Company.

Ahmad, Akbar S., 1997, *Jinnah: Pakistan and Islamic Identity*, London: Routledge.

Ahmed, Dr Ishtiaq, 'Splitting India-iii', *Friday Times*, 4 October 2013, Lahore.

Akbar, M.J., 1988, *Nehru: The Making of India*, London: Viking.

Akbar, M.J., 1991, *Kashmir: Behind the Vale*, New Delhi: Viking.

Albinia, Alice, 2009, *Empires of the Indus*, London: John Murray.

Ali, Mahir, 'A case of mistaken identity', *The Hindu*, 11 September 2009.

Ali, Tariq, 2002, *The Clash of Fundamentalists: Crusaders, Jihads and Modernity*, London: Verso.

Archives, Lok Sabha Debates.

Babar, Ayaz, 2013, *What's Wrong with Pakistan*, New Delhi: Hay House Publishers.

Baluch, Mir Ahmed Yar Khan, 1975, *Inside Baluchistan*, Karachi: Royal Book Company.

Bajwa, Farooq, 2013, *From Kutch to Tashkent: The Indo-Pakistan War of 1965*, London: Hurst.

Bass, Gary J., 2013, *The Blood Telegram: Nixon, Kissinger and a Forgotten Genocide*, New York: Knopf.

Baxter, Craig, 2007, *Diaries of Field Marshal Ayub Khan, 1966–1972*, Karachi: Oxford University Press.

Bhasin, Avtar Singh, 2013, *India–Pakistan Relations, 1947–2007: A Documentary Study*, vols 1–7, New Delhi: Geetika Publishers.

Bhatia, B.N., 'Army as an instrument of national power', *Tribune*, 29 August 2011.

Bhutto, Benazir, 1988, *Daughter of the East, An Autobiography*, London: Hamish Hamilton.

Bhutto, Zulfikar Ali, 1994, *My Dearest Daughter: A Letter from the Death Cell*, Lahore: Classic Publishers.

Bourke, Richard and Raymond Geuss (eds), 2009, *Political Judgement: Essays for John Dunn*, Cambridge: Cambridge University Press.

Brulliard, Karin, 'Pakistan conflicted over targeting rising extremists in its heartland', *Washington Post*, 22 June 2010.

Carter, Lionel, 2011, *Partition Observed: British Official Reports from South Asia, vols I and II, 14 August–15 October 1947*, New Delhi: Manohar.

Chaudhuri, Nirad, 1987, *Thy Hand, Great Anarch! India 1921–1952*, London: Chatto & Windus.
Chitkara, M.G., 2004, *Rashtriya Swayam Sevak Sangh: National Upsurge*, New Delhi: APH Publishing Corporation.
Cloughley, Brian (ed.), 1999, *A History of the Pakistani Army, Wars and Insurrections*, New York: Oxford University Press.
Collins, Larry and Dominique Lapierre, 1982, *Mountbatten and the Partition of India*, vol. 1, New Delhi: Vikas Publishing House.
Contractor, Behram (Busybee), *Uday India*, 21 November 2013.
Correra, Gorden, 2006, *Shopping for Bombs: Nuclear Proliferation, Global Insecurity and the Rise and Fall of the AQ Khan Network*, New Delhi: Oxford University Press.
Dasgupta, C., 2002, *War and Diplomacy in Kashmir, 1947–48*, New Delhi: Sage Publications.
Davis, Donald E. and Eugene P. Trani, 2009, *Distorted Mirrors: Americans and their Relations with Russia and China in the 20th Century*, USA: University of Missouri Press.
Dhar, P.N., 'Kashmir: The Simla Solution', *Journal of Peace Studies*, vol. 2, March–June 1995.
Dikshit, Sandeep, 'How he and his men won those wars', *The Hindu*, 28 June 2008.
Duncan, Emma, 1989, *Breaking the Curfew—A Political Journey through Pakistan*, London: Michael Joseph.
Dutt, Vijay, 2010, *Times by the Thames: An Indian Cruise*, New Delhi: Konark Publishers.
Fukuyama, Francis, 2004, *State Building: Governance and World Order in the 21st Century*, New York: Cornell University Press.
Gandhi, Gopal, 2011, *Of a Certain Age: Twenty Life Sketches*, New Delhi: Penguin.
Gandhi, Rajmohan, 1986, *Eight Lives: A Study of the Hindu–Muslim Encounter*, New York: State University of New York Press.
Gandhi, Rajmohan, 2013, *Punjab: A History from Aurangzeb to Mountbatten*, New Delhi: Aleph Book Company.
Gandhi, Sajit (ed.), 2002, *The Tilt: The US and the South Asia Crisis of 1971*, National Security Archive, USA.
Gauhar, Altaf, 1996, *Ayub Khan: Pakistan's First Military Ruler*, Karachi: Oxford University Press.
Ghaus, A.S., 1988, *The Fall of Afghanistan: An Insider's Account*, London: Taylor and Francis.
Ghose, Sankar, 1993, *Jawaharlal Nehru*, Bombay: Allied Publishers.
Goldberg, Vicky, 1986, *Margaret Bourke-White—A Biography*, New York: Harper Collins.
Hasan, Mushirul, 2002, *The Partition Omnibus*, New Delhi: Oxford University Press.
Hasan, Mushirul, 2002, *Partition Narratives*, New Delhi: Jamia Millia Islamia.
Haqqani, Hussain, 2005, *Pakistan between Mosque and Military*, Lahore: Vanguard Books.
Haqqani, Hussain, 2013, *Magnificent Delusions: Pakistan, the United States and an Epic History of Misunderstanding*, New York: Public Affairs.
Herman, Arthur, 2008, *Gandhi and Churchill*, London: Hutchinson.
Hewitt, Vernon, 1995, *Reclaiming the Past*, London: Portland Books.
Hilaly, Zafar, 'So should we build walls?', *The News*, Pakistan, 2 February 2013.
Hodson, H.V., 1986, *The Great Divide*, Oxford: Oxford University Press.
Hopkirk, Peter, 1984, *Setting the East Ablaze*, Oxford: Oxford University Press.
Hoodbhoy, Pervez, 'Faith and Nation: Reinventing Pakistan', *Ahmediyya Times*, Karachi, 24 March 2010.
Hoodbhoy, Pervez and Zia Mian, 'Pakistan, the army and the conflict within', *Middle East Report Online*, 12 July 2011.
Imtiaz, Saba, 'Wikileaks on 1998 nuclear tests', *The Express Tribune*, 3 September 2011.
Jalal, Ayesha, 1985, *The Sole Spokesman*, UK: Cambridge University Press.
Jha, C.S., 1983, *From Bandung to Tashkent: Glimpses of Indian Foreign Policy*, Hyderabad: Sangam Books.

Jha, Prem Shankar, 1996, *Kashmir 1947: Rival Versions of History*, New Delhi: Oxford University Press.

Kanwal, Gurmeet, 2010, 'Lost Opportunities', *CLAWS*, New Delhi.

Kaul, B.M., 1971, *Confrontation with Pakistan*, New Delhi: Vikas Publications.

Khairi, Saad R., 2006, *Jinnah Reinterpreted: The Journey from Indian Nationalism to Muslim Statehood*, Lahore: Ferozesons.

Khan, Ayub, *Friends Not Masters: A Political Autobiography*, Karachi: Oxford University Press.

Khan, Mohammad Asghar, 1983, *Generals in Politics: Pakistan, 1958–1982*, New Delhi: Vikas Publishing House.

Khan, Roedad, 1999, *The American Papers: Secret & Confidential: India, Pakistan & Bangladesh Documents, 1965–1973*, Karachi: Oxford University Press.

Khan, Roedad (ed.), 2002, *The British Papers: Secret & Confidential: India, Pakistan, Bangladesh Documents, 1958–1969*, Karachi: Oxford University Press.

Khan, Samin, 1989, *A Strategic Doctrine for Pakistan*, Karachi: Tehreek Nazariya Pakistan.

Khan, Sultan M., 1997, *Memories and Reflections of a Pakistani Diplomat*, London: The Centre for Pakistan Studies.

Khan, Wali, 1987, *Facts are Facts: The Untold Story of India's Partition*, New Delhi: Vikas Publishing House.

Khosla, Justice G.D., 1950, *Stern Reckoning*, New Delhi: Bhawnani.

Kissinger, Henry, 1979, *The White House Years*, New York: Little Brown & Company.

Kumara, Kranti and Jones Keith, 'US threatened to bomb Pakistan back to stone age', *World Socialist*, 27 September 2008.

Kwarteng, Kwasi, 2011, *Ghosts of Empire: Britain's Legacies in the Modern World*, London: Bloomsbury.

Langton, Robert, 'The wartime raid that shamed Mountbatten', *Daily Express*, London, 20 August 2012.

Lapierre, Dominique and Larry Collins, 1975, *Freedom at Midnight*, New York: Simon & Schuster.

Lieven, Anatol, 2011, *Pakistan: A Hard Country*, London: Allen Lane.

Logevall, Fredrik and Andrew Preston (eds), 2008, *Nixon in the World: American Foreign Relations, 1969–1977*, New York: Oxford University Press.

Malhotra, Inder, 'The collapse of Shimla accord', *Indian Express*, 9 June 2014.

Mansergh, Nicholas and Penderel Moon, 1981, *Constitutional Relations between Britain and India: The Transfer of Power, 1942–47: The Mountbatten Viceroyalty, Formulation of a Plan, 22 March–30 May 1947*, London: HM Stationery Office.

Masroor, Mehr Nigar, 1980, *Ra'ana: Liaqat Ali Khan—A Biography*, Karachi: All Pakistan Women's Association.

Mazari, Sherbaz Khan, 1999, *A Journey to Disillusionment*, Karachi: Oxford University Press.

Meyer, Karl E., 2003, *The Dust of Empire: The Race for Mastery in the Asian Heartland*, New York: Public Affairs.

Milton, Giles, 2013, *Russian Roulette: A Deadly Game—How British Spies Thwarted Lenin's Global Plot*, London: Bloomsbury.

Mirza, Humayun, 1999, *From Plassey to Pakistan: The Family History of Iskander Mirza*, USA: University Press of America.

Moon, Penderel (ed.), 1997, *Wavell: The Viceroy's Journal*, Oxford: Oxford University Press.

Morgan, Janet P., 1991, *Edwina Mountbatten: A Life of Her Own*, London: Harper Collins.

Morrice, James, 1993, *Pakistan Chronicle*, UK: Palgrave Macmillan.

Mountbatten, Louis, 1948, *Time Only to Look Forward*, London: Nicholas Kaye Ltd.

Mountbatten, Louis, 1968, *Reflections on the Transfer of Power and Jawaharlal Nehru*, Cambridge: Cambridge University Press.

Mukerjee, Madhusree, 2010, *Churchill's Secret War: The British Empire and the Ravaging of India during World War II*, New York: Basic Books.
Musharraf, Pervez, 2006, *In the Line of Fire: A Memoir*, London: Simon & Schuster.
Nanda, B.R., 2010, *Road to Partition: The Life and Times of Mohammad Ali Jinnah*, New Delhi: Routledge.
Nawaz, Shuja, 2008, *Crossed Swords: Pakistan, its Army and the Wars Within*, Karachi: Oxford University Press.
Nehru, Jawaharlal, 1987, *Selected Works of Jawaharlal Nehru*, vol. 4, New Delhi: Oxford University Press.
Nehru, Jawaharlal, 1989, *Letters to Chief Ministers, 1947–1964*, New Delhi: Oxford University Press.
Nixon, Richard, 1988, *The Memoirs of Richard Nixon*, USA: Easton Press.
Noorani, A.G., 'Bhutto's treachery', *Frontline*, 15 June 2007.
Noorani, A.G., 'Vajpayee's foreign policy', *Frontline*, 24 May 2003.
Padgaonkar, Dileep, 'Open the Pandora's box at your own peril!', *Outlook*, 9 June 2014.
Page, David, 1989, *The Partition Omnibus*, Oxford: Oxford University Press.
Page, David, 1989, *Prelude to Partition: The Indian Muslims and the Imperial System, 1920–1932*, Oxford: Oxford University Press.
Payne, A.M., 2012, *The Durand Line: History and Implications of British Imperial Policy in Afghanistan*, Ohio: Ohio State University.
Punjabi, Riyaz, 'Indus Waters Treaty, Human Security vs Military Sercurity', *Journal of Peace Studies*, 11(4) October–December 2004.
Rajghatta, Chidanand, 'Pak on track to being named terrorist state', *The Times of India*, 7 December 2008.
Rashid, Ahmed, 2001, *Taliban: The Story of Afghan Warlords*, London: Pan Books.
Rashid, Ahmed, 2002, *Jihad: The Rise of Militant Islam in Central Asia*, Lahore: Vanguard.
Rashid, Ahmed, 'Beware Pakistan's small nuclear weapons', *Financial Times*, 22 October 2013.
Rehman, Altika, 'Work harder to squeeze Haqqanis...', *Express Tribune*, 21 October 2011.
Rice, Condoleezza, 2011, *No Higher Honor: A Memoir of My Years in Washington*, New York: Crown.
Riedel, Bruce, 2011, *Deadly Embrace: Pakistan, America and the Future of Global Jihad*, Washington: Brookings Institution Press.
Rose, Leo and Richard Sisson, 1990, *War and Secession: Pakistan, India, and the Creation of Bangladesh*, Berkley and Los Angeles: University of California Press.
Ryan, Frank, 1992, *Tuberculosis: The Greatest Story Never Told*, Sheffield: Swift Publishers.
Saiyad, Matlubul Hasan, 1970, *Jinnah: A Political Study*, New Delhi: Elite Publishers Ltd.
Salim, Ahmed (ed.), 2001, *Lahore 1947*, New Delhi: India Research Press.
Schofield, Victoria, 2000, *Kashmir in Conflict: India, Pakistan and the Unending War*, London: Tauris.
Schmidt, John R., 2012, *The Unravelling: Pakistan in the Age of Jihad*, London: Macmillan.
Scott, Paul, 1976, *Raj Quartet*, London: William Marrow & Company.
Shaikh, Farzana, 2009, *Making Sense of Pakistan*, London: Hurst & Company.
Sharma, Hari Dev (ed.), 2007, *100 Significant Pre-Independence Speeches—1858–1947*, New Delhi: Rupa Publications.
Shirer, William L., 1980, *Gandhi: A Memoir*, New York: Simon & Schuster.
Smith, Michael Shane, 2007, *Windows of Opportunity and Military Escalation: Bringing Diplomatic Factors Back In*, USA: Pro Quest Online Publishers.
Sri Prakasa, 1965, *Pakistan: Birth and Last Days*, Meerut: Meenakshi Prakashan.
Swami, Praveen, 'Beating the retreat', *Frontline*, 8 November 2002.
Syed, G.M., 1992, *Sindhu Desh: A Study in its Separate Identity through the Ages*, Karachi: G.M. Syed Academy.

Talbot, Ian and Gurharpal Singh, 2009, *The Partition of India*, Cambridge: Cambridge University Press.
Tendulkar, D.G., 1951, *Mahatma: Life of Mohandas Karamchand Gandhi*, vols 1–8, India: Vithalbhai K. Jhaveri and D.G. Tendulkar.
Tunzelmann, Alex von, 2007, *Indian Summer—The Secret History of the End of an Empire*, London: Simon & Schuster.
Warikoo, K., 2007, 'Indus Waters Treaty: View from Kashmir', *Journal of Himalayan Research and Culture*, vol. 2, New Delhi.
Wilson, A.N., 2006, *After the Victorians: The World Our Parents Knew*, London: Arrow.
Wolpert, Stanley, 2010, *India and Pakistan—Continued Conflict or Cooperation*, California: California University Press.
Woodward, Bob, 2011, *Obama's Wars: The Inside Story*, New York: Simon & Schuster.
Yadav, K.C., 1998, *India Divided*, India: Hope.
Yousaf, Mohammad and Mark Adkin, 1992, *The Bear Trap—Afghanistan's Untold Story*, Lahore: Jang Publishers.
Zaidi, Z.H. (ed.)., 1993, *Jinnah Papers: Pakistan Struggling for Survival*, Karachi: Oxford University Press.
Zakaria, Rafiq, 2002, *The Man Who Divided India: An Insight into Jinnah's Leadership*, Mumbai: Popular Prakashan.

Acknowledgements

Ironically, the 'divide' made this book possible. Had that line in blood not been drawn, there wouldn't have been any need for this book or a reason for my parents to shift home. In that event my father would have been the writer; it was his dream and he had the imagination. But the partition was the spoiler. Like millions of other people, on both sides of the divide, my parents sacrificed their present to make my sister's, Dr Neera Ummat and my tomorrows. If there is a way for him to look from up there, I hope my father has a reason to smile in satisfaction.

My sister has been a great support all my life and has given me affection in abundance. My uncle B.K. Goswami believes stars were perched high on purpose for people to aim at. I have nodded reluctantly in agreement sometimes.

My son-in-law Amarendra Swarup sets a daily example of reaching for them through ability and perseverance. Seeing him at work often led me to the computer table.

Ram, my son, has the gift to focus on the big picture. He has been a consistent support all through the writing of this book, often leaving everything else to get me just the right word.

My friends Ashok Mirza and Surjit Das, each blessed with a discerning eye and an honest tongue, gave useful suggestions, encouraging me all the way through the writing of this book. Surjit generously gave me the use of his house in Dehradun, so I could soak in the salubrious surroundings as I thought of the next chapter.

The Indian Foreign Service (IFS) provided me the opportunity to explore and enquire. As colleagues, we might have an occasional bone to pick with each other, but in the end camaraderie overwhelms the odd sour note. Had it not been for the IFS, this book may not have had the insight of an insider.

Dharini Bhaskar, the Acquisitions Editor at Rupa, has been a model of efficiency, anticipating needs and staying two steps ahead of every contingency. She has been a great asset all through.

My grandchildren Maanas and Anaia monitored the progress of this book with a loving but firm eye on the deadline they had set for me. The need for their approval, more than anything else, made me spend countless hours at the writing desk.

Finally, huge thanks are due to the book itself and to the fond memories of the time spent dreaming, thinking and the actual writing of it. Interestingly, it took just about nine months from the time I wrote the first words of the manuscript on 20 August 2013 to 21 May 2014 when the book contract with Rupa was formalized. I can now appreciate better the agonies and the many ecstasies that 'nine months' can bring about.

Index